Black
Critics
& Kings

BLACK CRITICS & KINGS

The
Hermeneutics
of Power
in Yoruba
Society

ANDREW APTER

The University of Chicago Press
Chicago & London

Andrew Apter is assistant professor of anthropology at the University of
Chicago.

The University of Chicago Press, Chicago 60637
The University of Chicago Press, Ltd., London

Library of Congress Cataloging-in-Publication Data

Apter, Andrew H. (Andrew Herman)
    Black critics and kings : the hermeneutics of power in Yoruba
society / Andrew Apter.
        p.   cm.
    Includes bibliographical references and index.
    ISBN 0-226-02342-7. — ISBN 0-226-02343-5 (pbk.)
    1. Yoruba (African people)—Politics and government.   2. Yoruba
(African people)—Rites and ceremonies.   I. Title.
DT515.45.Y67A56   1992
306'089'96333—dc20   91-21791
                                                              CIP

This book is printed on acid-free paper.

Ọgbọ́n ò pin síbi kan,
Ọmọdẹ́-gbọ́n-àgbà-gbọ́n ni a fi dá Ilé-Ifẹ̀.

Knowledge has no limit.
Children-are-wise-elders-are-wise is the origin of Ile-Ife.

CONTENTS

ILLUSTRATIONS

PREFACE AND ACKNOWLEDGMENTS

In the summer of 1990 I returned to Ayede, the Ekiti Yoruba town and kingdom where I had conducted dissertation research nearly six years earlier (1982–84) and which appears in the ethnography of this study. I will not indulge in a description of the familiar tragicomedy of ethnographic homecomings—the tears, laughter, gifts, embraces, and emphatic recriminations which represent one of the highest expressions of Yoruba affection—save only to mention the equally familiar story that much had and had not changed. After Babangida's 1985 military coup, Nigeria continued down the road of post–oil boom decline. The naira had been devalued about 900 percent against the dollar within those six years, placing imports out of common reach, precipitating drastic inflation unmatched by salaries, and virtually wiping out an urban middle class previously accustomed to business, travel, and education abroad. The country is preparing for a return to civilian rule in 1992, but the political exhilaration of the 1979 and 1983 elections (an exhilaration fueled by petro-naira) has been replaced with resigned cynicism. The domestic economy is still vibrant, even if the stakes have dwindled. Business goes on, money and credit circulate in complementary flows, cars are repaired with salvaged parts, and night markets illuminate the stalls in Lagos, Ibadan, and Ilesha as children, traders, and—if you are unlucky—spirits of the dead hawk their goods to get by on narrow profit margins. Life continues with its predictable unpredictability, and many are seeking strength in the mushrooming industry of new religious prophets.

Within Ayede itself—like all Yoruba towns, a permeable microcosm of the Nigerian state—these national trends have had a visible impact but no drastic or devastating effects. True, the price of bread and yams has soared, and this complaint has become a common allegory of how one must manage during hard times. Public transport is more expensive, due less to increases in the price of petrol than to the cost of maintaining vehicles on debilitated roads, and this has added to the sense of insularity in the countryside. But in many ways life is easier in the rural areas than in the big cities, where traffic jams and power failures make it difficult to get anything done. Not that life is idyllic in towns like Ayede. But neither has it lost its vitality. I had expected to be shocked by the post–oil boom decline, but I was happily surprised. The Anglican Church and central mosque had been refurbished into monuments of extravagant glory—red carpets, paneled doors, and generators to bring forth the light of God when NEPA (the National Electric Power Authority) took a rest (which was most of the time). A new Aladura "cathedral" had also gone up. Old buildings were well maintained and new ones had been built, some with brightly painted cinder blocks and modern conveniences. Costly imported clothes had given way to less expensive "traditional" outfits, now worn by the style-conscious youth as well as their elders. And the busy social schedule of parties, naming ceremonies, burials, memorials, religious services, òrìṣà-cult rituals, and interminable social calls was as intense as ever, even if the scale of expenditures was slightly reduced. If many of my younger friends had left to work in larger towns and cities, many had also returned to the less glamorous but more reliable opportunities at home.

Some of the elders had died. Pa Fagboun—the oldest man in Ayede—had finally "kicked the bucket," at what people said was 130 years of age. He was the senior member of the Erokesin age-set, which was formally established in the 1890s, by my calculations; and he took to his grave an unparalleled knowledge of the lineage-based òrìṣà cults in Isaoye quarter, which declined under colonialism (see chapter 6). Baba M. B. Ayeni had also passed away—historian of Ayede, the first local magistrate, and a practicing Catholic until the end. His son Jide gave me some of his personal papers, including a diary written in 1905 which describes his first marriage and his Catholic conversion; and a school notebook with meticulous entries about modern health and hygiene, incipient markings of a colonial cosmology. Baba Babalola—olórí awo and priest of Osanyin—had also died, unsurpassed in the linguistic pharmacology of medicinal leaves, incantations, and Ifa divination. How well I remember my first session with him, as he sat on the floor with his diviner's tray (ọpọn ifá) and chain (ọ̀pẹ̀lẹ̀) before him, calmly explaining that just as medical school in America is expensive and takes many years, I shouldn't expect to learn his secrets too easily.

The day I returned to Ayede, Yeye, one of the oldest female diviners and my former personal advisor, also died. Respected in witchcraft, crippled from birth, she was the widow of the former king Gabriel Osho (see chapter 3) and the mother of the paramount Oshun priestess. Her predictions never failed, and her reputation extended to Ibadan and Lagos. Was this a bad omen, that she died that very day? On the contrary, it confirmed the bond between us, since I had arrived to help bury her. Yeye was known to talk to her birds, which nested in clay pots suspended on an inside wall and which enjoyed free flight in and out of the house. For two days they gathered on the mound above her corpse. Her funeral lasted for three weeks, ensuring safe passage for a spirit as powerful as hers.

But if these deaths are irrevocable losses, they are not tragedies. Their lives were long, their households full; and their wisdom passes on. To the priests and priestesses of Ayede, both living and dead, I owe the greatest respect and thanks. They alone could open the doors to provide glimpses into the subject matter of this study, and if earning their trust was challenging, receiving it has been an honor. I am particularly indebted to the *Yèyéolókun, Ìyá Ṣàngó,* and *Ìyàwó Ọ̀ṣun* priestesses of Yemoja; the *Ológun* priestess of Orisha Iyagba; and the *Olúwo, Apena, Ìyábíye,* and *Ìyáìdíàqbà* of Iledi Omowumi Odua (Ayede-Ekiti) for their love and support; for teaching me that, whatever I may know, "Secret surpasses secret, secret can swallow secret completely" (*Awó j'awo lọ, awo lè gb'áwo mí torí-torí*)—perhaps the central axiom of Yoruba hermeneutics; and finally, for the privileged access which this Yoruba insight indicates.

After nearly six years, my own thinking had also changed when I returned to Ayede. The more structural concerns of my dissertation had given way to the interpretive themes which emerged only in the reworking of my material; thus I confronted an earlier epistemology which had guided my research and which to some extent still informs it. It was difficult not to fall back into previous routines, building on what I knew to demonstrate what I had already demonstrated. But it was also refreshing to shift research registers and test some of the "deep" interpretations which had emerged after years of reflection. I had lived with this material in my head, and here it was, once again, a living reality, less confusing and intimidating, much easier to cope with and further explore. I tried to expand my agenda to include more on Christianity, Islam, everyday life, the body, local markets, the current economic crisis, and so on. But the *òrìṣà* cults drew me back like a magnet, and eventually I gave up trying to escape their magic.

I tried my interpretations out on the priestesses, and the effect was startling. Who had told me these things, particularly the deeper readings of the Yemoja festival (discussed in chapter 4)? Clearly Yemoja had visited me in my dreams to instruct me further. My return, it seems, was the final confirmation that I was trustworthy, and a new level of learning began. One herbalist gave me three notebooks full of medicinal formulae so that I could cure people overseas (I had explained that the ingredients could be obtained at the better Shango botánicas in America). This was an exceptional gift. My *jùjú*-medicine collection became a cumbersome burden (and required a lot of explaining to the customs officer at O'Hare Airport). I was also permitted free rein with a video camera, and I covered the Yemoja and Orisa Iyagba festivals over six weeks from start to finish. When a newly stationed policeman tried to stop me from filming, the town rallied behind me, and he quickly changed his tune. Thus, despite the passing of years, ritual remained the central prism which reconfigured my thoughts and energies, as well as my relationships within the community.

Ayede's king, the Àtá Samson Omotosho II (installed in 1948), is still alive as I write these words;* but he is old and ill, and the kingship will soon be up for grabs. Rival factions have already mobilized, demanding a new era of "progressive," literate leadership and courting the òrìṣà cults to represent their political claims. The wounds of the 1983 election riots (chapter 8) are slowly healing, although the event remains a common reference point in local politics and recent historical memory. A new shrine (Iyakere) in the marketplace, authorized by the Ọ̀ni of Ife and constructed with the assistance of his priests, represents Ayede's final reconciliation of the former warring political parties (Unity Party of Nigeria and National Party of Nigeria) under the Second Republic, although hostilities and loyalties still linger under military rule. Ritual idioms have continued to shape Ayede's internal balance of powers and its external articulation with the Nigerian state, a theme developed throughout this study.

My thanks extend to all who helped to foster and realize my Yoruba research: to Fulbright-Hays and the Social Science Research Council for their generous funding; to Jacob Ade Ajayi—my official advisor and unofficial guardian in Nigeria—who arranged my affiliation with the Institute for African Studies at the University of Ibadan and whose very name released me from bureaucratic obstructionism; and to his wife, Christie Ajayi, who made their home mine as well. Equally generous was Karin Barber, who taught me the foundations of the Yoruba language at the University of Ife and who has set a standard of linguistic fluency and scholarship impossible to match. Within Ayede, special thanks go to the Àtá and his civil chiefs for tolerating my inquisitive presence in their town and for sanctioning my efforts. Of my friends and assistants, I am particularly indebted to Olusanya Ibitoye, Joseph Oluwafemi Abejide, and Toyin Balogun. And for my Yoruba name (Ogundele), I cannot adequately thank Taye Bamisile—hunter, herbalist, musician, diviner, and currently a sideman for the jùjéú-music superstar King Sunny Ade.

*The Àtá Omotosho passed away in February 1991.

My intellectual debts trace back to Robert F. Thompson, who first introduced me to Yoruba culture and taught me how to learn from it. My title echoes his *Black Gods and Kings* to signify the flash of his spirit and to invoke the revisionary impulse of Yoruba aesthetics and ritual discourse so cogently illustrated by Skip Gates, my longtime friend and guiding light. At Cambridge University, I learned a traditional social anthropology which gave me an indelible respect for an older generation of Africanists, including Malcolm Ruel, Ray Abrahams, and Jack Goody, all of whom supervised my essays and set exacting standards of argument and research. I also had the good fortune of meeting K. Anthony Appiah, whose technical interest in formal semantics extended to African philosophical debates. From M. G. Smith, my dissertation advisor and now colleague and friend, I gained a powerful analytical perspective which runs throughout this study, although he might not agree with its more interpretive twists. John Middleton, who encouraged my more sober reflections on Yoruba symbolism, has also helped me bridge the sociocultural divide. In addition, Robert Harms first stimulated my historiographic interest and helped me identify the role of symbolic ambiguity in Yoruba political maneuvering. This brings me to the multiplicity of methods deployed and debates addressed in this study—old-fashioned functionalism, corporation theory, conflict theory, event history, historical practice, semiotics, textual exegesis, deconstruction, and finally, reflections on Africanist discourse. If the list reads like a bad postmodern joke, it is not intended as such, but rather seeks a contemporary synthesis of anthropological traditions and tools with Yoruba interpretive practices, and it develops an argument about conceptualizing power. There is a certain amount of autobiography built into this sequence, but it is also motivated by the conviction that a more critical anthropology should not reject its history but should build on it by taking it into account.

This has been the strategy of my own textual revisions. At the Smithsonian Institution, a predoctoral fellowship supported the writing of my dissertation (1985–86) under the challenging guidance of Ivan Karp, who encouraged me to think more about agency and subversion. Two postdoctoral years at Columbia University's Society of Fellows in the Humanities (1987–89) allowed me to rewrite the manuscript along more interpretive lines. There—and in the wider anthropological community—I gained greatly from discussions with George Bond, Lambros Comitas, Joan Vincent, Harvey Pitkin, Elliott Skinner, Constance Sutton, Richard Andrews, Peter Sahlins, Susan Manning, Gauri Viswanathan, and Loretta Nassar, many of whom encouraged me to tackle larger issues in critical theory and cultural studies. In addition, Roland Abiodun offered exegetical insights into ritual symbols, while Michael Afolayan transcribed and translated many of my ritual-language recordings, including the selections in chapter 5. For this Yoruba expertise and generous assistance I am grateful. Thanks to David Brown I enjoyed an initial introduction to Santería in New York and New Jersey, followed by many comparative ethnographic and theoretical discussions. Most recently, at the University of Chicago, I have gained much from the cartographic skills of Carol Saller and from sharing work and ideas with Jean and John Comaroff, Ralph Austen, Michael Silverstein, William Hanks, Raymond Fogelson, Bernard Cohn, Sharon Stephens, Marshall Sahlins, Nancy Munn, David Brent, Christopher Taylor, Marilyn Ivy, Milton Singer, and Robin Derby. All of these latter friends and colleagues offered constructive criticisms and comparative insights which have helped to shape this study in its final stages—of course the usual disclaimers apply.

Finally, my deepest gratitude goes to my parents: to my mother, whose personal, intellectual, and aesthetic qualities remain the greatest gift; and to my father, whose Africanist contributions, political perspectives, intellectual passion, and critical spirit pervade the subtexts of these pages.

Chapter 1 has appeared as "The Historiography of Yoruba Myth and Ritual" in *History in Africa* 14 (1987): 1–25, while chapter 8 was published as "Things Fell Apart? Yoruba Responses to the 1983 Elections in Ondo State, Nigeria" in *The Journal of Modern African Studies* 25, no. 3 (1987): 489–503. An abbreviated version of chapter 4 appears as "The Embodiment of Paradox: Yoruba Kingship and Female Power" in *Cultural Anthropology* 6, no. 2 (1991): 212–29. Permission to reprint this material is gratefully acknowledged.

A NOTE ON ORTHOGRAPHY

Yoruba terms and texts in this study follow contemporary Yoruba orthographic conventions. All vowels (including the nasalized *n*) are either high-tone (marked by an acute accent), mid-tone (unmarked), or low-tone (marked by a grave accent). Tonal glides can be inferred from their context—a rising glide occurs when a low tone precedes a high tone, while a falling glide occurs when a high tone precedes a low one. The close vowels *e* and *o* are unmarked and are pronounced like the "long" English vowels *a* and *o*, as in *fate* and *rope*; while their open forms, marked by a dot underneath (*ẹ* and *ọ*) are pronounced like the "short" English vowels *e* and *o*, as in *pet* and *pot*. The voiceless sibilant *ṣ*, also marked by a dot, is pronounced like the *sh* in *ship*.

In English text, Yoruba proper names remain unmarked, including names of deities—such as Shango, Eshu, Oshun, Yemoja, and even orisha (the term for deity) when used in the name of a cult. In Yoruba text, the same terms are marked with accents (*Ṣàngó, Èṣù, Ọ̀ṣun, Yemọja,* and *òrìṣà),* as are other Yoruba terms used within English text (including cult, kingship, and chieftaincy titles). I have separated English from Yoruba orthographies to avoid the confusing mixes (e.g., Sango, Osun) one often finds in the literature and to facilitate recognition for the English reader.

Certain texts also reflect dialect variation in ritual as well as ordinary language use. These variations represent actual speech as it was recorded, and they should be taken as sociolinguistic facts—even when Oyo and Ekiti dialects are mixed in the same phrase—rather than as transcription errors.

INTRODUCTION

C ritical approaches to Africanist ethnography question its methods, categories, and epistemological claims as inventions of a colonial mentality, or what Mudimbe (1988:69) calls "a philosophy of conquest." This critique is pitched directly against the classic ethnographies that were produced as much for colonial officers as for growing numbers of anthropologists, but it challenges the very possibility of ethnography itself. In British social anthropology, for example, functionalism incorporated the practical units of administrative overrule into its theoretical lexicon. "Tribes," chiefdoms, lineages, and kinship systems represented the "patterns of authority" that were officially sanctioned—even as they were altered—by the British Crown. Moreover, ethnographic fictions occluded the politics of the colonial situation, with societies depicted as ethnically "pure," located in a timeless world of an ethnographic present which generally excluded the colonial state. But even as this ethnographic vision expanded to embrace history, change, and imperial intervention, the "colonial gaze" endured. And, as the more radical argument goes, it still endures, implicitly, in any ethnography which treats Africans as objects of science, symbols of alterity, or even victims of oppression, rather than as agents of their own histories and sociocultural transformations.

The present study of Yoruba religion and politics—what I have recast as a *hermeneutics of power*—responds to this challenge by focusing on indigenous forms of knowledge and understanding which structure and restructure the Yoruba world. This study is not an exercise in ethnophilosophy, seeking mystical participation in some Yoruba "soul" or "mind," but offers rather a corrective to such hypostasizing illusions.[1] The Yoruba are not ruled by timeless traditions, but—like any people—have, make, and write their own history in different idioms and registers and from multiple perspectives. Nor is Yoruba culture restricted to Yorubaland, or even to modern Nigeria and the Republic of Benin; it has been disseminated through the New World trade in human cargo to construct Yoruba visions of ritual empire abroad. The Candomblé and Macumba religions of Brazil, practitioners of Santería in Cuba, Puerto Rico, Venezuela, and North America, Shango worship in Trinidad, Grenada, and Barbados, and aspects of Haitian

Vodoun are only the most explicit manifestations of Yoruba culture within the black diaspora.[2]

THE GLOBAL VILLAGE

Scholars of contemporary Yoruba culture must recognize that the Yoruba belong to the modern world—or, perhaps more accurately, to the postmodern world. Today, Yoruba language and culture is taught in Nigerian high schools and universities, "traditional" herbalists are licensed by the state, and physics professors consult diviners, while businessmen, "cash madams," army officers, and politicians protect themselves with *jùjú* medicines and educate their children abroad (if they can muster the foreign exchange). Nor are "traditional" practices lost on Yoruba Christians and Muslims, despite their sometimes-explicit disavowals of "paganism." Even the Yoruba diaspora is taking new turns. Practitioners of *òrìṣà* worship in Brazil, the Caribbean, and the United States, including Jews and gentiles as well as Hispanics and African-Americans, charter flights to Nigeria and converge on Ile-Ife (the cosmographic center of the Yoruba world) to attend world conferences on Yoruba religion, where they read papers, make sacrifices (*ètùtù*), and reflect on their transnational identities. And in complementary rotation, well-connected Nigerian practitioners attend similar conferences in the Americas, flying to such cities as Bahia, New York, and Miami. This larger community has also generated new internal schisms, with some African-Americans breaking ranks with the Santería *cabildos* (temples of worship). Today John Mason runs a Yoruba theological arch-ministry in Brooklyn. And the former civil-rights activist H. R. H. Oba Ofuntola Oseijeman Adelabu Adefunmi I (aka Walter Serge King) heads Oyotunji Village in South Carolina.

Clearly the Yoruba world is no "traditional" ethnographic object, but has taken on truly global proportions. The writings of Nobel Laureate Wole Soyinka have entered the mainstream of great literature and criticism. In music, King Sunny Ade and Fela Anikulapo Kuti pack European and American concert halls with expatriate Africans, hip-hop blacks, and turned-on whites. And within the moral and conceptual architecture of Christianity and academia, Yoruba scholars have developed a monumental tradition. Western scholars since Leo Frobenius (1913) and A. B. Ellis (1894) have established the Yoruba as a *locus classicus* of African "civilization" and philosophical achievement, drawing parallels with ancient Greece and Rome and tracing dubious origins from ancient Egypt. This discourse was appropriated by Yoruba proto-nationalists to establish a noble ethnic pedigree in colonial Nigeria, and the genealogy persists among the Yoruba elite today. In a parallel discourse, Yoruba Christians who were commanded to forswear the religion of their ancestors have "rewritten" Christianity into òrìṣà worship by revising myths of origin (as I argue in chapter 9) or by perceiving nascent Christian intuitions in Yoruba religion (e.g., Idowu 1962; Awolalu 1979). And within the more secular contexts of Nigerian nationalism and independence, Yoruba scholars repossessed the riches of their culture in what have become classic studies. Jacob Ade Ajayi's Ibadan History Series, Wande Abimbola's exegetical compendia of Ifa divination texts, Roland Abiodun's insights into Yoruba aesthetics, S. A. Babalola's analyses of *ijálá* chants, and N. A. Fadipe's and G. J. A. Ojo's books on Yoruba sociology and culture are among the invaluable exemplars of this trend.[3]

Thus for many decades it has not been possible or conscionable for non-Yoruba scholars to write "about" or "for" the Yoruba, but rather with the Yoruba, within a complex discursive field. Today the field of Yoruba studies, however, is ideologically divided and at times hotly contested, and any serious study is bound to draw fire. Some Yoruba scholars in Nigeria understandably resent the encroachment of foreigners with insatiable appetites for cultural plunder. As the financial resources of Nigerian universities dwindle, these tensions inevitably intensify. Furthermore, studies of òrìṣà worship are politically compromised from the start, since practitioners resent the betrayal of secrets—a charge which can apply to the most superficial account of a myth or sacrifice. And indeed, as the talking drummers warn, the ethnographer must "walk cautiously" and with respect, since the officializing consequences of documenting traditions, including something as basic as a dynastic genealogy, can unleash political havoc in a local community over access to titles and resources. I have taken a number of risks which I hope will be forgiven, and I protect myself and others with the methodological disclaimer—meant with full sincerity—that all ethnographic facts are literary fictions and cannot be used as reliable evidence in a Nigerian court of law.

Within the larger and more "applied" reaches of Yoruba scholarship, different cleavages divide the field. In America, practitioners of Santería—many of whom read and even write about their religion—are grossly misrepresented by the popular media (including the television show "Miami Vice") and are sometimes prosecuted by animal-rights activists who buy meat from butchers but are somehow offended when the slaughter and consumption of animals is endowed with more than secular intent. Although I have not yet studied Santería as such, my Yoruba photographs of animal sacrifices may violate norms of privacy in the American *cabildos*, which recognize their kinship with Yoruba *òrìṣà* cults.[4] This extreme sensitivity to the public gaze is important because it shows how ritual idioms and boundaries are invested with new political meanings in different ethnic, historical, and national contexts. In addition, American racial politics has intensified intellectual debate, with some African-American scholar-practitioners "purging" Yoruba religion of its New World "corruptions." I do not take sides on this sectarian issue, but I recognize its significance in contemporary North America as an emerging black-nationalist discourse.

And finally, in the groves of American academe, Yoruba culture has inspired fundamental challenges to the canonical taxonomies of African and African-American art and literature established by more conventional scholarship. Robert F. Thompson's pathbreaking research on Yoruba aesthetics in West Africa and the black diaspora cultures has revolutionized the meaning of "African art," by taking "objects" out of descriptive typologies and throwing them back into metaphysical motion. His exceptional sensitivity to interior visions and voices has shifted the locus of explanation away from "us" and onto the "other," tapping the wellsprings of Yoruba knowledge and the critical power of its interpretive traditions. In a similar reversal of commanding rhetorics, Henry Louis Gates's use of Yoruba religion as a model of black textuality and signification has revolutionized research in black literature and literary theory, by privileging *vernacular* strategies of figuration and revision. Conventional scholarship resists these approaches because it is otherwise transformed by them—turned upside down, revalued, and restructured. This is, my study will argue, just how Yoruba ritual and cosmology transform dominant discourses and the authority structures which they uphold.

The dissemination of the deities and the building of new *cabildos* and shrines, the attributes of Yoruba identity and the transnational construction of ritual genealogies, new principles of recruitment and new boundaries of exclusion, the polyvocalities of ritual symbols and the political implications of Yoruba scholarship—all generate powerful debates in the contexts sketched above. It is not my intention to merely acknowledge these larger issues, but to lay an ethnographic foundation which will illuminate their growing significance.

THE HERMENEUTICS OF POWER

The interpretive strategy developed in this study follows the methodological reversals of Thompson and Gates by working toward those indigenous or vernacular forms of knowledge and understanding which render Yoruba politics, history, and religious experience intelligible—not only to "us," but to the Yoruba themselves. Similar approaches are not new to anthropology. Marcel Griaule's (1948) "conversations" with Ogotemmeli, the blind Dogon sage of Mali, offered esoteric visions of the Dogon social universe which dazzled the West with their philosophical complexity.[5] Clifford Geertz's (1973) "thick descriptions" of Balinese (and Javanese) cultural and aesthetic sensibilities elevated the role of symbolic exegesis and phenomenology in understanding social life. Their approaches offered valuable alternatives to scientistic reductions of religious phenomena "into terms of social function and of the social structure which they serve to maintain" (Fortes and Evans-Pritchard 1940:17). But ultimately, these more interpretive approaches reverse the same arrows, reducing social reality to meaning. For Griaule, Dogon cosmology provides "a demonstration, summary but complete, of the functioning of society" (quoted in Clifford 1983:144). And even Geertz's seminal study (1980) of the Balinese "theatre state" concludes with political actors seeking religious ends—that is, with politics, in the last instance, serving ritual experience.

The hermeneutical approach developed in this study seeks to transcend the "function" vs. "meaning" antinomy (cf. Augé 1979) by building on the insights of both anthropological traditions without privileging either "society" or "culture." What I suggest is that both sets of paradigms illuminate different fields of knowledge/power relations within their sociocultural "objects" of analysis. One does not become a vulgar functionalist by recognizing that, *from an official point of view,* royal ritual maintains political authority. Only when one claims that this perspective subsumes and explains all others does the reductionist epithet apply. For example, from the perspective of a Yoruba king and his palace officials, successful ritual fructifies women and land, neutralizes witches and enemies, purifies the kingdom, and protects the king, ensuring his sovereignty from one year to the next. But this perspective cannot account for the "deeper," hidden discourses which inform the logic of ritual empowerment within the royal òrìṣà cults and from competing ritual centers and political points of view. Needed is an interpretive frame which accounts for both the superficiality of official discourse (what Griaule called exoteric knowledge or "paroles de face") and the secrecy surrounding those deeper understandings (Griaule's esoteric knowledge or "la parole claire") which sustain possibilities of radical revision and are invoked, at critical moments, to precipitate political change.

Neither does one become a cultural reductionist by recognizing that certain master tropes and narratives (or what Pierre Bourdieu [1977:96–158] calls "generative schemes") *configure* social and political relations—between men and women, indigenes and strangers, allies and enemies, kith and kin, or between a king, his chiefs, and the national state. If cultural models shape material relations, including those of local and regional production and exchange, they do not do so in a strictly determinate sense, but dialectically, under historical conditions of political and economic competition and transformation. In both the ordinary contexts of everyday life and the ritually marked contexts of cosmological renewal, such Yoruba idioms are continuously contested, either openly, in heated debate, or implicitly, in deeper interpretations of royal icons and ritual symbols. As this study will illustrate, cosmological meanings are never simply fixed, but shift between deep and official levels to *index* the power which renders them efficacious and dangerous or the authority which establishes them as orthodox and safe.

Where, then, do we stand? With one foot in "society" and the other in "culture"? How can we avoid the dialectical tautologies which plague such mediating concepts as Bourdieu's (1977) "habitus" or Anthony Giddens's (1979:69–73; 1984:1–40) "structuration"—concepts which, by presupposing the objective structures which agents actively reproduce, forsake any explanatory power? I do not wish to belittle these contributions toward de-essentializing what should remain heuristic concepts of social structure and toward retheorizing the significance of agency. The idea that social (including political and economic) structures are instantiated through practical activity highlights our awareness of different subjective orientations to the world, revealing the social significance of embodied forms of knowledge and power in "natural" taxonomies and everyday routines. Such perspectives open up vistas of implicit meanings which are otherwise buried within bodies personal and social. But what, in the last instance, do concepts like "habitus" and "structuration" explain? Bourdieu's social actors remain Giddens's cultural dopes, "doomed to reproduce their world mindlessly, without its contradictions leaving any mark on their awareness—at least until a crisis (in the form of 'culture contact' or the emergence of class division) initiates a process of overt struggle" (J. Comaroff 1985:5). For Bourdieu, practical consciousness is a form of tacit knowledge, lacking discursive articulation, apperception, and critical reflection. If it embodies and reproduces its "objective" conditions, it lacks—barring external intervention or internal class formation—the critical power to change them.

A hermeneutical focus addresses these problems by examining how indigenous forms of knowledge and power constitute the critical conditions of social reproduction and change.[6] Embedded—as this study argues—in Yoruba cosmology, these conditions are critical in several important and related senses of the term. First, they are critical in the ordinary sense of being crucial, "essential," and fundamental to the Yoruba world. Deep truths *(imọ jinlẹ̀)*, secret mysteries *(awo)*, even history *(itàn)* and tradition *(àṣà)* gloss the sacred foundations of Yoruba social life into divisions of an archive of knowledge. Second, they are critical in the transcendental sense that they render Yoruba politics and social experience possible—according to an official set of cosmological categories that are semantically revalued by "deeper" knowledge-claims. Third, they are critical in the evaluative and deconstructive sense that the deeper meanings of ritual signs and discourses contradict, destabilize, and even subvert official orthodoxies. As we shall see, deep knowledge is by definition dangerous and heterodox because it opposes official charters of kingship and authority and reconfigures hegemonic taxonomies of the natural and spiritual world.[7] And fourth—at the deepest (and most controversial) level—cosmological conditions are critical in the self-reflexive sense, affording self-conscious awareness of the contradictions underlying effective government and of the role of human agency in "rewriting" official illusions of legitimacy. It is not, I should emphasize, the "contents" of these levels of knowledge which remain stable—these, as we shall see, are quite fluid—but their more pragmatic levels of articulation into public (exoteric) and restricted (esoteric) forms, and the interpretive possibilities which such distinctions maintain.

The critical dimensions of this hermeneutical system sustain potentials for sociopolitical change within deeper and necessary visions of the truth. If these restricted interpretations are intrinsically powerful, the empirical question which this study addresses is under what conditions such power is actualized. Here I break ranks with more sensitive scholars who are content to locate resistance within the imagination. To be sure, meaningful change requires visions of alternative worlds which challenge the dominant sociopolitical order, but such visions do not in and of themselves qualify as effective strategy. Plenty of lunatics have utopian dreams, but only certain heterodoxies mobilize popular support and collective action. If the deeper dimensions of Yoruba ritual and cosmology safeguard a space for hidden histories and subversive claims, they do so under the cloak of enshrined traditions which only exceptionally restructure the sociopolitical order in radical ways. These exceptions prove the interpretive "rules," demonstrating that the power invoked by deep knowledge-claims is real and must be taken seriously.

The hermeneutics of power in Yoruba society reconstructs our vision of a social totality and reveals the forms of knowledge and, indeed, critical consciousness which render the Yoruba world possible and intelligible.[8] It is, I maintain, a *vernacular* hermeneutics which relates knowledge to power in all of the ways sketched above—as public definitions of the given world, as sectional heterodoxies of rival historical memories, and at the hidden cosmological center, as critical reflection on the political contradictions and pragmatic constraints which make esoteric knowledge powerful. The hermeneutics of power is a critical theory which is put into ritual practice. If it "functions" to maintain political authority, this study will also illustrate how it has invoked the power to depose kings, initiate new dynasties, precipitate political fission, establish military alliances, and bring Christianity, colonialism, and national party politics within its ritual fields of command. To understand how such interpretive practices can reproduce and transform authority structures or effectively resist hegemonic interventions, we must characterize them not simply on their own terms, but in relation to each other. We thereby preserve the holism of Yoruba society while "excavating" (as Foucault would say) its deeper voices, revealing how the construction of political authority is contested from below.

STRUCTURE AND HISTORY, HEGEMONY AND RESISTANCE

The hermeneutical principles outlined above bear a family resemblance to Sahlins's (1981, 1985) work on the cultural production of history and to the Comaroffs' studies of hegemony and resistance (J. Comaroff [1985]; Comaroff and Comaroff 1991). I will return to this connection in the Conclusion, where a more general theory of ritual, power, and history will develop some wider implications of the Yoruba material. Here I can only signpost, in abbreviated and somewhat dismembered form, the relevance of Sahlins's concepts of "practical revaluation," "symbolic risk," and "conjunctural structure" to the tripartite organization of my study.

Part 1 examines the history and politics of Yoruba "traditions," introducing the classic myths and rituals of ancient Ife and Old Oyo as they were reviewed and revised by contesting polities and renewed by the Ekiti kingdom of Ayede (where I conducted my field research). The first chapter is mainly historiographic, illustrating how rituals of subordinate kingdoms preserved subversive historical memories vis-à-vis the expanding Oyo empire. Such "preservation" should not be taken too literally, since it was the claims of historicity rather than historical accuracy which, I argue, were sustained by an Ife-centric ritual field. Nonetheless, as my research on contemporary ritual confirms, òrìṣà cults do preserve indigenous (and carefully archived) records of former migrations and allegiances to rival kings—in their praises, songs, iconography, dialects of spirit possession, and even in their talking-drum texts. These idioms possess historical significance in the conventional sense of the term, and the piecing together of historical events with recorded traditions and their narrative conventions is plausible for eighteenth- and nineteenth-century Yorubaland, given the quality of written histories available (e.g., Ajayi 1974; Johnson 1921; Law 1977).

Chapters 2 and 3 focus more intensively on the history and politics of Ayede, a military kingdom which sprang up during the nineteenth-century wars to become a significant player in regional and local power politics. Given its relatively recent arrival (c. 1850) as a "traditional" Yoruba kingdom, and its highly strategic location along the eastern border of the former Ibadan empire (see map 2), it provides an ideal case for pinpointing shifting ritual configurations and for documenting the practical role of òrìṣà cults in shaping major political events and transformations. These chapters illustrate—in specific political and historical contexts—how certain cultural categories and mytho-historical narratives *(itàn)* were ritually deployed to restructure power relations.

If Part 1 represents the "practical revaluation" of cultural categories within and between Yoruba kingdoms, Part 2 examines the hermeneutical principles which make such revaluations possible. Here I explore the "deeper" and more "dangerous" dimensions of Yoruba ritual and knowledge within Ayede, focusing on sacred kingship (chapter 4), ritual language (chapter 5), and the "unstable" pantheon of the òrìṣà (chapter 6). In a sense, these chapters are about "symbolic risk" and "selective reification" (Sahlins 1985:xiv)—i.e., the semantic revision of symbolic reference and the pragmatic privileging of specific interpretations—and they explain why ritual is in fact such a risky business for all who manipulate and receive its regenerative powers. And it is here that the power of hidden forms of knowledge is made explicit, *contra* authority, as a form of political action.

Finally, Part 3, on hegemony and resistance, shows how the hermeneutical dimensions of Yoruba cosmology shaped initial Christian and colonial encounters, as well as effective protest against the 1983 gubernatorial elections in Ondo State.[9] The chapters of this section deal with "the structure of the conjuncture" between two world orders at different moments of confrontation—between "pagans" and Christians, the colonized and the colonizers, as well as between the local community and the Shagari government. Chapter 7 examines how violent clashes between Ayede's Christians and "pagans" *extended* the critical horizons of òrìṣà worship to encapsulate the colonial state. Chapter 8 reveals how the ritual construction of national party politics within Ayede informed the logic of popular protest as symbolic drama and effective political action. And in chapter 9, I reflect back on the "vernacular" strategies of Bishop Samuel Ajayi Crowther and Rev. Samuel Johnson, two nineteenth-century Yoruba Christians who transformed the church by "rewriting paganism" into missionary prose. In each of these encounters, moments of rupture signal the power of a hermeneutical vision at work, deploying those deep strategies of refiguration and renewal which continue to make Yoruba history.

ONE   HISTORY AND POLITICS

1

Traditions Reviewed:
Ancient Ife and Old Oyo

he historiography of Yoruba traditions—from mythic origins to the mid-nineteenth century—begins with documenting, comparing, and interpreting variant texts. Whereas documentation is inscriptive and comparison descriptive, interpretation is notoriously complex, embracing a variety of approaches within two methodological extremes.[1] The functionalist extreme—what J. D. Y. Peel (1984:112) calls "presentism"—defines myth as a charter of political and ceremonial relations and interprets variant traditions as rival political claims. Myth is by this definition a false reflection of the past because it is continually revised to fit the present. The historicist extreme regards myth as testimony of the past in oral societies, incorporating history into a narrative which resists revision and remains historically valid through fixed chains of oral transmission. Variant traditions, according to this view, are dismissed as aberrations or contaminations of more authentic texts. Neither approach grasps the historicity of Yoruba myths unless the two are somehow combined, for as the historiography of African oral traditions reveals, myth is both political and historical (Miller 1980). This chapter combines functionalist and historicist approaches in an interpretation of Yoruba myths and their variants by examining the critical relationship between Yoruba myth and ritual. The review of mythic origins at ancient Ife and the imperial history of Old Oyo show how Yoruba charters of kingship and political autonomy were ritually "re-viewed" from contesting centers of power.

The prevailing approach to variant Yoruba myths follows Ulli

Beier's historicist readings. Beier (1953, 1955, 1956a, 1956b, 1959, n.d.) explains contradictory accounts of the same mythic events or cultural heroes by treating one of the variants, usually one associated with the more parochial traditions, as a holdover from a pre-Yoruba aboriginal culture which was modified and assimilated by immigrant Yorubas who descended upon ancient Ife to found Yoruba monarchy. Although some of his interpretations are plausible, Beier applies this approach indiscriminately to myth-ritual complexes which do not clearly support the aboriginal theory. A more "diagonal" (Harms 1983) approach to Yoruba myth recognizes the two tendencies in myth itself. The first, in line with classic functionalism, is that myth is indeed a social charter subject to political revision. Variants of Yoruba founding myths illustrate this quite clearly. But the second, historicist principle also obtains—that the more formalized the myth in its mode of transmission, the less easily it submits to political revision. As P. C. Lloyd (1955:28) advises: "Examine the methods by which myths are transmitted; those preserved in ritual or in praise songs are likely to have greater continuity in unaltered forms."

This latter principle is especially significant among the Yoruba, who reenact founding myths of lineages, quarters, towns, and entire kingdoms in installation ceremonies and annual òrìṣà festivals, using talking drums and gongs to communicate textual fragments in extremely formalized modes of transmission. In his monumental *History of the Yorubas*, the Yoruba scholar and clergyman Samuel Johnson recorded that the arọkin, or official Oyo historians—who figured prominently among his primary sources—were also the Aláàfin's (Oyo king's) "bards, drummers and cymbalists" (1921:3). These historians were court functionaries who performed historical narratives in the formalized languages of oríkì (praises), songs, and talking drums during royal and religious rituals. This does not mean that the official Oyo history was free of propaganda; rather, the consolidation and hegemony of the Oyo empire in the seventeenth and eighteenth centuries persists in Oyo ritual, long after the empire succumbed to Fulani *jihad* and internal collapse. The critical relationship between Yoruba myth and ritual, however, is stronger than an indeterminate "lag" effect implies. The thesis of this chapter is that the Yoruba *ritual system* illuminates the politics and history of Yoruba myths and their variant traditions.

The demonstration of this thesis develops in five parts: (1) an illustration of the revision of myth by politics; (2) a discussion of the preservation of myth by ritual to explain why mythic variants occur and why they endure over time; (3) the development of a rudimentary model of the Yoruba ritual system with complementary principles—

emphasizing the unity of the polity and the autonomy of its parts—which extend between kingdoms when an expanding kingdom subjects weaker ones to its authority; (4) the application of this model to Yoruba traditions of Oyo conquest and expansion; and (5) an argument (*pace* Beier) that the Obatala myth-ritual complex belongs to these traditions. I conclude that the Yoruba ritual system sheds new light on the "mystery" of ancient Ife's enduring sacred status.[2]

THE REVISION OF MYTH BY POLITICS

Because all Yoruba myths are to some extent politically motivated, there are no "original" versions with which "corrupt" variants can be compared. Founding myths of kingdoms, for example, are shaped to favor their kings. Even Yoruba traditions of genesis fall into two basic types: creation myths and myths of migration.[3]

Creation myths generally state that in the beginning, Olodumare, the Yoruba High God, had a son, Oduduwa, who climbed down a chain from heaven (*ọrun*, or sky) to an uninhabited world. Since the world was covered with water, Oduduwa placed a handful of earth on it and a rooster on top of the earth. As the rooster began to scratch the earth about, land spread out over the water. According to this myth, Ile-Ife (hereafter called Ife) is the sacred locus of Oduduwa's original descent, where he became the first Yoruba king and fathered future generations of Yoruba kings through sixteen sons. This basic narrative, found with minor variations, is generally thought to express the origin of Yoruba monarchy at Ife, or at least Ife's importance as an early center of political power.[4] Migration myths, on the other hand, tell how Oduduwa, founder of the Yoruba people, came from somewhere in the East. Some myths are vague about his point of departure; others cite Nupeland, Egypt, or Medina, while Johnson's *History* brings Oduduwa from Mecca (Law 1973). In this latter, Oyo version, Oduduwa, son of a Meccan king, rebelled against his father and Islam and fled with his children to Ife, where he founded Yoruba kingship. Of his seven sons in this Oyo account, the first six left Ife to found the kingdoms of Owu, Ketu, Benin, Ila, Sabe, and Popo, while the last born, named Oranyan (or Oranmiyan), succeeded his father at Ife. The myth finishes with an account of the founding of Old Oyo, and herein lies the clue to its political intent.

Once Oranyan was settled in Ife and became sufficiently strong, he set out to overthrow the "Meccan" dynasty of his forefathers. Delegating one of his father's slaves to worship the *òrìṣà* (deities) in his absence, Oranyan traveled northeast with an army through Nupeland, until he reached the banks of the Niger. Here his way was blocked, but rather than suffer the humiliation of failure, he settled in the bush and built the town of Oyo Ile, which later became the capital of the formidable Oyo empire. Whatever the historicity of this migration myth may be, its political intentions are clear. The idiom of migration, as opposed to cosmological descent, underplays the political and ritual authority accorded to Ife by the creation myth, for Ife figures as a place of arrival and temporary kingship, not as the locus of origin. In fact, the attribution of Oduduwa's paternity to a Meccan king places the founder of the Yorubas outside the Ife cosmological scheme altogether. Furthermore, the migration myth amounts to a flat denial of Ife kingship. When Oranyan left Ife to avenge his father (or grandfather, depending on the variant), he placed a slave to serve the òrìṣà and safeguard the kingship. The Oyo myths are quite explicit on this point. In Johnson's *History* (1921:12), the *Adímú*, as he was initially called, was the son of a female slave chosen for sacrifice but temporarily reprieved when discovered to be pregnant. This child was dedicated to the perpetual service of the gods, especially Obatala, to whom his mother was eventually sacrificed. Hence the renaming of his title as the Ọ̀ni of Ife, where Ọ̀ni allegedly is a contraction of ọmọ olúwọ ni, "he is the son of a sacrifice."[5] Since slaves as well as commoners were barred from highest office, this pseudo-etymology and its mythical basis effectively deny the Ọ̀ni's royal pedigree.[6]

Founding myths of other Yoruba kingdoms also contradict official Oyo traditions. Whereas local versions trace their origins from Ife, Oyo variants trace their foundings from Oyo. In Ondo, for example, just southeast of Ife and beyond the southern limits of the Old Oyo empire, local founding myths trace Ondo origins from Ife and make no mention of Oyo:

> The story is that one of Oduduwa's wives bore twins. Now in
> those ancient days twins were killed in Yorubaland and
> Oduduwa, fearing for the safety of his children and his wife,
> sent her away from Ife so she might settle in some distant place.
> At the head of the followers whom Oduduwa had given her, the
> woman wandered about in the forest for many years. The twins
> grew up and finally the senior one, a male child, founded the
> town of Epe, while the junior one, a woman called Pupupupu,
> founded the town of Ondo (Beier 1956a:238).

In addition to making several other claims, this myth validates Ondo's political sovereignty and unique identity in the idiom of dynastic de-

scent. The Oyo version in Johnson's *History* (1921:25), however, contradicts the Ife-centric genealogy:

> It happened once upon a time when the practice (of killing
> twins) still prevailed that one of the wives of the ALAFIN (king
> Ajaka) gave birth to twins, and the king was loth to destroy
> them, he thereupon gave orders that they should be removed—
> with the mother—to a remote part of the kingdom and there
> remain and be regarded as dead. So she left with a large number
> of friends and retinue to the site of the present Ode Ondo, then
> sparsely peopled by a tribe named Idoko, and there settled,
> hence the term "Ondo", signifying the "Settlers".

In this version, the *Aláàfin* Ajaka replaces Oduduwa as the father of
Ondo's founder within the same theme of saving infant twins. Since
Ajaka is one of Oranyan's sons, the twins would be Oranyan's grand-
children. Thus in the Ondo version, some equality between the founders of Ondo and Oyo is implied by their horizontal ties of siblingship
(both are Oduduwa's children); the Oyo version asserts Ondo's subordinate status and direct descent from Oyo through the vertical ties of
filiation between Oranyan, Ajaka, and the twins. At the same time, the
Oyo political perspective regards Ondo as "remote" and the twins as
"dead."

A similar tension exists between local and Oyo traditions of Ilesha
kingdom. Located east of Ife and Old Oyo, Ilesha remained independent enough to oppose Oyo policy (Mabogunje and Omer-Cooper
1971:13). A local tradition relates, in considerable detail, how
Ajibogun, a descendant of Oduduwa, left Ife to found Ilesha (Oni
n.d.:12–15). As in Ondo's local founding myth, there is no mention of
Oyo. According to Johnson (1921:22), however, Oyo designed the
Ilesha monarchy:

> When the town of Ilesha was to be laid out a special messenger
> was sent to the ALAFIN to ask for the help of one of the princes
> to lay out the town on the same plan as the ancient city of Oyo.
> That prince ruled for some years at Ilesha.

This Oyo tradition asserts Ilesha's subjection to Oyo leadership and
models of government. Similar divergencies exist between local and
Oyo versions of the founding myths of Ede, Egba, Ketu, Ijebu, and most
likely every Yoruba town or kingdom whose claims of political sovereignty and unique identity opposed the power and propaganda of
Old Oyo (see map 1).[7]

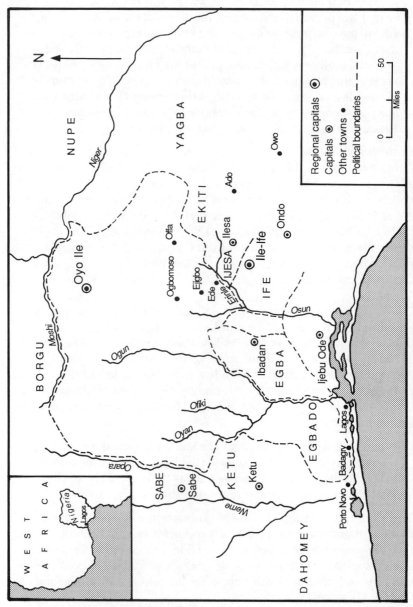

Map 1. The Oyo Empire, c. 1780 (after Law 1977:89)

THE PRESERVATION OF MYTH BY RITUAL

The comparison of local traditions with Johnson's Oyo-centric *History* shows that non-Oyo Yoruba founding myths were subject to imperial revision. The significance of ritual in this revisionary process is in one sense negative; ritual "preserves" local traditions in its formalized modes of performance and transmission. But it does so with respect to a local center of power which contests the hegemony of rival readings and claims. It also appears that Yoruba ritual communication is so highly formalized, particularly in the surrogate speech of talking drums and gongs, that the traditions encoded and conveyed outlast the political interests which they may initially serve.[8]

The preservation of myth by ritual is most clearly visible in royal installation ceremonies.[9] These ceremonies not only validate the right of a king (*ǫba*) to a beaded crown by tracing his descent back to Ife, but also emphasize the unique identity and corporate unity of his kingdom. This is accomplished partly by the reenactment of its founding, in which coveted details acquire the authority of political charters.[10] In the installation ceremony of the *Awùjalè* of Ijebu, for example, local founding myths are preserved by their reenactment, which was observed and described by Lloyd (1961:7):

> Ijebu myths relate that Obanta was born to a migrant from the east and a daughter of Oduduwa, the Yoruba progenitor and first Oni of Ife. When he set out to found his own kingdom, he travelled westward from Ibu, near Okitipupa, to Ogbere and thus to Itele . . . Here he turned southeast to reach Yemoji and then travelled northwards reaching the now famous market where he met the Oloko of Idoko. Moving westwards again he passed through Ilesha and reached Ijebu-Ode . . . This journey of Obanta is repeated in the installation of each new Awujale.

The ritual mimesis of Ijebu founding myths represents and actively constitutes the legitimate transfer of power to the new incumbent. Themes of Ijebu unity and identity are publicly exalted at these rituals of succession because at no other time is high office so vulnerable to appropriation by a rival faction. The political function of these rituals is to ensure a stable transfer of power by legitimizing the successor and elevating the unity of the kingdom over and above its parts.

What is politically unifying for Ijebu, however, is politically divisive for Oyo. If the *Awùjalè*'s installation rite neglects the *Aláàfin*'s claims of paramountcy, Oyo traditions tell another story. According to Johnson, the *Aláàfin* Jayin, who reigned in the early eighteenth century, sent an *ìlàrí* (a palace representative and often a Shango priest) to settle a land dispute between two towns in an area between Owu and Ife. The *Olówu* of Owu and the *Ọ̀ni* of Ife were unable to resolve the dispute, whereas the *ìlàrí* succeeded and remained to found Ijebu monarchy:

> As it was customary to pay royal honours to the King's messengers out of courtesy, this ilari was accorded royal honours in due form, and he remained there permanently and became King of that region over the Ijebus who up to that time had no tribal "king" of their own and rather held themselves aloof from their neighbours (Johnson 1921:20).

Johnson supports this tradition with a pseudo-etymology of *Awùjalẹ̀* derived from *aqbè-ja-ilẹ̀*, "arbiter of a land dispute"; but this pseudo-etymology and its associated story are rejected by the Ijebu themselves, who trace the title back to Obanta (Law 1977:136).

It is tempting to dismiss the Oyo myth of Ijebu kingship as the political propaganda that it was, but the myths preserved by the *Awùjalẹ̀*'s installation ceremony have their own bias as well. Although the Ijebu myths record a specific migration which the Oyo tradition represses, Ijebu historical memory can be equally selective. Law (ibid., 135–136) relates a tradition from Ondo which describes Oyo intervention in Ijebu under the *Aláàfin* Ajagbo during the latter half of the seventeenth century—how the Ijebu king Ayora was deposed by his people and appealed to Oyo for assistance:

> Ajagbo sent two ilari to Ijebu Ode, the Ijebu capital, to reinstate Ayora, but soon afterwards Ayora was assassinated. Ayora's partisans again appealed to Oyo, and Ajagbo dispatched an army which succeeded in entering Ijebu Ode through their treachery. The ring leaders against Ayora were seized and carried off to Oyo, and a certain Fasojoye was installed as king.

This tradition describes the deposition, reinstallation, and subsequent assassination of an Ijebu king, events which portray the vulnerability of the kingship to internal factionalism and external intervention and which detract from the credibility of Ijebu unity and political autonomy. It is just this type of political rebellion which an installation ceremony would suppress from the public record, favoring traditions of unity, stability, and continuity instead. The Oyo tradition of Ijebu kingship, on the other hand, may allude obliquely to these events. The *ìlàrí* who adjudicated the land dispute in the Oyo variant may refer to those sent by the *Aláàfin* Ajagbo to reinstate Ayora, for Oyo would recognize Ijebu kingship as properly beginning with Oyo intervention. The divergent traditions of Ijebu kingship, therefore, are both politically motivated; the Ijebu variant, preserved by ritual, is not in all aspects more faithful to fact, but selects its past to officially represent the corporate identity and unity of its present and presumptively perpetual kingdom.

THE RITUAL SYSTEM

The ọba's installation ceremony clearly illustrates how ritual preserves myth, but it should not be confused with the annual cycle of calendrical rites which propitiate the òrìṣà (deities) of the Yoruba pantheon. Yoruba òrìṣà worship represents, in its sacred and symbolic idioms, not just the unity of the kingdom but also the diversity of its parts; its cult organization and performance cycle articulate with the structure of Yoruba government. Variable bases of cult-group recruitment correspond to different levels of political segmentation: the king "owns" an òrìṣà for the town (ìlú) as a whole, chiefs for their quarters (àdúgbò), and subchiefs (often elders) for their lineages (ìdílé) clustered within (but sometimes crosscutting) quarters.[11] In Old Oyo, for example, the Shango cult was "owned" by the Aláàfin and associated with his sacred status; the central shrine within the royal quarter had secondary associations in nonroyal quarters, while cults of chiefs included Sopono and Jabata in Laguna quarter, Oranuan in Agbakin, Oya in Agunpopo. Oro in Jabata, etc., with secondary and domestic shrines distributed within and between them (Morton-Williams 1964).

Although Yoruba polities and pantheons vary widely between different subcultural groups—ritual organization, I will argue, covaries with political organization—the ritual system *in abstracto* highlights the complementary principles of Yoruba government, which are horizontal opposition between corporate political units (àdúgbò) and their vertical inclusion within the kingdom (ìlú) at large.[12] Whereas a king's òrìṣà festivals represent the town as cosmos and community, those vested under chiefs represent its complementary parts (J. D. Y. Peel 1979:131–133).

In its basic form the Yoruba kingdom is a town ruled by an ọba together with his ìwàrèfà council of civil chiefs, and it is surrounded by lineage-held lands and uncultivated bush. Powerful towns, however, often dominated weaker neighbors, creating "complex" kingdoms with metropolitan capitals and subordinate towns. Former kings of vanquished towns dropped in status from ọba to baálẹ̀, denoting their subjection to the metropolitan capital. The unity of these complex kingdoms was thus subject to a double tension. Within the capital, a powerful chief could break away with his quarter (and clients from other quarters) to establish his own kingdom; local Yoruba histories are full of such accounts. Beyond the capital, subordinate towns could grow powerful enough to assert their independence. These jurisdictions were contested in idioms of dynastic descent. If the *baálè* of a subordinate town traced his descent from Oduduwa and migration from Ife, he could challenge the *ọba*'s claim to a beaded crown and legitimize political competition for independent or dominant status. The *ọba*'s mythic charters of kingship were so important and jealously guarded that their "authenticity" was enforced.[13] How did subversive founding myths persist in the face of coercive censorship and repression? They were preserved, it seems, by rituals, in the hidden meanings of their symbols.

A brief description of a subordinate-town ritual supports this hypothesis. In the festival of Iya Mapo, the inhabitants of Igbeti, a subordinate town of Old Oyo situated twenty miles southwest of the early capital, worship four hill deities—Iya Mapo, Santo, Erugba, and Sino—which are identified with local landmarks.[14] The festival commemorates the founding of Igbeti with sacrifices to the *òrìṣà* and prayers for rain, fertility, and the general well-being of the town. The town's *baálè* (he cannot be an *ọba*, for that would contravene Oyo's metropolitan status) venerates his ancestors, whose history and notable deeds are recounted on talking drums and praised by the court bard (*akigbe*). The festival concludes with propitiations to Shango, the Oyo *òrìṣà* of the *Aláàfin*'s divinity, and a ritual "chase" by the Shango priest—perhaps an expression of Igbeti's surrender and ultimate subservience to Oyo. Local founding myths are at least partially preserved in this fashion. Not openly asserted by ritual, they are cloaked in the praises of the *òrìṣà* and baálè, in the secrets of symbols and in the language of the drums.

A widespread charter of subordinate-town rituals derives from euphemisms of conquest asserted by the capital.[15] Yoruba ideas of political authority require that a king rule by virtue of his royal genealogy and reputable judgment, not by the military power of his ancestors. For this reason, conquest is rarely mentioned in the official founding myths of kingdoms. Instead, conquest is "sweetened" by the fiction that the original ruler of a town invited the conqueror to assume leadership so that he—the former king—could thereby devote himself entirely to town rituals (Lloyd 1955:24). Such a euphemistic charter serves a double function: if it maintains the legitimacy of a conquering king, it also safeguards the rights of displaced rulers to preserve and worship their specific *òrìṣà*. Powerful kings could prohibit subversive myths, but could not, according to their own euphemistic charters of leadership, prohibit implicitly subversive rituals.

The Yoruba ritual system thus contains the contradictions of Yoruba government: within the town, ritual mediates between the king and his chiefs; within complex kingdoms, it mediates between the center and the periphery. From this principle of mediation emerges a model of the Yoruba ritual system which accounts for the heterogeneity of Yoruba founding myths. For every capital town and its subordinate towns, the rituals of the king—his royal installation ceremony and annual *òrìṣà* festivals—celebrate and objectify the unity of the kingdom as a whole. Conversely, rituals of the subordinate towns—the commemoration of local rulers *(baálè)* and the worship of their *òrìṣà*— implicitly challenge the unity of the kingdom by expressing the corporate autonomy of its parts. Whereas rituals of the metropole generate and sustain a unified body of official mythic traditions, rituals of the periphery generate and sustain an alternative corpus of their own distinctive founding myths. The strength of this model (a gross simplification of a complex empirical reality which will be examined later in greater ethnographic detail) is that it encompasses relationships between kingdoms as well as within them.[16] From this wider, more inclusive perspective, divergent traditions between Old Oyo and its vassal kingdoms can be located in the history and politics of imperial conquest and incorporation.

THE OYO EMPIRE

The development of Oyo into a major West African empire is already a subject of considerable research and debate.[17] Oyo's initial growth is usually attributed to its advantageous location along major trade routes. Close to the Niger River, Oyo participated in trans-savanna trade from Gonja to the Hausa kingdoms and in the kola trade from the forest to the savanna. In the latter decades of the seventeenth century, Oyo began to export slaves to the coast, using routes which necessitated subjugation and control of Dahomean territories and which extended further to the east as well. Cavalry and administrative bureaucracy combined commercial expansion with imperial conquest and rule (Lloyd 1971:9; Law 1975).

As Oyo expanded its frontiers, the subject kingdoms brought under its authority fell, according to Law (1977:84–185), into three categories:

1. The area that, to use Ajayi's phrase, 'owed direct allegiance to the Alafin', and was subject to a relatively centralized

administration from the capital. The Oyo Yoruba formed the core of this area, but it also came to include some of the Igbomina and Ekiti Yoruba to the east and some of the Egbado, Awori and Anago Yoruba to the south.

2. The kingdoms whose dynasties were traditionally supposed to be descended from Oduduwa, the legendary king of Ile Ife, and over whom the *Alafin* claimed authority as the legitimate successor to Oduduwa's kingship. Of these perhaps only the Egba were in any real sense subject to Oyo, but others (such as Ijesa) were prepared to acknowledge loosely the suzerainty (or at least the senior status) of the *Alafin*.

3. States outside the Ife dynastic system which paid tribute to Oyo, such as Dahomey.

In the analysis of divergent founding myths, towns and kingdoms of category 3 are largely irrelevant, for they lay outside the Ife ritual field entirely. Kingdoms of category 2 were most likely to openly acknowledge founding myths which contradicted Oyo claims of seniority, for as discrete polities they possessed greater autonomy from Oyo rule than those of category 1. Since these latter were most fully incorporated into Oyo administration, they were more likely compelled to pay official lip service to Oyo-centric founding myths, restricting Ife-centric rival traditions to esoteric ritual knowledge. Local deviations from Oyo myths at this level were politically most subversive.

In order to administer its empire, the Oyo capital developed a uniquely complex palace organization. Beneath the *Aláàfin* were three titled eunuchs: *Ọtún Ìwèfà*, *Ọnà Ìwèfà*, and *Òsì Ìwèfà*, whose respective spheres of competence were religious, judicial, and political (Lloyd 1971:10). The *Ọtún Ìwèfà* controlled the Shango cult, the *Ọnà Ìwèfà* heard disputes between vassal kingdoms, and the *Òsì Ìwèfà* represented the *Aláàfin* in public. Of these three offices, the *Ọtún Ìwèfà*, heading the Shango cult with a staff of *ajẹlẹ* (the king's resident overlords) and *ìlàrí* (the king's messengers), was most closely involved with the empire's administration. Among the duties of the *ajẹlẹ* and *ìlàrí* in vassal kingdoms was the maintenance of general order and compliance with Oyo overrule, including the supervision of local installation ceremonies. The Shango cult was thus fused with Oyo's imperial administration to distribute the *Aláàfin*'s ritual power and political authority.[18] Whereas resident *ajẹlẹ* were sent out from the capital, Shango priests from the provinces traveled to the metropole for final initiation and instruction by the *Mọ́gbà* priest at the royal shrine in Koso (Morton-

Williams 1964:258). Thus the Shango cult established an Oyo-centric ritual field: a dangerous cult of thunder, lightning, and the *Aláàfin*'s authority which sanctioned the unity of the empire through the power of Shango's divinity and the threat of his curse.[19]

The Shango cult was not the only ritual basis of Oyo kingship. The annual *Bę́ę̀rę̀* festival was also associated with sovereignty. Whereas the Shango cult sent out the *Aláàfin*'s representatives to supervise vassal kings, and if necessary to overrule them, the *Bę́ę̀rę̀* festival called in local leaders to the capital to pay tribute to the *Aláàfin*, both material, in the form of taxes, and symbolic, in the form of *bę́ę̀rę̀* grass, which was used to thatch the palace roofs (Law 1977:99, 112). The act of giving *bę́ę̀rę̀* grass was a symbolic homage which added, both literally and figuratively, to the strength of the palace. Ogunba (1973:97) relates how, during this festival, representatives of vassal kingdoms "annually re-enacted the historical fact of their defeat and inferiority." The *Aláàfin*'s annual *Bę́ę̀rę̀* ceremony thus promoted, quite explicitly, a repertoire of Oyo-centric founding myths which reflected and reinforced Oyo unity and hegemony.

The Shango cult and *Bę́ę̀rę̀* festival reflect political centralization in seventeenth- and eighteenth-century Oyo. In the center and periphery these ritual institutions upheld the king's growing power with charters of authority. Vassal kingdoms within the empire, however, maintained their structural opposition to the *Aláàfin* within a complementary set of ritual institutions which sustained mythic charters of their corporate autonomy. If subversive founding myths were not openly asserted by subordinate rulers, they found muted expression in calendrical rites.

These rituals of "opposition" to Oyo hegemony generated an Ife-centric ritual field which commemorated the "original" ties of kingdoms to Ife and the descent of their founders from Oduduwa. The cults of Oduduwa and Ifa, with their central shrines in Ife, established with other Ife *òrìṣà* this Ife-centric ritual field. The cult of Oduduwa worshipped for the benefit of all kingdoms founded by his descendants, with Oyo's vassal kingdoms participating in its rituals. Quite literally, the annual Oduduwa festival at Ife drew these kingdoms away from Oyo, since their representatives journeyed to Ife to participate. Very likely, these representatives of Oyo's vassal kingdoms invoked their Ife-centric founding myths, with historical allusions coded into *oríkì* and talking-drum repertoires, protecting them against Oyo revision. The fact that Shango had no organized cult in Ife supports this hypothesis, indicating the absence of *ajęlę̀* and *ìlàrí* representing Oyo authority (Bascom 1944:37).

• In addition to the cult of Oduduwa, the Ife-centric nature of the cult of Ifa—the òrìṣà of divination and revealed truth—is illustrated by its origin myths. These relate how Ifa, personified as Orunmila, came to Ife from heaven (Abimbola 1975:2–4). Dennett (1910:88–90) cited a popular tradition in which Orunmila was the first Ọ̀ọ̀ni of Ife, clearly associating the power of the cult with original kingship in Ife. The central cult shrine, headed by the Àràbà, is located in Ife, from which secondary associations branch throughout the kingdoms. The myths which justify this branching invert rather neatly the myths of princely dispersion which describe the origins of Yoruba kingdoms. Whereas Oduduwa sent out sixteen sons (according to Ife traditions) to found the first kingdoms, Ifa selected sixteen apprentices, one from each of the kingdoms, to come to Ife for training and to return with the powers of Ifa divination.

The Ifa corpus of divinatory verses (ẹsẹ)—numbering in the thousands—divides into sixteen categories (odù) which correspond to the sixteen "original" Yoruba kingdoms, the sixteen Ifa apprentices selected from the kingdoms, and the sixteen palm kernels cast in divination (McClelland 1966). Each odù reveals to the diviner a "true" account of what happened in the past, but their poetic contents are opaque to the public (Bascom 1969:130). The interpretation of these condensed poetic fragments is restricted to Ifa priests (babaláwo, lit. "fathers of secrets"). Although somewhat hidden from public understanding, the form and content of these odù "give order to Yoruba myths, establish the relationships between the various deities and organise them into something like a pantheon" (Beier 1959:56). They also establish relationships between kingdoms, as an unambiguous fragment from the first odù (Ogbè-Méjì) proclaims: "No king is as great as the Ooni" (Bascom 1969:141).

Ifa divination is the subject of many formal and detailed studies. The neglected point I wish to argue is that the highly coded form of its traditions and their restriction to specialized Ifa priests insulated them—at least in principle—from political revision by Oyo, thereby preserving charters of autonomy for Oyo's vassal kingdoms. Even in non-Oyo areas, their formalized mode of oral transmission militated against revision and modification over time, according to felicity conditions imposed by the iyèrè chanting technique.[20] During the annual Ifa festival in major Yoruba kingdoms, the babaláwo would convene in the palace, sacrifice to their òrìṣà, and sing selections from the sixteen odù throughout the night, accompanied by the àrán talking drum, agogo gongs, and the king's dancing after each recitation (Beier 1959:56–62). In this fashion, strings and fragments of mythic and poetic narratives validated the king's authority, identifying his office with Ife spirituality rather than Oyo overrule.

If Ifa preserved a corpus of traditions which discreetly challenged Oyo hegemony, what of the Ifa festival in metropolitan Oyo—the very capital and center of its empire? Johnson (1921:48) dismisses the festival in three sentences, although he describes the *Bèèré* festival at great length. McClelland (1966:424n) notes with surprise that Old Oyo is not included at all among the *odù*, but that Oko, a subordinate town, holds a prominent place. Abimbola (1975:6) describes a unique development within the Ifa cult in Old Oyo which represents the danger it posed to the *Aláàfin*. There the cult had two leaders, the *Ọ̀nàilémọlẹ*, or political head, and the *Àràbà*, or religious head:

> The political head of the cult represents the interests of the state within the cult while the religious head is the final arbiter on religious matters. The political head is however regarded as senior to the religious leader and he is the link between the cult and the king. It is his duty to see that the cult does not engage in any matter detrimental to the interests of the state. He also arranges an Ifa festival on behalf of the king . . . Whenever the king needs the support of the Ifa cult either to perform sacrifices or to perform divination on matters affecting the interests of the state, the Onailemole and his immediate deputies make all the arrangements on behalf of the king.

The *Ọ̀nàilémọlẹ̀* thus mediated between the Ifa cult and the *Aláàfin*, protecting the king's person, office, and empire from the cult's religious leaders and their subversive wisdom. The Ifa cult in metropolitan Oyo required political supervision precisely because its Ife-centric *odù* resisted textual revision, implicitly preserving charters of autonomy for subordinate kingdoms within the empire.

THE IMPRISONMENT OF OBATALA

The development of two ritual fields in response to Oyo conquest and expansion generated a divided repertoire of founding myths; Oyo-centric rituals supported hegemonic claims which Ife-centric rituals implicitly opposed. Not all myths preserved by rituals of this period, however, are founding myths; some allude to Oyo's conquest and incorporation of less powerful kingdoms into its empire. According to the development of two ritual fields, Beier's "aboriginal" interpretation of the Obatala festival can be pushed up and located in the period of Oyo expansion.

Beier describes an Obatala festival in Ede, an early Oyo military outpost that protected its southern territory against Ijesha raids.[21] Although most of Ede's òrìṣà came from Oyo, Obatala came from Ife, where his central shrine still stands (Beier 1959:7, 12). The festival begins with a sacrifice performed by the Àjàgẹmọ, or high priest, and distributed to the Tìmì (the Ede king) and his chiefs sitting in state. The highlight of the festival occurs on the second day, when the Àjàgẹmọ and another priest perform a brief ritual drama, or mock battle[22]:

> The story is of a fight between the Ajagemo and another priest, bearing the title Olunwi. Ajagemo is taken prisoner by Olunwi and carried off from the palace. The Oba, however, intervenes for his release. He pays ransom to Olunwi, and Ajagemo is liberated and allowed to return to the palace . . . The ability to suffer and not to retaliate is one of the virtues every Obatala worshipper must strive to possess (ibid., 14).

The scheme of this story—the fight, imprisonment, and release of the Àjàgẹmọ—represents, according to Beier, a historical event which the people of Ede have forgotten. Beier ventures an interpretation based on two quite different traditions, one presumably from Ifon, the other from Ife.[23]

The Ifon myth tells how Osalufon—the local name for Obatala—decided to visit his friend Shango and consulted Ifa before departing. Ifa advised him not to go, that he would meet with suffering and misfortune. Osalufon insisted on going, so Ifa told him to be patient on the journey, never to complain, and never to refuse any service requested of him. Osalufon set out and met Eshu—the Yoruba trickster deity and messenger of the other òrìṣà—sitting by the road with a great pot of palm oil. He attempted to help Eshu by lifting the pot to the carrying position on his head, but Eshu maliciously spilled the oil all over him, spoiling his white cloth. Osalufon did not complain, but went to the river and changed his cloth. This happened three times, and still he did not complain. Finally he came to Shango's kingdom and saw Shango's horse, which had run away. He caught the horse to bring it back to its owner, when Shango's servants appeared and seized Osalufon as a thief. He was cast into prison, where he remained for seven years. During those years Shango's kingdom became infertile—women were barren and crops failed. Ifa was consulted, and he announced that an old man was unjustly imprisoned. The prisoner was found to be Osalufon, who was released, reunited with Shango, and sent home with gifts.[24] According to Beier (ibid.), this myth (1) "explains the peculiar friendship and understanding which exists today between Obatala's worshippers and those of Shango," and (2) "expressed clearly the Obatala belief that retaliation and violence do not always achieve their ends." Beier uses the myth to illuminate the moral message of the dramatic ritual sequence, which he likens to a passion play.

Beier's historical interpretation derives from Ife oral traditions which refer to Obatala as "Orisha Igbo" (not to be confused with the Igbo of eastern Nigeria), whom Beier believes were the original, pre-Oduduwa inhabitants of Ife. If the Igbo were the aboriginal inhabitants and if Obatala was their òrìṣà, then, Beier reasons, the Obatala festival represents their defeat by Oduduwa and his followers:[25]

> Was Obatala, perhaps, an Igbo cult later adopted by the Yoruba conquerors after a period of persecution? This myth explains why Obatala asserts his superiority, not through his military prowess as do the invader gods like Ogun and Shango, but through his moral integrity, through patience and through wisdom. It is interesting to note that Johnson records a tradition that the early Obatala priests were the "sons of slaves". If the Ede play refers to this, the capture of Ajagemo would signify the defeat of the original worshippers of Obatala. His release and triumphant return would record the homage later paid by the victors to the god of the defeated (ibid., 15).

Beier's aboriginal theory sheds no historical light on the Osalufon (Obatala) myth, nor does it begin to explain why the defeat of the "Igbo" should be commemorated in Ede, an Oyo military outpost that worshipped the Oyo òrìṣà. The "ritual field" theory of Oyo conquest and expansion, however, provides an alternative and historically more consistent interpretation of the fragmentary Obatala data.

In the Ifon myth Obatala is called Osalufon—a contraction of Òrìṣà-Olú-Ifón—because he is the òrìṣà of their king, the Olúfón, and is thus associated with the kingship. Osalufon went to visit his "friend" Shango against Ifa's advice. His problems began when he met Eshu, who maliciously tipped oil on him. This opening scene establishes an Ife-Oyo polarity through a set of binary contrasts:

Ife : Oyo
Obatala : Shango
Ifa : Eshu

Whereas Obatala (represented by Osalufon, the òrìṣà of Ifon kingship) has his central shrine in Ife, Shango, the òrìṣà of Oyo kingship, has his central shrine in Oyo. The Ifa-Eshu opposition is basic to Yoruba culture, and in this context it restates the Ife-Oyo opposition. Whereas Ifa reveals order and truth from the random toss of palm nuts in divination, Eshu, the òrìṣà of misfortune and indeterminacy, turns order into chaos. In terms of the myth, Ifa, associated with Ife kingship and esoteric wisdom (odù), helps Osalufon, while Eshu thwarts him.[26] Osalufon proceeds to Shango's kingdom, which is of course Oyo, where he sees Shango's runaway horse. Read as an allegory of Oyo conquest, the horse refers to the Oyo cavalry which expanded the empire's frontiers; Osalufon's attempt to return the horse represents Ifon's military resistance; and his capture by Shango's servants (ajẹ́lẹ̀, ìlàrí, or soldiers) represents the subjugation of Ifon kingship.

The rest of the myth fits Oyo conquest to Yoruba ideas of political legitimacy. The imprisonment of "Obatala" is indeed unjust, and Oyo suffers from famine and infertility. Shango consults Ifa, thereby recognizing Ife as the locus of truth and esoteric insight, and learns the cause of Oyo's affliction. Shango releases Osalufon from captivity and Oyo is consequently freed from its plight.[27] Osalufon returns home with gifts and much rejoicing. When read as a euphemism of Oyo conquest, the Osalufon myth locates Beier's "passion play" in a historical process. The "peculiar friendship" between Shango and Obatala devotees may well be a joking relationship buffering the potential explosiveness between victors and vanquished. The values of patience and humility which Obatala generally represents and "the belief that retaliation and violence do not always attain their ends" (Beier 1959:14) repress and dignify the shame of subjugation to Oyo. The Ifon myth represents one variation on this theme; nearby Ejigbo, where Obatala is called Ogiyan and Eleejigbo (the king of Ejigbo's title), has a similar festival and traditions.[28] Most of Obatala's local names are in fact modified place-names and kingship titles from areas that fell to Oyo.[29] Obatala, a paradigmatic white deity, or òrìṣà funfun, is thus the òrìṣà of political displacement: his ritual power, cool and controlled, dignifies surrendered political authority and discourages rebellion.[30]

If the Oyo conquest theory is correct, the imprisonment of the Àjàgẹmọ in the Ede drama refers not to the conquest of an aboriginal population in the remote past, as Beier proposes, but to the subjection of independent kingdoms to Oyo overrule, which began no earlier than c. 1600.[31] Ransom paid by the ọba for the Àjàgẹmọ's release represents the payment of tribute by conquered kings. And Johnson's reference to the early Obatala priests as "sons of slaves," which Beier cites to support his aboriginal theory, represents, as we have seen, Oyo's effort to discredit Ife kingship, for it is an Oyo tradition which portrays the first Ọ̀ọ̀ni as the son of a slave and dedicated to Obatala's service. The Obatala festival dignified Oyo overrule for the victors as well as the vanquished, diminishing Ife's political status while validating its ritual primacy. This would explain why Ede, an Oyo military outpost which defended the empire and waged many campaigns, incorporated an Ife òrìṣà into its Oyo-centric ritual calendar.

THE MYSTERY OF ANCIENT IFE

Thus far I have developed a very crude and general model of the Yoruba ritual system to account for (1) the pattern and persistence of variant mythic traditions in both simple and complex Yoruba kingdoms; (2) the development during Oyo expansion of two ritual fields— Oyo-centric and Ife-centric—which generated and sustained a divided mythic repertoire; and (3) specific historical references in the Obatala festival. I have argued that when local founding myths are revised to legitimize more powerful centers, they are simultaneously "preserved" by local rituals which sacralize their meanings in secret symbols. The critical relationship between ritual and myth, however, is more than one of formal preservation. Openly subversive to Oyo authority, the "original," Ife-centric founding myths contested the claims of their political overlords in restricted codes during sacred occasions. Such ritual knowledge is considered "deep" *(jinlẹ̀)* and powerful. Too dangerous for the public, it is confined to cult specialists. The hermeneutics of ritual is thus discursively structured to publicly and openly uphold and revitalize what it privately and secretly denies and subverts. Beier's own testimony unwittingly bears this out. The highlight of the Obatala festival in Ede—the Àjàgẹmọ's fight, imprisonment, and release—is based not on forgotten myth, as Beier concluded, but on the restricted, unspeakable, forbidden knowledge that the Aláàfin of Oyo was never their true king. Extended to the limits of the Oyo empire, this indigenous hermeneutics sheds new light on the "mystery" of ancient Ife.

Briefly stated, the mystery is this: why, after Ife's eclipse by successor states and the rise of the powerful Oyo empire, did an Ife-centric corpus of traditions persist? What kept traditions of Ife dynastic origin alive? In his comprehensive reassessment of ancient Ife, Horton (1979:118–28) reviews Akinjogbin and Law before presenting his "elder-statesman" solution to the puzzle. According to Akinjogbin, post-fifteenth-century Ife exerted a continuing influence over its successor states *because of* their enduring reverence of Ife as a "spiritual capital" or "father kingdom." The character of such influence, however, is moot. As Law points out, Akinjogbin cites as evidence "a rather thin array of beliefs, rites and gestures; the acceptance in the successor states of the story of Ife origins; the request for confirmation from Ife at the accession of a new Oba; and little else besides" (ibid., 80). Law, on the other hand, interprets the "beliefs, rites and gestures" of successor states which assert links with Ile-Ife as charters of dynastic legitimacy and nothing more. According to his view, Ife was preserved by traditionalistic piety as the locus of sacred kingship, but it retained no significant political influence over successor states as a "father kingdom" or "spiritual capital."

Horton accepts Law's critique of Akinjogbin—that Ife rites and dynastic claims do not, by themselves, represent significant Ife influence. But he finds Law's recourse to "the inertia of traditionalistic piety" lacking as well. Given our knowledge of the revision of myth by politics, Horton argues that there must have been some political influence at Ife which sustained its dynastic traditions. Otherwise they would have reverted to themes of autochthonous origins or would have been revised by a more powerful center. Horton (ibid., 92) explains that "Ife *did* continue to exercise region-wide influence even after losing the more obvious trappings of power, and it was this continuing influence which kept traditions of Ife dynastic origin so vigorously alive in the other major states of the region." To substantiate this claim, he develops the "elder-statesman" thesis of Ife.

Horton proposes that when Ife was eclipsed by Benin, Oyo, and remaining "filial" successor states such as Ilesha and Ijebu, it became an important buffer and mediator between them. He reasons that there was some sort of tacit geopolitical consensus: "By the mid-seventeenth century . . . it would seem that most of the inheritors of Ife power, with their economic and political energies concentrated along their outward-facing frontiers, preferred to maintain a state of peace and inertia at their respective rears" (ibid., 119).[32] Owing to its central geographic location, its recently faded glory, its mythic identification as the locus of dynastic origins, and its fatherly status vis-à-vis its successor states, Ife was ideally suited to perform a mediatory role. The fact that Ife was too weak to influence an outcome by taking sides in any conflict, Horton argues, would have enhanced its credibility as a mediating center. In the absence of explicit traditions or concrete evidence referring to such a role, Horton invokes the Ifa oracle.

Observing that "in pre-industrial societies with predominantly religious world-views, political 'elder statesmanship' and mediation is often carried on through religious institutions, and in particular through oracles," Horton adduces evidence that (a) Ife was the center of Ifa activity, and (b) "such activity was directed toward giving advice of a political nature to the successor states" (ibid., 121). Horton clearly illustrates the Ife-centricity of Ifa, but this by itself proves nothing of Ife's mediating role unless we allow a *hysteron proteron*. Evidence of *(b)* is equivocal at best. With due respect to its venerable practitioners, we cannot accept what Ifa says (in the *odù* of Ifa) as historically valid. Yet Horton uses a few Ifa traditions as *prima facie* evidence of Ife's mediating role. One such tradition, he tells us, recounts how Ifa's advice ended a period of Ife subjugation to Oyo (which sounds just like the Osalufon myth). Another cautions against ignoring Ifa's political advice. Such traditions are not without political and ideological significance—as I shall soon argue in an alternative interpretation— but they still beg the question which Horton believes they answer.

Horton (ibid., 124) summarizes his argument as such:

1. Post-fifteenth-century Ife *was* the center of the Ifa divination cult.

2. As such, it exercised regionwide political influence of an "elder-statesmanly" and mediating character.

3. Its role in this respect almost certainly developed in response to a situation in which all the major powers of the region were concentrating on holding or expanding their outward frontiers and had a strong interest in peace at the center.

4. It was their awareness of the importance of this role which encouraged all parties concerned to preserve memories of the city's ancient glory and dynastic creativity.

This argument relates the persistence of Ife-centric dynastic traditions to Ife's political influence as the locus of *entente*.[33] The argument's weakness, however, lies in the lack of convincing evidence in support of the central "elder-statesman" thesis. Whereas (1) is well established, (2), (3), and (4) remain articles of well-reasoned faith. In my own solution to the "mystery" of Ife's enduring traditions, based on a theory of ritual fields, I vindicate Law's position that Ife-centric traditions persisted after Ife ceased to exert any significant political influence, but I do so without recourse to mystifying notions of traditionalistic piety, which Horton also correctly rejects.

According to the ritual-field theory, Ife-centric traditions were preserved by rituals which emphasized the autonomy of Ife's successor states vis-à-vis Oyo's imperial interests. *It was not traditionalistic piety for Ife's past grandeur which kept its founding myths and dynastic traditions vigorously alive, but the political opposition of its successor states to Oyo's growing hegemonic claims.* There is no need to assume Ife's political influence at this time, either as an "elder statesman" or in any other way, save that Ife remained an ideological foil to Oyo revisionism, a foil which grounded subversive traditions in the cosmographic center of a pan-Yoruba cosmology. The Ife-centric character of Ifa divination relates not to Ife's hypothetical role as a political mediator, but to the ritually sanctified association between .cosmological origins and Ifa's "true," explicitly antirevisionist, "history" *(itàn)*. Whereas Horton assumes that the *odù* of Ifa are in fact homogeneous texts with little variance (and a glance at the published editions reveals just the opposite), the ritual-field theory maintains only that Ifa ideology asserts this to be the case. Hence we cannot accept Ifa at face value; what it says relates to divination itself by upholding the authority of its portentous texts. The cautionary tales Horton alludes to about heeding Ifa's political advice "explain" political turmoil in retrospect and keep the *babaláwo* in business. The tradition of how Ifa's oracular advice ended Ife's subjugation by Oyo asserts the unassailability of Ifa's Ife-centric texts to Oyo revision and overrule. Ifa's "historical" claims are ideologically meaningful in their opposition to emerging Oyo-centrism. They may or may not be historically accurate.

If the ritual-field theory is correct, we would expect Ife's importance as a "ritual center" or "spiritual capital" to intensify at the height of the Oyo empire. Horton (ibid., 128) argues from his theory of *entente* that "Ife and its *Oni* would have been neither more nor less 'religious', 'spiritual' or 'holy' than Benin and its *Oba* or Oyo and its *Alaafin*," and he recommends the more secular label of "father state." I would prefer Ife's more sacred descriptive labels and idioms. This is not to deny Ife's political influence, but to interpret it in a new light. Ife *was* politically important, not for what it did, but for what, in the ritual domain, it came to represent.

2

Traditions Renewed:
The Founding of Ayede

The preceding historiographic review of ancient Ife and Old Oyo
reveals how Yoruba myth and ritual structured shifting fields of
power. The spectacular rise of the Oyo kingdom into a ten-
thousand-square-mile empire—supported by a cavalry, long-distance
trade revenues, a complex administrative empire, and the royal
Shango cult—generated two dominant ritual fields which have shaped
the very writing of Yoruba history. Ife-centric dynastic traditions persisted in opposition to Oyo hegemony to establish two major historiographic themes: the invocation of Ife as the locus of Yoruba creation
and political authority, and the identification of the Oyo empire as a
model of Yoruba statecraft and political economy. If the elders of Ife
possessed incomparable wisdom and privileged access to the secrets of
Ifa, the leaders of Oyo achieved power and glory through military
prowess, political cunning, the control of trade, and the worship of
Shango.

By 1836 the Oyo empire succumbed to Fulani *jihad* and the internal
disaffection of its civil chiefs, creating what Ajayi (1964:63) has called a
"power vacuum" which rival kingdoms sought to fill. From 1837 to 1878,
wars between Oyo's successor states—primarily Ibadan, Ilorin, Ijaye,
and Abeokuta—established new military strongholds and centers of
influence which redefined the political topography of Yorubaland.
Old Oyo was shattered; the town resettled south at Ago Oja, where "a
conscious attempt was made to re-create the glories of the old capital
and to preserve the rituals of its kingship" (R. Smith 1969:160). The *Al-*

\tiba provided nominal leadership and ritual authority for the emerging Ibadan empire. Initially charged to protect the new Oyo kingdom's north and northeast boundaries, Ibadan became a powerful military state, waging successive military campaigns into Ekitiland, where it consolidated its eastern empire and undermined Ilorin's control (Akintoye 1971:33–75). Like Old Oyo before, Ibadan placed its subject kingdoms under the coercive and exploitative *ajélè* system of imperial administration (Awe 1964). Since Ibadan was founded as a military camp with no recognized king or dynastic claims to a beaded crown, it appropriated the essentially Oyo-centric pantheon of *òrìṣà* (with the important addition of the "arch-deity" Oke-Ibadan) and consequently sustained Ife's sacred status as the locus of opposition to hegemonic overrule (cf. Awe 1964:58). If Ibadan lacked the symbolic resources to rewrite official dynastic history, it possessed the political power to "renew" the traditions of Old Oyo.

The history of Ibadan's rise to power is a bloody one, involving wars against the Egba Yoruba to the West, the Ijebu Yoruba to the south, and the Ijesha and Ekiti Yoruba to the east. It is not the battles themselves, however, which this chapter examines, but strategies of shifting centers and alliances established by ritual networks and articulated by ritual fields. The founding of Ayede on the eastern fringe of the Ibadan empire (see map 2) and the social history and organization of its dominant *òrìṣà* cults illustrate how myth and ritual were officially restructured to establish a "traditional" Ekiti Yoruba kingdom c. 1850.[1] The kingdom of Ayede stands out for several reasons. Its rapid development into a military autocracy under the infamous warlord Eshubiyi distinguished it politically from the fragile and decentralized "ministates" more typical of the region. Since Ayede began as a refugee settlement with questionable claims to a beaded crown, its founding myths and rituals of state reflect competing visions of legitimate kingship which are incorporated into its dominant *òrìṣà* cults. But if Ayede's ritual system vividly illustrates the strategies and tactics of its own traditions—how some political charters were renewed and others repressed—it also epitomizes the *multiplicity* of meanings and claims enshrined in every Yoruba town.

THE BRICOLAGE OF WAR

North Ekiti kingdoms in the nineteenth century endured the disruptive violence of three competing centers of power: the Ilorin champions of Fulani *jihad* from the northwest, the encroaching Ibadan empire from the west, and chronic Nupe raids from the northeast in which "all

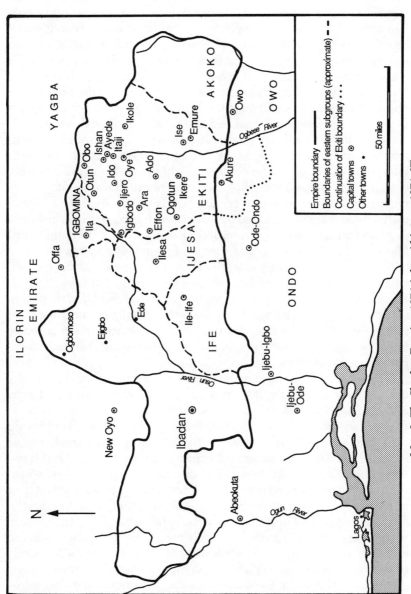

Map 2. *The Ibadan Empire, 1874 (after Akintoye 1971:67)*

captured places were looted and burned" (Nadel 1942:112). The periodic decimation and reorganization of the fragile Ekiti kingdoms produced a kind of sociopolitical "bricolage," with fragments of shattered communities relocating in new towns. Nineteenth-century warfare affected the North Ekiti polity in three basic ways. First, it established "fused" patterns of political segmentation based on the resettlement of refugees into compact defensive enclaves. Second, it created new opportunities for men of humble origin to become Big Men, take military and political titles, and even found their own kingdoms. And third, it militarized the region's highly elaborated age-set systems, which became associated primarily with town defense.

In addition to military incursions from outside, an influx of immigrants from Igbomina, Iyagba, Akoko, and Ijumu towns into the North Ekiti region during the nineteenth century (and perhaps earlier as well) brought sociocultural and ethnic variety to resettled warfare states. Immigrant groups to this day remain highly aware of their ancestral towns, which are represented by distinctive dialects, praises, and marriage and burial practices, but most of all by the òrìṣà of the immigrants' forebears. Their northeastern towns of origin were what Obayemi (1971:205–9) calls "mini-states," or loosely federated villages and village clusters segmented into patrilineages and stratified by age-sets. The top grades of such age-sets, such as the Oróta and Olólú, held senior titles including the headship (Olú) itself, forming rotating title associations which regulated community affairs. The acquisition of senior titles combined gerontocracy with descent to ensure that each major patrilineage was officially represented.

The characteristic form of the nineteenth-century north Ekiti polity derived from the amalgamation of mini-states with local Ekiti towns into compact defensive settlements. Survivors of devasted towns regrouped as "quarters" (àdúgbò) within refugee kingdoms, reproducing their former social, political, and ritual structures on a smaller scale while preserving their unique identities in praises, rituals, and traditions of common provenience. The one institution, however, which could not be reproduced in each immigrant quarter was the kingship of its former town. This was either relinquished entirely or reduced to the status of town chief or high priest (àwòrò) in exchange for the military protection of the ruling ọba. At least these are the official terms of the exchange recalled in palace testimonies. But preserved in the traditions of each immigrant quarter and in the mythic charters of their unique identities are historical memories of political autonomy and allegiances to former kings. As we shall later see, the subversive implications of such unofficial immigrant histories remain hidden in the secrets of

their òrìṣà cults or erupt during violent efforts to appropriate the kingship. For now, we can examine how the dynamics of defensive resettlement established the political context of Ayede's early history.

FROM IYE TO AYEDE

The genesis of Ayede and its development into a powerful military
kingdom began with the rise of Eshubiyi, the *Balógun* (senior military
officer) of Iye, during the first half of the nineteenth century. Iye was at
that time a fairly typical northeast Yoruba mini-state, or village
cluster—a loose federation of four major quarters (*àdúgbò*) segmented
by lineages, stratified by age-sets (*àrẹ*), and united by the "supreme
head," or *Olú*, of Iye, who traced his dynastic ties to Ile-Ife through one
of Oduduwa's daughters.[2] Each lineage (*ìdílé* in "standard" Yoruba, *akù*
in the regional dialect) had an *ighárẹ* chief whose title was usually
formed by adding the prefix *ọba* (king) to the lineage name, as in the
Ọbasákan of Osakan lineage or the *Obalési* of Ilesi lineage. In each quarter, one such *ighárẹ* chief ranked *primus inter pares* as representative to
the *Olú*.

According to idealized reconstructions elicited from Iye elders, the
Olú met with his chiefs in the palace to discuss town affairs, but he exercised little power himself. Before any decision could be taken, the
chiefs would return to their respective quarters and call the heads of
each age-set for a meeting. There they would discuss the issue and
reach a decision for the quarter; the head chief would take the decision
back to the palace council, which would determine a final course of action. In the event of serious problems or emergencies, no single quarter
would take a decision. Rather, the age-set representatives (*olórí àrẹ*)
from Owaiye—the senior of Iye's four quarters and "owner" of the
king—would summon the other representatives from Isaoye, Ejigbo,
and Ilaaro quarters to debate the issue and agree on a final decision.
This decision, representing the will of Iye's age-sets as one body,
would then be sent to the chiefs for ratification, who in turn would submit their decision to the *Olú*—whose consent and approval was a fore-
gone conclusion. If an *Olú* overruled the decisions of his chiefs, he
could be deposed, killed, or sent into exile.

Like most north Ekiti towns, Iye was already a composite of indigenes and resettled strangers. Its population grew with the influx of
refugees from the neighboring towns of Egbe, Ere, Ogbe, Obo, and
parts of Iyagba. It is said that the walled trench which surrounded the
town was two and a half miles in diameter, and that Owaiye quarter
had its own walled trench equal to the one surrounding the other three

quarters. Owaiye was thus a town within a town; owner of the king, greatest in population, even surrounded by its own wall, it ranked first among the four quarters of Iye, followed by Isaoye, Ejigbo, and Ilaaro quarters.

The Age-Set System

Within each quarter, an elaborate system of age, or generation, sets (àrẹ) organized the freeborn men into corporate sections which performed military, civic, and religious duties and which moved through the social structure over time. Their major responsibilities included defense of the kingdom against invading Nupe, Ilorin, and Ibadan enemies; cleanliness of the town; clearing of bush paths to neighboring towns; contribution of yams, goats, and hens for certain public rituals; detection and punishment of criminals and witches; building decoration, and renovation of the Olú's palace and of important town shrines; prevention of untimely and careless burning of the bush (forest and farmland) during the dry season; and advising their lineage and quarter representatives on matters of general concern. Not all àrẹ performed these tasks in the same capacity, for junior sets carried less clout and worked on matters more mundane than the middle and senior sets, whose decisions and labors were more politically engaged. But each set had its collective life cycle within the town. The most junior group, founded at the bottom rung of a generational ladder, would ascend to the second rung after sixteen years while a new group of juniors was initiated, and to the third rung sixteen years after that, until it eventually became the most senior àrẹ, disappearing with the death of its last surviving member. Although the system "condensed" somewhat during the nineteenth-century upheavals, when the Iye people migrated twenty-five miles southwest to found the kingdom of Ayede, the ideal àrẹ system consisted of sixteen named generation-sets of sixteen years each, with six àrẹ functioning at any given time (spanning a period of ninety-six years) and twelve "outstanding", waiting to be filled by future generations (fig. 2.1).

The ideal model of the àrẹ system, with sixteen generation-sets of sixteen years each, relates to the esoteric numerology of Ifa divination, with its sixteen odù, or divinatory verses; its sixteen palm nuts cast in the divinatory process; and its association with the mythic histories of the sixteen "original" Yoruba kingdoms founded by Oduduwa's progeny in Ife creation myths. In theory, the entire cycle of sixteen generation sets takes 256 years to complete. In practice, some generation-sets were dropped and the initiation of others delayed due to politics and

Figure 2.1. A Model of the Àre Generation-Set System

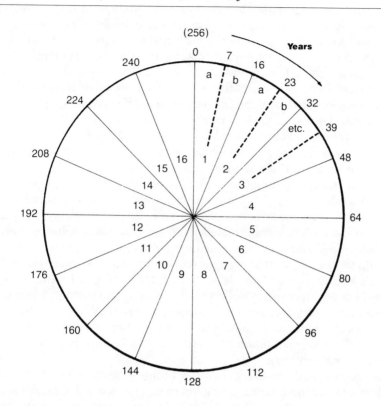

Key

1. Mimiyo	9. Iye-Madiyan	a = iwájú ("in front")
2. Amogunran	10. Kemoke	b = ehin ("behind")
3. Edo-Kegba	11. Kemajo	
4. Keloko	12. Erokesin	
5. Keyena	13. Kemeyo	
6. Kemogba	14. ?	
7. Kelote	15. ?	
8. Kedijo	16. ?	

warfare, while still others have been fused.[3] Of the sixteen *àrɛ* at Iye, thirteen are still remembered: Mimiyo, Amogunran, Edo-Kegba, Keloko, Keyena, Kemogba, Kelote, Keijdo, Iye-Madiyan, Kemoke, Kemajo, Erokesin, and Kemeyo. Each name reflects circumstances in the town when the group was initiated, and each has its own attributive praises *(oríkì)*. Thus Iye-Madiyan means "Iye people, don't worry," for the group would protect them in war; while Kemajo refers to those who were initiated after the *Pax Britannica* in 1896. Although subject to change and revision, the *àrɛ* system provides a rough historical framework in the oral testimonies of local historians *(òpìtàn)*.

As a concrete membership unit, each *àrɛ* is internally differentiated into two sections: those who are "in front" *(iwájú)* and those who are "behind" *(ɛhin)*. Although members of the *ɛhin* section can be older than members in *iwájú*, *ɛhin* is behind *iwájú* in seniority because its initiation takes place seven years later. Thus, seven years after Iye-Madiyan *iwájú* were initiated, Iye-Madiyan would initiate its *ɛhin* section. Nine years after that, the next *àrɛ* (Kemoke, in the Iye system) would be organized, making a gap of sixteen years between the incorporation of successive age-sets. In war, the *àrɛ* formed fighting battalions in which *ɛhin* and *iwájú* sections relieved each other: when the front section was tired or suffered heavy losses, they would retire and the back section would replace them. Hence, some elders explain, *iwájú* and *ɛhin* refer to military formations on the battlefield as well as to generational seniority.

The essentially military character of the *àrɛ* groups, in which "the elders commanded the juniors what to do" (as one elder explains it), may account for their otherwise-puzzling principles of recruitment. The first, a proscription, is that no man can join the *àrɛ* immediately following that of his father. He can in unusual cases join the *ɛhin* section of his father's *àrɛ* if his father is *iwájú*, but membership in the second *àrɛ* after the father's is preferred. A second proscription is that no two sons of the same mother *(ɔmɔìyá)* can join the same *àrɛ*, even if they have different fathers, unless they are twins. This principle is summarized by the apothegm *a kìí rí ɔmɔ ìyá méjì ní ìsɔ̀ igi* (we never see two children of one mother on the same slab of wood). Rather, the senior brother must always belong to a senior *àrɛ*, creating complications for families with many sons. In principle, sons of the same father *(ɔmɔkùnrin baba kan)* in a polygynous household determine their *àrɛ* membership according to their maternal birth order. The firstborn of the first wife and the firstborn of the second wife join the second *àrɛ* after their father's; the second sons of both wives join the following *àrɛ*; and the third sons join the *àrɛ* after that. Even if the firstborn of the

Figure 2.2. Generational Seniority in the Àre System

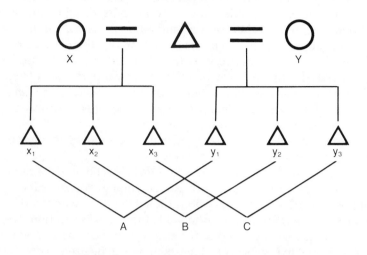

Key

Àrẹ A (x_1 + y_1) is senior to àrẹ B (x_2 + y_2)

Àrẹ B (x_2 + y_2) is senior to àrẹ C (x_3 + y_3)

second wife is younger than the second or third sons of the first wife, he will be senior to them in the *àrẹ* system (fig. 2.2). This generational seniority carries significant weight. If x_2 is older than y_1 and commits an offense against him, the *àrẹ* of y_1 can apply pressure on x_2 and order him to prostrate himself *(dobálẹ)* to y_1. If x_2 refuses, the *àrẹ* can then fine him. The same principles apply to the sons of a man's additional wives, preventing the strong loyalties between full brothers (who also inherit their father's property together) from generating conflict and division within the *àrẹ* group. From a military perspective, the two restrictions on recruitment safeguarded the continuity of the lineage. The principle of alternating generations ensured that if two adjacent *àrẹ* set out to battle, fathers and sons would not both be killed in defeat. The half-sibling principle ensured that the sons of one mother would not be wiped out in the same *àrẹ* regiment. Assigning them to different *àrẹ* maximized the likelihood of some survivors.

At the apex of the *àrẹ* system stood a title society, called *Empé,* which members of the senior *àrẹ* could join provided (1) that they had distinguished themselves in battle; (2) that four or five *àrẹ* had been initiated after their own *àṛẹ*; (3) that they were over fifty years of age; and (4) that they could pay the expenses of the *Empé* initiation. The *Empé* council organized the initiation of new *àṛẹ*, persecuted criminals and Big Men who abused their power, and advised the *Olú* on important matters of state. Like the civil *igharẹ* chiefs of Iye, the *Empé* carried an independent voice in the community: they did not take advice from any other authority and they needed no special permission from the *Olú* to execute their decisions. But unlike the civil chiefs, the *Empé* belonged to a hierarchy of military chiefs and functioned, as one local historian described it, "like the supreme military council." Even the choreography of the dance performed at the funeral of an *Empé* member recalled the movements of military combat.

Iye's elaborate age-set and title systems reflect one of the more decentralized patterns of political power among Yoruba subcultural groups (cf. Forde 1951:79–80). Both the *Olú* and his commanding officer, the *Balógun*, were quite vulnerable to public disaffection. Iye traditions relate how one *Olú* (known as *ọmọ ẹsàn*) possessed a powerful *jùjú* (medicine) in the form of a long chain which he used to protect the town. When the enemy attacked, the *Olú* would draw his chain around Iye's four quarters. When the enemy reached the chain, "they would drop like flies." The Iye people were afraid of so much power concentrated in their leader's hands. They felt that if there was trouble within the town, the *Olú* could draw the chain around them. They called a big meeting to tell the *Olú* "to give the Iye people a chance," and they deposed him. The *Olú* gathered his household together and said, "You my wives and children, see what Iye people have done, they want me to go, and I shall go, so all of you go back to your parents' compounds"; whereafter he stood on a flat stone with one leg raised, and he disappeared, leaving one footprint behind.[4] Whatever the actual cause of the *Olú*'s deposition, the idiom of dangerous power concentrated in his hands indicates a violation of his authority. A similar tradition tell show Shankaniwon, an infamous Iye *Balógun* (c. 1777–1830), alienated himself from his warriors and lost his life. Born into the Idofin-Egbe lineage of Ejigbo quarter, he distinguished himself in many battles against the Ilorin and exploited his mother's Nupe ties to learn about the Nupe enemy. He was a ruthless and fearless war leader, whose lust for women—including his officers' wives—and persecution of rivals cost him his support. Shankaniwon was betrayed and killed on a rock, where, Iye people maintain, his footprints can still be seen.

Iye traditions relate how Shankaniwon's apprentice and successor, Eshubiyi, followed his mentor's example, kidnapping innocent people and selling them into slavery, fighting the Nupe, and blocking Ilorin's southern trade routes. But where Shankaniwon succumbed to his disaffected officers, Eshubiyi used his military power to consolidate political control, to found a new kingdom, to break with the *Olú* ruling dynasty, and finally to proclaim himself king. The story of this remarkable warrior-king and his Machiavellian statecraft reveals how far charters of legitimate authority could be manipulated and stretched to accommodate the realities of power politics.

The Rise of Eshubiyi

The official story of Eshubiyi narrated by the Ayede chiefs (and alluded to in his *oríkì*) begins with his exceptional birth. Eshubiyi's father, Onimogun, was a native of Ikole (Ilotin quarter), where he became a respected hunter, herbalist, and practitioner of Ifa divination *(babaláwo)*. He also belonged to Ikole's royal family and held a senior post—some say the *àwòrò*, or high priest—of the royal cult of Orisha Ojuna. For reasons unstated, Onimogun left Ikole and settled as a stranger in Iye, residing in Osakan's compound in Isaoye quarter. There he divined that the *Ọbasákan* (the chief of Osakan lineage) had a barren daughter whose husband would reject her. When this occurred, Onimogun took her as his wife, and they bore several children. Here traditions diverge; some say that his wife remained pregnant for seven years and went to Eshu's shrine in the town of Ijelu to propitiate him for a successful delivery. She bore a son with a full set of teeth and named him Eshubiyi, meaning "Eshu bore this." Other traditions say that at the time of her delivery, Iye was raided by the Ilorin army, and she hid in the Eshu shrine and gave birth. Hence in his *oríkì*, Eshubiyi is "*ọmọ Elékọ̀lé,*" or "child of the *Elékọ̀lé*" (the title of Ikole's king) through his patriline and "*ọmọ Ọbasákan,*" or "child of the *Ọbasákan*," through his matriline. Even this official history raises questions about Eshubiyi's eligibility for the kingship. As *Ọmọ Elékọ̀lé*, he had a royal Ikole pedigree but had no business ruling the Iye people. As *Ọmọ Ọbasákan*, he was a native of Iye, but through matrifiliation and not patrilineal descent. Some variants try to resolve this embarrassment by reversing Eshubiyi's parents—his father, they state, was *Ọmọ Ọbasákan* and his mother *Ọmọ Elékọ̀lé*.

In actual fact, Eshubiyi's paternity is something of a scandal. According to "secret" traditions, it was not the *Ọbasákan*'s daughter but his wife, Oni Abake, who was barren and subsequently impregnated by Onimogun's "powers"—a dubious achievement alluded to in the older Oroyeye songs of abuse against adulterers. The *Ọbasákan* accepted the son as his own, but the Iye people knew otherwise. He was thus *Ọmọ Ọbasákan* through his pater and *Ọmọ Elékọlé* through his genitor, hardly the pedigree of a future Iye king.[5] Eshubiyi grew up to be a respected herbalist, *babaláwo,* and warrior. Through his natural father he inherited Orisha Ojuna, and he sent his Ifa clients in Iye to offer sacrifices at the shrine in Ikole. The Ikole cult was pleased to receive new devotees from Iye, but the Iye cults, particularly Oroyeye, resented Orisha Ojuna's encroachment and abused Eshubiyi with song, translated as:

Baálẹ Otunja is sending to inform you that the festival for *ote-muru* is near.
Olú Iye never wears calabash crown, are you not preparing to fight?
You had better return home in time.

Otunja was the owner of Orisha Ojuna in Ikole and was the *Elékọlé's* "brother." *Ote-muru* is the sacred water carried by the Orisha Ojuna devotees from the bush shrine, where the *baálẹ* of Otunja wore a "calabash" crown in contrast to the *Elékọlé's* beaded crown. By singing that the *Olú* of Iye never wears a calabash crown, Oroyeye proclaimed that unlike the *baálẹ* of Otunja, he was not subordinate to the *Elèkọlé.* The Oroyeye cult was correct to note that the Orisha Ojuna cult threatened the *Olú's* authority because, as we shall see, Eshubiyi later promoted the cult to consolidate his position in Ayede.

Eshubiyi's military career was one of shifting fortunes and alliances. He was seized by the Ilorins and taken as a slave, but was redeemed, according to Johnson (1921:308), "for 12 heads of cowries" and was given a wife from Offa. He then joined the Ibadans to fight against Ilorin and was received as a war chief by the *Baṣọrun* Oluyole, who gave Eshubiyi a war standard and initiated him into Ibadan's Yemoja cult. The *Balógun* Ali of Ilorin set out to recapture Eshubiyi at Opin and held the town under siege for three years before it finally succumbed. Eshubiyi escaped from Opin, seeking refuge at Ishan, Oye, and Ikole with the Ilorins in hot pursuit. He finally found safety in Omu, located high on a hill and surrounded by a protective thicket which the Ilorin cavalry could not penetrate. Eshubiyi was again besieged by the Ilorins at Otun c. 1854, when the Ibadan army came to his rescue. Eshubiyi immediately thereafter joined Ibadan's campaign against Ikoro, where a united Ekiti army surrendered in 1855. Eshubiyi was Ibadan's strong ally at this time. He was also a reputable war chief with a newly established base, which he founded between Ishan and Itaji kingdoms and called Ayede. The people of Iye were the first to resettle and seek Eshubiyi's protection, for their town was devastated by Ilorin's *Balógun* Ali c. 1845. But Eshubiyi also attracted "strong men" and "war boys" from Opin and Ikole.

In 1858 Daniel May became the first European to visit Ayede, put it quite literally on the map (map 3), and meet Eshubiyi, whose reputation as "a great war chief" he had already encountered in Ibadan (May 1860:221).[6] May journeyed to Ishan, where he visited the resident *ajẹlẹ̀* and was summoned by Eshubiyi to Ayede. As he wrote in the *Journal of the Royal Geographic Society* in 1860:

> E'shon and A'iedi are nominally or politically one town; really they are two, and about two miles apart. In the former the Ajele resides; in the latter the chief E'shu is to be found, and, as its formation is recent and it is now very select, I imagine it is a compromise with the feelings of the reported fighting man who governs, subject, however, to Ibadan. I remained at this place during Saturday the 26th June [1858], in the forenoon of which I was summoned to E'shu at A'iedi. I found him and his assembled men waiting for me; he, a very black man, was seated on a dais, on a fine leopard's skin, under a piazza on one side of a spacious square, and a rather select crowd filling the other three sides. The salutations over, I was desired to seat myself under the piazza opposite him, and our conversation was then conducted by a party of three or four running between us. After the usual explanations, I had to approach the matter of my proceeding, when I had to learn (politely enough conveyed to me) that the road eastward to the confluence was shut to me; 'war in the road' was the farther information on my attempting to shake the chief's determination (ibid., 224).

May's observations of nascent Ayede reveal Eshubiyi's importance both as a war chief for Ibadan and as a leader among the northeast Yoruba. The fact that Ayede had no *ajẹlẹ̀* to administer Ibadan's overrule confirms that Eshubiyi was at the time an overseer and protector of the Ibadan empire's northeast border (Akintoye 1971:70). He was certainly a man of considerable authority, for it was Eshubiyi, and not Ishan's resident *ajẹlẹ̀*, who denied May access to the east and directed him north to Ladi instead. May also noted that Ayede's location two miles away from Ishan reflected a "compromise with the feelings of the reported fighting man, subject, however, to Ibadan," indicating an incipient tension which was soon to erupt in the vindictive Wokuti expedition (Johnson 1921:403). For even by 1858 Eshubiyi was behaving like a king and asserting his independence. Although lacking the beaded crown which he later attained, he resembled an *ọba* in state, seated on a

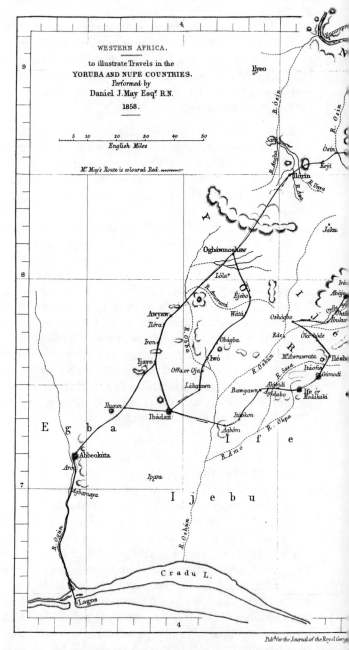

Pub.ᵈ for the Journal of the Royal Geog.

Map 3. Daniel May's Journey through Ayede, 1858 (from May 1860)

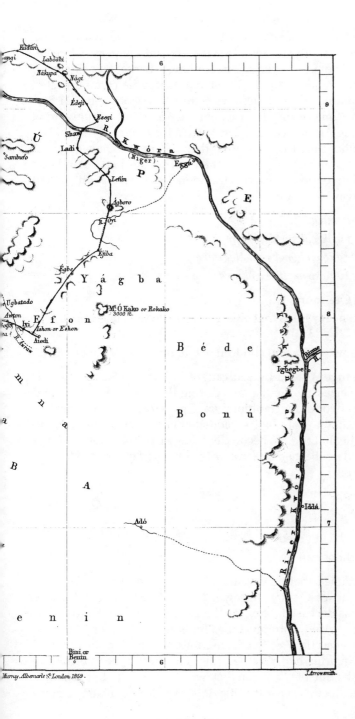

Kudan
angi   Laboshi
    Nakupa   Nagi
                        6   9
        Edeji

        Esegi
        Shar   R.
Ú   KWÓra
    Ladi   (Niger)
Sambufo   Eggá
            Lefin   P
        Ágboro   E
        E. Oyi

            Éjiba
    Égbe
        Yágba
                                            8
Ugbatado   Mt Ó Kako or Rokako
Awton   3000 ft.
ogó, Iyi Ishon or E'shon
a ?   Aiedi   Bimme
E. kwraw   Béde   Igbegbe   R.

    m   n
                Bonú
a   a
B
    A

        Adó   Iddá
                                            7

e   n   i   n

        Bini or
        Benin
                        6
Murray Albemarle St London 1859.   J. Arrowsmith.

"dais," or throne; on a leopard's skin—the prerogative of kings and certain high priests only; under a "piazza," or rudimentary palace veranda; at the side of a spacious square, or king's market (*qua* extension of the palace's foreground [Ojo 1966a:35]), where he communicated with May through intermediaries—as befits a king (Johnson 1921:51).

It was sometime during the following decade that Eshubiyi took the kingship title Àtá of Ayede and initiated a new ruling dynasty. The Iye refugees who came to Ayede with their *Olú* in 1845 never trusted their powerful war chief, who by their own traditional standards should have been deposed. An oral tradition recalls a song which they sang on their way to Ayede:

Èyin Ọmọ Ote-muru,
Òjó gìrìgìrì tó ńgba ẹjà ńlọ sínú agere,
Òjó gìrìrì ti ó bá rọ oń lọ ńgba ẹjà ńlọ sínú agere,
Òjó gìrìrì ti ó bá rọ kò mọ itìbí ẹ ńko wa lọ ẹyin ọmọ Ote-muru.

Children of Ote-muru,
Sudden and heavy rains that sweep fishes into the fisherman's net,
We don't know where you children of Ote-muru are taking us.[7]

The Iye refugees were indeed caught in Eshubiyi's "net." Their own *Olú* was seized by the Ibadans during the Aye war of 1847 and held captive in Iwo (other traditions say Ogbomosho), where his fate remained unknown. Eshubiyi exploited this lacuna by filling it in stages. When he first tried to become *ọba*, the Iye people protested that a new *Olú* could not be installed in case the captured one was still alive, citing a proverb:

Tí ọba kò bá kú,
Ọba kò gbọ́dọ̀ jẹ.

When a king hasn't died,
We cannot choose another.

Eshubiyi replied that he was not taking a title of the whole town, but only as head of Osakan lineage, that is, *Ọba Osákan*, which he claimed from his deceased pater. As the captive *Olú* from Ejigbo quarter was still recognized, Eshubiyi called himself Olu-Odo, or Olu of the "river," or "lower section" of Ayede, in contrast to the "upper section," where Ejigbo quarter had resettled. He told the Iye people that he would return the title of *Olú* when they were ready for it, but of course he never did. Instead, he took the title Àtá of Ayede with Ibadan's political backing and consent, and he proclaimed himself king during the Yemoja festival.[8] During the ritual sacrifice, Eshubiyi went to the sacred grove—*igbó Yemoja*—where a crown (seized from Irun, an Akoko town against which he fought with the Ibadans) was hidden, and he announced that Ayede was allowed to be an *ilú aládé*, a town with a beaded crown. When the put it on, his supporters cried, "Kábíyèsí, Àtá Ayédé," addressing him as a king. There was an outcry of protest that was silenced by his followers, and the Yemoja cult concluded its ritual. The Yemoja cult, brought from Ibadan, remains to this day the guardian of the *Àtá*'s "Olokun" beaded crown, although Iye, which remains today as a small hamlet, has kept the *Olú*'s "original" beaded crown hidden away from Ayede's royal gaze.

As Eshubiyi's power grew, his relations with Ibadan deteriorated. The newly crowned warrior-king used his position as Ibadan's watchdog to build up his own kingdom in the northeastern reaches of the Ibadan empire, sacking towns and taking prisoners as his slaves. Johnson (1921:403) refers to Eshubiyi at that time as "lord of the Yagba and Akoko tribes in the confines of the Yoruba country Northeastwards," and Akintoye (1971:65) describes his military expansionism:

> Eshubiyi was himself a very ambitious man, and surely one of the greatest warriors among the Ekiti and Ijesha. From his town of Ayede he was for ever leading out expeditions into the Iyagba and Akoko countries and subjecting town after town to Aiyede. By the middle seventies he ruled over a large and heterogeneous kingdom made up of some Ekiti, some Akoko and some Iyagba. Sooner or later such a man was bound to excite the suspicion and hostility of the Ibadan chiefs.

In 1875 the Ibadan army launched its last major offensive into Ekitiland to capture Eshubiyi and regain control of its northeastern territories in what became known as the Wokuti expedition, meaning "pile the corpses out of the way" (ibid., 68). Eshubiyi was taken to Ibadan, where he allegedly impressed his captors with his *jùjú* medicine and ability to divine the outcome of battles, and thence he returned to Ayede as ruler of Ibadan's "protectorate." By 1878, however, the Ekitiparapo military confederacy united independent Ekiti kingdoms against Ibadan overrule, and Eshubiyi joined the Ekiti in the famous Kiriji war (1879–86). By the time he died c. 1880, he had developed Ayede into a centralized military autocracy.

It is difficult to define the limits of the *Àtá* Eshubiyi's kingdom because many of his military expeditions sought war bounty rather than

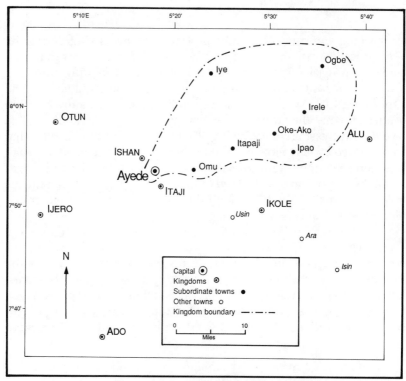

Map 4. The Kingdom of Ayede, c. 1878

lasting political conquest. Among the towns he conquered were Irele, Ipao, Oke-Ako, Ogbe (now in Kwara State), Itapaji, and Omu. These became subordinate to Ayede, supplying labor to build the walled trench around the capital as well as coconut-palm planks to build the *Àtá*'s palace (map 4). During major *òrìṣà* festivals in Ayede, they also contributed agricultural products, such as palm oil, and palm wine, yams, kola nuts, goats, and fowl, for sacrificial offerings and general public consumption. Unlike the Old Oyo and Ibadan empires, however, the *Àtá* did not administer his subordinate towns through appointed officers. With the exception of Ogbe, where the *Àtá* appointed a *Balógun* as a liaison (in contact with Irele and Oke-Ako as well), Ayede's subordinate towns enjoyed considerable independence. Links between the capital and its periphery developed through marriage alliances between royal families and the more important chiefs rather than through administrative overrule. Eshubiyi also sacked and plundered towns such as Irun and Ogabaji in Akoko and Ejuku in Iyagba, but these remained beyond his political control. Refugees seeking protection came to Ayede from Itapa, Ileje, Eda, Iyé (not to be confused with Iyè, which has been discussed so far), and Iporo; but many returned after the British *pax*, leaving place-names such as Omi Itapa (Itapa stream) and Okuta Ileje (Ileje rock) where they first had resettled. They also generated networks of kinship and affinity with resident Ayede families.

The Suppression of Civil Chiefs

Iye refugees were the first to settle Ayede with Eshubiyi. Virtually the entire town moved, reproducing the four quarters—Owaiye, Isaoye, Ejigbo, and Ilaaro—and the *àrę* age-set system in the town's new location between Ishan and Itaji. The arrival of "strangers" from Ikole and Iyagba led to the creation of two new quarters, Egbe-Oba and Omole-Akodi, segmented into "lineages" based as much on common provenience as on common descent. Refugees and immigrants from Ikoyi, Otuna, Itapa, Ara, Usi, and Osi in and around Ikole town formed segments of Egbe-Oba, while refugees from Iyagba and Kwara towns such as Alu, Ejuku, Ilafin, Idofin, and Iyara formed segments of Omole-Akodi quarter.[9] Such resettlement patterns of strangers around an indigenous core were quite typical of the nineteenth-century Ekiti kingdoms. Much less typical was Eshubiyi's system of government. In what amounted to a structural revolution, he deliberately suppressed Iye's dominant civil chieftaincies and elevated his military chieftaincies—war lieutenants and strongmen—into positions of political authority, recruiting mostly from strangers to counterbalance disaffection within the Iye quarters. An Iye chief whose title was only recently resuscitated in Ayede vividly describes (and perhaps overstates) Eshubiyi's unconventional statecraft:

> He had no political administration. He only ruled the people by
> military government. He purposely refused to resuscitate all
> chieftaincies as we had in Iye. He had no council of chiefs. He
> had a council of war chiefs and he made sure he had a majority
> of these chiefs selected from either his household, or from the
> stranger elements and a few other Iye war chiefs. Indeed, he did
> not trust the Iye people. He leaned more confidently on the
> strangers than the natives. Several times the Iye nobles
> complained of his treatment. On many occasions they made him
> [Eshubiyi] know that his method of administration was alien
> and unconventional. But that was the height they could go with

this man. He was not actually a tyrant or a dictator, but he never made anybody a civil chief. There was always a silent suspicion on both sides.

Eshubiyi's dynastic break with the old Iye order—his suppression of the *Olú* and *igharẹ* chieftaincies—elevated a new order of military power brokers into the political domain, patterned largely after the Ibadan army (cf. Ajayi and Smith 1964:14). In Omole-Akodi quarter he installed the *Balógun-Èkìtì* (from Opin), the *Balógun-Àòfin* (from Alu), the *Sẹ́ríkí* (an Ibadan title), the *Aládé* (from Oke-Idofin), and the *Asíwájú*, the latter as an "information officer." From Egbe-Oba quarter he installed the *Òtún-Balógun* (of Ikoyi), the *Òsì-Balógun*, and the *Ésinkin* (from Ikole). Lesser war chiefs from the Iye quarters included the *Òtún* (Osinkolu) and the *Alágbáìye* from his own Osakan lineage within Isaoye quarter, and the *Elégùnmi*, a warrior title from Ejigbo quarter. Beyond this inner circle of war chiefs, the *Àtá* Eshubiyi ruled through the heads of the military age-sets *(olórí àrẹ)* in each quarter. Thus the heads of the senior age-sets in each quarter became de facto quarter chiefs, advising the *Àtá* in disputes and town affairs; but their titles were vested in the age-sets themselves and not in specific lineages or "ruling houses."

The centralization of political power into a military autocracy under the *Àtá* Eshubiyi generated complementary revolutions in the ritual domain. Whereas the major *òrìṣà* in Iye was Olua, worshipped by the whole town to revitalize the *Olú*'s powers of leadership, the *Àtá* Eshubiyi relegated Olua to Owaiye quarter in Ayede and elevated Orisha Ojuna from Ikole and Yemoja from Ibadan into Ayede's royal *òrìṣà* cults. These cults, however, belonged to Isaoye quarter, and there was a ritual-power vacuum among the strangers of Omole-Akodi quarter, who worshipped other gods. To enshrine the political power of the war chiefs from Omole-Akodi and to counterbalance the ritual power of the *Àtá*'s dominant cults, Ayede's strangers, mostly from the Iyagba region, fused their *òrìṣà* into the cult of Orisha Iyagba, thereby consolidating the ritual powers of Ayede's "other half." To clarify the ritualization of changing political relationships, we can examine Ayede's *òrìṣà* cults not as isolates but as corporate factions promoting rival interpretations of power within the kingdom.

THE INCORPORATION OF TRADITION

Òrìṣà cults are ritual corporations possessing—as well as material and symbolic resources—the structural features of any corporate group.

These are (1) unique identity, (2) determinate membership, (3) presumptive perpetuity, and (4) rules of closure (M. G. Smith 1975:94). A cult's unique identity is expressed by the name of the dominant òrìṣà which it serves and is elaborated with specific oríkì which refer to the deity's attributes and origins. Determinate membership is established by initiation. Initiation requires payment of fees; rituals of seclusion involving defilement, hair cutting, and treatment with jùjú medicines; and rituals of "rebirth" and incorporation into the cult, which include instruction in esoteric traditions and modes of worship. Different membership categories within the cult represent specialized ritual functions and orders of seniority. The presumptive perpetuity of an òrìṣà cult is an important principle of religious dogma. Not only are all òrìṣà cults presumed to have originated in Ife before branching out to different towns, they are also presumed to continue *ad futurum*. Ifa divination provides one important safeguard against cult excorporation by revealing when an òrìṣà is "calling" a person to its cult. It is believed that failure to comply with the òrìṣà's demands results in serious misfortune and premature death. Another such safeguard is the belief that the òrìṣà must be tended by the cult; if the cult dwindles in size, the òrìṣà will become angry and punish the quarter which owns it.[10] Cult membership itself is governed by rules of closure, which define reciprocal rights and duties inclusively (between members) and exclusively (between members and nonmembers) and which also define principles of recruitment to the cult.

In addition to possessing these structural features, òrìṣà cults also own property and control socially recognized resources. Ritual technology such as masks, effigies, staffs of office, medicines, iron rattles and instruments used to contact the òrìṣà, and sacrificial altars are kept within a town shrine *(ipara)* located in the quarter associated with the cult, generally close to the chief's house. The initiated members meet at the shrine every two markets (i.e., every nine days) to offer sacrifices, to discuss cult finances and affairs, and to treat private clients who "beg" the òrìṣà for personal assistance. Quarter cults also have a bush shrine *(igbó imọlẹ̀)* cleared near sacred water *(omi imọlẹ̀)* where the òrìṣà dwells. This area lies beyond the residential bounds of the town and is symbolically marked off-limits to outsiders because it is the locus of the òrìṣà's spiritual power. More important than the shrines themselves, however, is the ritual power *(àṣẹ)* which they house and the body of techniques which access and control it. The most highly valued cult property consists of secrets *(awo)*, such as incantations *(ọfọ̀)* uttered in medicinal formulae and specialized sacrifices which harness the òrìṣà's power and direct it toward specific ends. Such property is not only restricted to the cult, but is differentially incorporated and distributed within it.

Cults in Ayede

Ayede's dominant *òrìṣà* cults consist of Orisha Ojuna, which Eshubiyi's natural father had brought to Iye from Ikole; the Yemoja cult, which Eshubiyi brought from Ibadan; and Orisha Iyagba, which Yagba immigrants brought from Alu c. 1880. Lesser cults include the *òrìṣà* Olua and Oroyeye of Owaiye quarter, Orisha Oniyi of Ejigbo quarter, and the "bull-roarer" cult of Babatigbo of Ilaaro quarter, all brought from Iye by "original" settlers; and the *òrìṣà* Oloke, brought by a final wave of Ikole immigrants who formed Egbe-Oba quarter. Many of these lesser cults were at one time dominant in Iye, where they ritualized the corporate autonomy of its quarters. Thus the *Olú* of Iye owned the Olua cult in Owaiye quarter, where it served as the town's royal cult. The *Olú* himself did not participate in the *òrìṣà* cults of other quarters. In Ayede, however, the royal Orisha Ojuna and Yemoja cults overwhelmed the resettled Iye cults in three ways: (1) by recruiting members from different quarters; (2) by merging some membership categories of lesser cults with dominant cults; and (3) by establishing ritual networks between central and peripheral cults, networks which did not previously exist in Iye.

Orisha Ojuna

The *Àtá*'s cult of Orisha Ojuna was brought to Ayede by Eshubiyi; he claimed it from his genitor, who belonged to the cult in Ikole. Whereas Orisha Ojuna in Ikole is associated with the *Elékọ̀lé*'s (the *ọba* of Ikole) royal power and authority, in Ayede, the cult associates these powers with the *Àtá*. The *Àtá* of Ayede is thus perceived as a "ritual descendant" of the *Elékọ̀lé* of Ikole, a connection which some royal kinsmen claim is genealogically correct as well. Although owned by the *Àtá*'s royal lineage, Ayede's cult of Orisha Ojuna has incorporated other *òrìṣà* from nonroyal quarters to increase its membership and broaden its ritual jurisdiction. Within Orisha Ojuna's town shrine *(ipara)*, four inner chambers contain specialized shrines for the deities Olua, Osanyin, Ado, and Elekole, each with titled representatives and recruits from different quarters (fig. 2.3).

It is said that when Eshubiyi became the first *Àtá*, he engineered this fusion of different cults. The inner shrine of Olua, represented by the warrior chief *Ògúnjọbí* (who is represented today by a patrilineal

Figure 2.3. Centralized Recruitment to the Orisha Ojuna Cult in Ayede

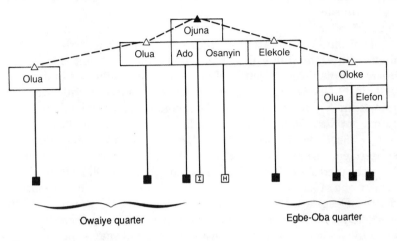

Key

■ Devotees

[I] Devotees from Isaoye quarter

[H] Herbalists and devotees from Ilaaro quarter

▲ Àwòrò of Orisha Ojuna

△ Priests of branch cults

descendant), incorporates the followers and ritual powers of Owaiye quarter's Olua cult—the òrìṣà of the former *Olú* of Iye—into Orisha Ojuna's cult. Formerly dominant in Iye, the Olua cult was repressed and co-opted by Eshubiyi in Ayede. Members of the Olua cult in Owaiye quarter cannot participate in Orisha Ojuna's annual festival until they are formally invited by the Ògúnjọbí to attend. Although the àwòrò (high priest) of Olua maintains a separate town shrine in Owaiye quarter with distinct sacrificial rites, he receives ritual respect (*ìjúbà*) from the Orisha Ojuna devotees during their festival, as well as meat from their sacrifices. They also share the same spiritual water (*omi* Olua) in the bush. The shrine of Ado within the Orisha Ojuna cult also recruits devotees from Owaiye quarter; these are led by the priestess *Olórí Ijegbede* and include followers of two lineage cults—Orisha Emuyin and Osanyin Aiku. Ogun's shrine within Orisha Ojuna's cult was founded by the military chief *Alágbayé*, head of the Agbeta branch of the royal lineage, who recruits from among hunters and herbalists in the town.[11] The shrine of the òrìṣà Elekole within Orisha Ojuna ritualizes the cult's spiritual continuity with past Ikole kings. It is led by the Olóka priestess, whose title means "owner of Oka," the Elékọlé's "street" in Ikole.

In addition to these four sacrificial chambers within Orisha Ojuna's town shrine, the cult is also "married" to the Oloke cult of Egbe-Oba quarter, which was settled by Ikole immigrants. Whereas in the town of Ikole, Orisha Ojuna and Oloke exist as separate cults under different priests, in Ayede they are partially merged. The Oloke cult does perform a separate Oloke festival with Egbe-Oba quarter, but this the Àtá must himself avoid since, I was told, his attendance would signify his subservience to the Elékọlé of Ikole. The Àtá is represented, however, by his beaded staff of office, which is brought to the Oloke festival, and also by one of his daughters in the Orisha Ojuna cult, who attends and dances. Despite such distance between the cults, Oloke's town shrine is located within Orisha Ojuna's, and their members share the same basic food taboos.[12] Whereas Owaiye's Olua cult shares the same spiritual water with Orisha Ojuna but maintains a separate town shrine, Egbe-Oba's Oloke cult shares the same town shrine but maintains a separate source of spiritual water. The Orisha Ojuna and Oloke cults are described as "both of one body" (ará kan ni méjèjì), as "fragments" of a calabash, and as "affines" (ànọn). Chief Òsì of Egbe-Oba quarter, the officiating priest of Oloke, is in fact married to the priestess of the female hunters (Olórí Ọlọ́ọ̀mẹyin) in Orisha Ojuna, compounding real with fictive affinity.

Like any major òrìṣà cult, Orisha Ojuna is organized as a town or polity unto itself. The àwòrò, or high priest, leads all of the deity's devotees and is described as their "king." It is through him that the devotees, whether individually or collectively, can most effectively invoke the deity. Even non-initiates advised by the Ifa oracle to sacrifice to Orisha Ojuna must present their offerings to the àwòrò. The same applies to the Àtá of Ayede and by extension to the entire town. The àwòrò is a ritual-power broker. It is through him that the òrìṣà receives major sacrifices, and it is also through him that the òrìṣà can reply, possessing the àwòrò directly or indirectly through oracles, to indicate whether or not sacrifices are accepted, what further sacrifices are required, and what problems the future holds. The Èyémọlẹ̀ priestess, or "grandmother of the imọlẹ̀," is the "second in command" within the Orisha Ojuna cult, and she leads the women. She should be present whenever the àwòrò offers a major sacrifice. Proscribed from carrying anything on her head, she wears a simple white head tie, beads, and white cloth and holds an expensive white horsetail fly whisk in her right hand to symbolize her "chieftaincy" title within the cult. She never goes to the bush when the devotees carry spiritual water, but remains in the town shrine. Her power is "cool" (*ìtútù*), as her color is white; she represents civic hierarchy and control within the cult.

The two most senior titles within the Orisha Ojuna cult—the *àwòrò* and the *Èyémọlè*—are followed by two membership grades, the *ọlóòtun* and the *ọlóòmẹyin*, whose members are ranked according to their seniority. Although both men and women can belong to the *ọlọọtun* grade, only women carry revitalizing water (*òtun*) from the bush to the town shrine in vessels on their heads. The *Olórí Ijegbede* leads this procession carrying a white calabash which contains the spiritual water of the cult as a whole, followed by devotees carrying their individual vessels of water. Wherever this water is placed upon the ground, the deity will arrive from the sky (*òrun*) and speak. The men of the *ọlóòtun* grade carry not water, but fire. This event occurs five days prior to the carrying of water (*ọjó iponmi*) and takes place at night, indicating that the *Àtá* has provided a goat for the yearly sacrifice and indicating the place where Orisha Ojuna should arrive from heaven, rather like airport runway lights. The *Amáṣa*, leader of the male *ọlóòtun*, embodies the "hot" power of Eshu and utters incantations (*ofò*) to defeat enemies of the cult. Like the *àwòrò* and the *Èyémọlè*, he is recruited from the royal lineage, preferably from among the king's own sons.

The *ọlóòmẹyin* grade of devotees represents "hunters" and is also sexually differentiated. The men do not go into trance or perform conspicuous roles in public rituals. The women, however, perform male ritual roles. Like men, they cannot carry water on their heads. Instead, they wear red peacock feathers (*ìkó odídẹ*) in their hair—as emblems of ritual danger and potency, wield warrior cutlasses, and dance in "hot" male styles to clear the path of enemies and bad medicine for the *ọlóòtun* carrying water. After the "hunters," a general category of ordinary members, or "children" (*ọmọdẹ*), includes the newer and untitled recruits. In the past, members of a subcategory of "wives" of the cult were selected from among the "children" to fetch water from the stream and run errands for senior members, but this subcategory no longer exists in Ayede.

The Orisha Ojuna cult's links with other towns illustrate the variable bases of *òrìṣà*-cult networks. Unlike the centralized Shango cult of the Oyo empire, which extended to subordinate towns and installed Shango priests with politico-ritual authority over local rulers, the *Àtá* of Ayede's Orisha Ojuna cult never dominated his subordinate towns. Except in Iye, where Eshubiyi's natural father established a shrine called Ojule-ile-oba, Ayede's subordinate towns have no Orisha Ojuna cults of their own. Members of subordinate towns who are related to cult members through kinship or marriage come to "support" the festival in Ayede, dancing, singing, and sharing food and palm wine, but they hold no positions in the cult. Initiated devotees come from other towns such as Ikole, Osin, and Ijelu; women join Ayede's devotees wearing similar cult uniforms and beaded panels (ìkólàbà), while men may be invited to beat gongs (agogo) for the ritual procession. The towns of Osin and Ijelu, however, belong not to Ayede but to Ikole kingdom. When Eshubiyi promoted the Orisha Ojuna cult to usurp the Olú of Iye's ruling dynasty, it was at a cost—he established ritual links with Ikole, links which ironically threatened his political independence. One senior cult member explained that to establish Orisha Ojuna in Ayede's subordinate towns would invite divided loyalties, for they would be drawn toward the Elékọlé of Ikole. Relations between the Àtá and the Elékọlé were in fact problematic from the start, when they fought over territories for their respective kingdoms. Even in 1934, the Elékọlé petitioned the district officer that Ipao, Oke-Ako, Irele, and Itapaji were originally his and should be returned to him from Ayede district. It was thus in Ayede's political interest not to promote Orisha Ojuna in its subordinate towns, but to consolidate the cult's power within the kingdom's capital.

Yemoja

Whereas the Orisha Ojuna cult represents the Àtá Eshubiyi's patrilineal connection with Ikole, the Yemoja cult represents his political alliance with Ibadan in the idiom of marriage. The idiom is appropriate, for if Eshubiyi inherited Orisha Ojuna from his father Eshukolo Onimogun, he literally married into Ibadan's Yemoja cult by incorporating it into his family through wives. According to local traditions, Eshubiyi was initiated into the Yemoja cult after his capture by the Ibadans, who wished to secure an alliance with the belligerent "Lord of the Ekitis." Included in this initiation were the sanctions of Ibadan's powerful Ogboni cult, which extended politico-ritual networks throughout the empire. That Eshubiyi soon forswore himself by joining the Ekitiparapo against the Ibadan army did not diminish his interest in the Yemoja cult. Eshubiyi needed the Yemoja cult to legitimize his own ruling dynasty. It provided a valuable charter of independent kingship which the Ikole-centric Orisha Ojuna cult could not achieve by itself. As we noted, traditions relate how Eshubiyi first crowned himself king during the Yemoja festival in Ayede.

The affinal character of Ayede's Yemoja cult is visible in the structure and history of its major offices and titles, which are reserved mostly for women. Two exceptions are the *àwòrò* Yemoja, who offici-ated as the head *(Aṣípa)* of Eshubiyi's family Ogun cult, and the *Baba Mógbà,* or male priest of Shango. Both are *ọmọ ọba,* that is, "children of the king," and their titles have passed from fathers to sons. The major-ity of cult titles, however, were incorporated into Eshubiyi's family through marriage and devolved through cognatic descent lines.

The high priestess of Yemoja, for example, married Eshubiyi and brought her *Yèyéolókun* title from Ibadan to Ayede. The title devolved through their son Abolokefa, who reigned as the second *Àtá* of Ayede, to his daughter and afterwards to her brother's daughter (fig. 2.4). The same Abolokefa married an Oshun priestess from Offa, whose title de-volved through Orishagbemi—their son, who was the fourth reigning *Àtá*—to his daughter. The title of *Ìyá Ṣàngó* has a more controversial his-tory. Before the arrival of the Yemoja cult, Shango was worshipped by Ilisa lineage in Owaiye quarter. With the advent of the Yemoja cult, a new *Ìyá Ṣàngó* title was introduced to Eshubiyi's Adodo lineage seg-ment and passed to Abolokefa's daughter. Since Yemoja is the mother of Shango in Yoruba myth, and since, I was told, a child cannot precede its mother, Owaiye's Shango cult fused with that of Yemoja under the new *Ìyá Ṣàngó.* The new title, however, passed laterally to her brother's wife, Iyelola, who descended from Oshogbo immigrants and devotees of Oshun, and then lineally from Iyelola to her daughter, a full member of the Eshubiyi patriline. The royal Yemoja cult thereby absorbed Owaiye's Shango cult and recruited Oshogbo immigrants without re-linquishing control of its titles.

The Yemoja cult, like that of Orisha Ojuna, houses a complex clus-ter of different deities. The core subcults within Ayede's Yemoja cult today are Orisha Oko, Shango, Ogun, Oshun, and Oya, each with its priestess, sacrifices, drum rhythms, and devotees. In the past they in-cluded Orishanla, Osanyin, Olokun, Oke, Kinkofo, Erinle, and Bayoni as well. The relations between Yemoja and these subordinate *òrìṣà* are expressed in idioms of kinship and affinity (fig. 2.5). In local myths, Yemoja is married to Orisha Oko, a "king" and deity of the farm. Her two most important sons are Ogun and his junior brother Shango, who are among the "hot" *òrìṣà* of the Yoruba pantheon. Ogun married Oya, but Shango stole her away. Shango also married Oshun. The additional *òrìṣà* of Ayede's Yemoja cult are either "tacked on" to this core model or remain "free." Bayoni is placed between his brothers Ogun and Shango, while Erinle is identified as Oshun's junior brother. Eshu, Konkofo, Oke, and Osanyin, however, are "free" spirits associated with Yemoja.

Figure 2.4. Devolution of Yemoja Cult Offices

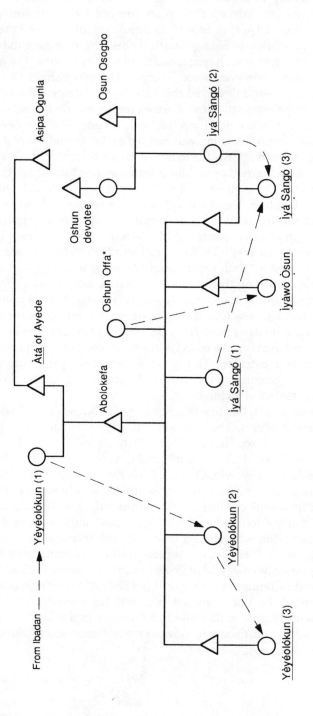

*Alternative traditions say that Ajayi Abolokefa's mother, not his wife, was the Oshun priestess from Offa.

Figure 2.5. Kinship and Affinity in Ayede's Yemoja Cult Pantheon

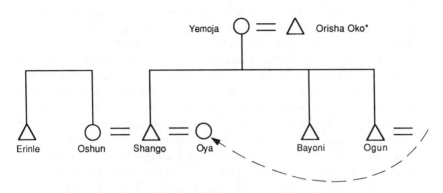

*Orisha Oko's affinal relationship to Yemoja is emphasized in Ayede over and above patrifilial relations to her children.

The precise genealogical and affinal configuration of Yemoja and her associated òrìṣà differs from models found elsewhere in Yorubaland for reasons discussed in chapter 6. In Ayede it expresses relations between shrines, priestesses, and devotees within the cult. The *Yèyéolókun* is the high priestess of Yemoja—it is she who carries the ritually potent calabash *(igbá Yemọja)* from the bush through the town to the king's palace. On her head, in the dense and key symbol of the calabash, rests the spiritual welfare of the town and kingdom; hence her paramount authority in the town shrine. The *Ìyáolókun* priestess of Olokun is the *Yèyéolókun*'s ritual counterpart in the bush. There she sacrifices a white pigeon to Olokun at the sacred water where the spirit and "power" of Yemoja dwells. The titled priestess next in rank—*Ìyá Ṣàngó*—officiates for Shango devotees within the Yemoja cult. Also called *Ìyàwóòsà*, or "wife of the òrìṣà", she paradoxically occupies a male ritual role representing deified Oyo kingship and unconstrained power, and she holds an extremely high title in the Ogboni society. Shango's popular *oríkì*, "the king didn't hang" *(ọba kò so)*, refers to the fourth *Aláàfin*'s abuse of authority, suicide, and subsequent deification as an òrìṣà. Studded with mirrors, the *Ìyá Ṣàngó*'s fulgurous dress represents the "hot" power and danger of lightning. When possessed by Shango (as we shall discuss in chapter 5), she foresees imminent dangers and prescribes remedial sacrifices for the *Àtá* and his townspeople. Her choreography and drum rhythms are also "hot" and unconstrained. After *Ìyá Ṣàngó* ranks the Oshun priestess, *Ìyàwó Ọṣun*, who belongs with Yemoja to the "cool" white òrìṣà of female composure and control.

Unlike the Orisha Ojuna cult, which houses separate chambers in its town shrine for its subordinate òrìṣà, the Yemoja cult priestesses sacrifice together before one altar in their town shrine. In the bush shrine, however, they sacrifice to their separate òrìṣà at different locations within a walled enclosure. The high priestess of each òrìṣà leads a group of titled followers and devotees. Whereas the high priestesses of Yemoja and of the subordinate òrìṣà belong to the Àtá's royal lineage within Isaoye quarter, devotees from commoner lineages and from Owaiye, Ejigbo, Ilaaro, and Omole-Akodi quarters can join the Yemoja cult, allying with one of the òrìṣà within the cluster, and can ascend to titled office through serial succession. The most senior posts, however, are restricted to members of the royal lineage. When such a priest or priestess dies, he or she is replaced by a junior representative or "regent" until a new incumbent is "called" by the òrìṣà or is selected through divination.

Within Ayede, the Yemoja cult is vested in the royal lineage but recruits its members through a web of cognatic ties which spread across all quarters of the town. Women predominate as ritual-office holders, and they establish cognatic bases of recruitment through children who follow them into the cult. Whereas the Orisha Ojuna cult is historically related to Ikole and recruits from among Ikole "strangers" and tenant lineages in Ayede, Yemoja "married" into the royal lineage and recruits from among the "Oyo" refugee and tenant lineages from Ibadan, Offa, and Oshogbo. The Yemoja cult, however, like Orisha Ojuna, is not institutionalized in Ayede's subordinate towns. Today, as before, subordinate towns send relatives, age-set representatives, and gifts to the cult and the palace during Yemoja's annual festival, but they have never incorporated the cult for themselves. Iye, Ayede's relocated town of origin, is the one exception. Tradition relates how Shango went to Iye to fight the townspeople during Ayede's Yemoja festival. When Shango hurt them, the Amùwágún, or first chief under the Olú, told his people to establish the cult in their town. When the cult established itself in Iye, the Amùwágún was elevated to the political status of baálę, thereby institutionalizing Iye's subservience to Ayede and displacing the Olú. Just as the Yemoja cult initially allied Ayede with Ibadan by elevating Eshubiyi into a proper king, so it reinforced political loyalty between Ayede and Iye's elevated Amùwágún.

The absence of Yemoja cults in Ayede's remaining subordinate towns does not rule out ritual networks between the kingdom's center and periphery. Ritual links between Ayede's Shango cult, which is embedded within the Yemoja cult, and the Shango cult of Itapaji, a subordinate town, are mobilized in their respective festivals, as are links between Yemoja's Oshun in Ayede and the Oshun cult in Omu. In such networks, a subordinate òrìṣà within the dominant Yemoja cult links with a dominant òrìṣà in a subordinate town. Thus the subsidiary òrìṣà clustered within the Yemoja cult not only attract followers from different quarters within Ayede, but establish links with devotees in subordinate towns as well. The rationale for restricting Yemoja proper to the Àtá's metropolitan capital may well have been the same as of Orisha Ojuna. Just as the cult of Orisha Ojuna extended a ritual field centered in Ikole, the Yemoja cult extended an Oyo-centric ritual field based in Ibadan. Ayede emerged at the intersection of the two ritual fields, lying on the eastern periphery of Ibadan's influence and on the northwestern periphery of Ikole's. If subordinate towns with Orisha Ojuna would be pulled away from Ayede and toward Ikole, so subordinate towns with the Yemoja cult could be pulled into the Ibadan empire. As if to hold Ayede in place, a third ritual field, the cult of Orisha Iyagba, extended from the Yagba town of Alu to include Ayede in its southeastern periphery, making Ayede the center of a triangle of forces. If from an external viewpoint the cult of Orisha Iyagba balanced Ayede against Ibadan and Ikole, internally, it balanced Yagba immigrants within Ayede against royal cults and Iye quarters. Orisha Iyagba is not a royal cult in Ayede, but it belongs to the lineage of a powerful town chief. It rivals the Orisha Ojuna and Yemoja cults in size and importance, and it maintains strong links with Ayede's subordinate Yagba towns.

Orisha Iyagba

The development of the Orisha Iyagba cult in Ayede reflects the promotion of military chiefs under the Àtá Eshubiyi. The cult is officially associated with the *Balógun Àáfin*, a military chief of Yagba origins whose career as a Big Man altered the political and ritual distribution of power in Ayede. The "story" *(itàn)* of Orisha Iyagba in Ayede, provided by a senior cult priestess, is worth recounting in some detail, as it illustrates the politics of changing ritual relations.

Orisha Iyagba was brought to Ayede by Yagba immigrants who settled in Omole-Akodi quarter during the nineteenth-century wars. Cult elders relate how the principal Yagba chief, the *Ésinkin*, cofounded Ayede with Eshubiyi and was second to him in rank. According to one tradition, Eshubiyi was going to Ilokoja and the *Ésinkin* was on his way to Akoko when they met at a crossroads *(orítà)* after the town of Omuo and greeted each other.[13] The *Ésinkin* followed Eshubiyi to war, and together they plundered towns and captured slaves. On returning to Iye, both wanted to settle, but Eshubiyi could not remain because his brother Elegunmi wanted to kill him.[14] They left for Ekiti looking for water and saw verdant growth at Okuta Metigberan. There they looked for water but could not find it. The *Ésinkin* told his son to penetrate the thick bush and find water. The son reached Olosoro (Orisha Iyagba's sacred water) and saw that the ground was wet. He placed an antelope horn beneath the root of an Eku tree, so that water dripped from the root into the horn until it was full.[15] He then carried the horn to Eshubiyi and the *Ésinkin*. The *Ésinkin* said he would settle at Olosoro and Eshubiyi said he would settle at Oju-Oja, where Ayede's market is today. A native of the Yagba town of Aaye, the *Ésinkin* brought the Yagba immigrants to Ayede. He was the head of Omole-Akodi quarter, and his junior chiefs included the *Balógun Ààfin* from Alu, the *Balógun Èkìtì* from Opin, the *Séríkí*, and the *Asuwájú* from Irele. The *Balógun Ààfin* at that time was no more than a messenger for the king. As a palace chief, he mediated between Eshubiyi and his military advisors.

According to this tradition, the *Ésinkin*'s wife, Olubintan, first saw Orisha Iyagba in Ayede's marketplace and took it to her husband's house. The *òrìṣà* "chose" the *Ésinkin* as its priest because he was second in rank to Eshubiyi. At that time, the Yagba immigrants combined their various *òrìṣà* with Orisha Iyagba into a single, powerful cult. Soon afterward, the cult drummer built a house near the shrine. An epidemic folloed—a sign that Orisha Iyagba was angry—so the devotees moved the shrine to a new site, near the *Balógun Ààfin*'s house. That was how the *Balógun Ààfin* took over the cult.

In a variant tradition which also supports the *Balógun Ààfin*'s appropriation of the cult, Orisha Iyagba appeared at *ìdìyá* in Ayede's marketplace, where he started fighting people.[16] The townspeople recognized that the *òrìṣà* came from Alu, which was also the *Balógun Ààfin*'s town of origin. The king went to the market to see for himself, and he called the *Balógun Ààfin* as his second in rank to pacify the *òrìṣà*. The *Balògun Ààfin* seized the *òrìṣà* in the marketplace and took it to the Olosoro bush, where it dwells today. The *Balógun Ààfin* became a popular and powerful chief. He married sixteen wives, built a large walled compound, and acquired countless slaves. He also attracted devotees from eight Yagba towns to worship Orisha Iyagba in Ayede; these were Alu, Ejuku, Ipao, Irele, Itapaji, Oko-Akom, Igbo-Ele, and Iife. Each town sent a senior cult representative to participate in Ayede's annual festival.

These oral traditions are clearly about political change, and they deserve a closer and more critical reading. Whereas the first tradition associates the origin of Ayede and the advent of Orisha Iyagba with the *Ésinkin*, the second shifts the cult's focus to the *Balógun Àáfin*. Even a cursory comparison reveals common motifs: (1) the *òrìṣà* is associated with Ayede's locus of origin (Olosoro, Idiya), and (2) the *òrìṣà* arrived in the king's market, where it was pacified and appropriated by a Yagba military chief (*Ésinkin, Balógun Àáfin*) who in both cases is second to the king. We can reasonably infer from both traditions that the *Balógun Àáfin* eclipsed the *Ésinkin* in political power and rank, took control of the cult, and extended ritual networks to Yagba towns both within Ayede's kingdom and beyond.

The internal organization of the Orisha Iyagba cult in Ayede recapitulates this history. Like the cults of Yemoja and Orisha Ojuna, it is a central cult containing a cluster of subordinate *òrìṣà* owned by different lineages and settlers of Omole-Akodi quarter. The *òrìṣà* Ereo ranks first in the cluster; the name refers to the *Balógun Àáfin*'s family name before he received his title. Although his parents worshipped different Yagba *òrìṣà*, the *òrìṣà* Ereo passed to the children of the *Balógun Àáfin* in the Iletogun lineage. After Ereo follow Ogbon-Ilele and Oloye from Ipao, Ore from Irele, Iroko from Ejuku, Olooke and Okutaaro from Itapaji, Orisha (the nonspecific name for Orishanla, or Obatala, whose local provenience I could not determine), and Agiri from Ogbe. As these *òrìṣà* within the cult belong to lineages in a quarter of "strangers," they are, like their devotees, identified by their town of origin. In addition to these clustered *òrìṣà*, devotees of Orisha Iyagba worship a water spirit, Yeyetomi, which speaks to them at the bush shrine in an esoteric "Yagba" language.

As with Orisha Ojuna, Orisha Iyagba's allocation of ritual roles crosscuts lineage-based *òrìṣà* within the cult. The *àwòrò*, or high priest, is followed in rank by *Ẹkùn*, a man who represents the dangerous and unpredictable power of a leopard. Possessed by the *òrìṣà*, he grunts and gestures like an animal, appears suddenly in trees and on rooftops, dances in a heated frenzy, rolls in dirt, and decapitates a chicken with his teeth to drink its blood and restore his senses.

The *Èyémọlẹ̀*, in "cool" contrast to the "hot" leopard, represents the women of the cult. These divide into the *ọlóọtun* grade of ritual-water carriers and the female "hunters" (*ọdẹ*), who hold spears and cutlasses (*àgàdà*) while dancing like men to clear the path for the *Olóọtun*. The present *Ológun*, or head of the female hunters, is the great-granddaughter of the powerful *Balógun Àáfin* who aggrandized the cult, and she represents him as a "warrior." She is also the present *Àtá*'s fifth wife, bringing the cult of Orisha Iyagba into the palace, where she maintains a personal shrine. Thus the Orisha Iyagba cult belongs to "strangers" in Ayede but attaches to the royal lineage through networks of kinship and affinity. As a ritual corporation, it articulates with the major cleavage of Ayede town into "natives" of Iye and "strangers" from the Yagba region, a cleavage which extends through the kingdom at large, distinguishing the Yagba subordinate towns—Irele, Oke-Ako, Ipao, and formerly Ogbe, which Ayede lost to Kwara District under the British—from Iye, Itapaji, and Omu, which are perceived to be more properly Ekiti. Cognatic principles of recruitment to the cult, however, help to bind these sections together.

Within Ayede, Yemoja, Orisha Ojuna, and Orisha Iyagba are described as "friends." Like the *Àtá* and the *Balógun Ààfin*, they live in different quarters, come from different towns, and exercise their powers for the good of the kingdom. But like all friends, they can also fight and go their separate ways. Implicit in the power of Orisha Iyagba, latent in its corporate organization, military iconography, and ritual choreography, are threats of armed insurrection or secession from the kingdom. As we shall see in chapter 3, such conflict erupted in 1934 between the *Àtá* Gabriel Osho, who ruled autocratically, and Ayede's Yagba towns, which petitioned to secede from the district. The development of Orisha Iyagba into a central, nonroyal cult in Ayede can therefore be seen as a strategic response to the *Àtá* Eshubiyi's consolidation of political and ritual power. The *Balógun Ààfin* extended the cult throughout Ayede's Yagba towns to expand his own political base. He appropriated a valuable resource of ritual power which, as an examination of political and ritual processes will reveal, harnessed potentially divisive political interests to revitalizing idioms of public good.

●●

The incorporation of multiple "traditions" into dominant *òrìṣà* cults within Ayede reveals how the "old" Iye order was displaced and reorganized into a centralized military kingdom. The four quarters of Iye—Owaiye, Isaoye, Ejigbo, and Ilaaro—were reranked by Eshubiyi, who promoted Isaoye above the others; and they were politically overwhelmed by immigrant refugees from Ikole, Oyo, and Yagba areas. Formerly dominant in Iye, the cult of Olua was restricted to Owaiye quarter, where it glorified its displaced dynasty in virtual quarantine within the town. In Ayede, the warlord Eshubiyi promoted new chiefs and new cults. The cult of Orisha Ojuna, associated with the king of

Ikole, elevated Isaoye to the status of a "royal" quarter and consolidated devotees of other deities within its inner chambers. The Yemoja cult, brought from Ibadan, provided Eshubiyi's beaded crown through real and fictive links of kinship and marriage with Oyo-centric cult representatives and refugees. The cult of Orisha Iyagba consolidated Ayede's power bloc of Yagba strangers and their military chiefs within one ritual corporation. Whereas Orisha Ojuna and Yemoja are royal cults of the *Àtá* of Ayede, Orisha Iyagba is a civil cult of "strangers" vested in the lineage of the powerful *Balógun Ààfin* and worshipped by his followers and clients in Omole-Akodi quarter and beyond.

The social history and corporate organization of Ayede's dominant *òrìṣà* cults, and the correlative repression of dominant cults from Iye, document with considerable precision how traditions are selectively renewed and reified to establish new political alliances and bases of power. More important, however, than the changing politico-ritual topography of Yorubaland, yet more difficult to grasp, are the interpretive frameworks of the power relations themselves. As external observers with historical hindsight, we see Ayede's *òrìṣà* cults as closed corporations allied to competing and shifting power blocs. The history of the cults can thus be plotted and traced within different Yoruba regions and towns. But seen within Ayede itself, cult histories *(itàn)* remain largely hidden within shrines which house secrets that are infinitely subversive and "deep."

Officially, all *òrìṣà*, like all kings, come from Ife. Off the record, they possess distinctive migrations and itineraries which are loaded with political implications and innuendos. Devotees in the cult of Olua ritually avoid the *Àtá* of Ayede because he is a usurper of power, and to them a false king. Within Orisha Ojuna he is praised with the *Elékọ̀lé* of Ikole, while the Yemoja cult identifies him with the *Olúlọ̀yé* of Ibadan and the *Aláàfin* of Oyo. Devotees of Orisha Iyagba recognize the *Àtá* but also divide their loyalties by glorifying their former Yagba rulers and kings. Within Ayede, as in every Yoruba town, *òrìṣà* cults enshrine rival interpretations of power which are ritually sanctioned and only secretly discussed. If the *ọba* represents the unity of the kingdom, he does so as a composite figure, embodying the multiple and often mutually exclusive visions and claims of its political segments and corporate parts. To grasp these multiple visions more clearly, and the power relations which they represent and articulate, we can look beyond Ayede's turbulent genesis to analyze the contradictions of kingship in local politics.

Dialectics of Power
in Local Politics

I t is one thing to found a Yoruba kingdom and another to regulate its
internal affairs. The exigencies of nineteenth-century warfare may
account for the diversity of Ayede's resettled population, but they
cannot explain the reproduction and modification of its "original"
groups and their traditions over time. As Lévi-Strauss's concept of bricolage suggests—when transposed from myth to military polities—it
is not the elements of dismantled structures that confer significance or
value, but the differential relations into which they recombine.
Ayede's resettled "indigenes" and "strangers" may have initially
aggregated for survival and defense, but they also engaged in competitive politics, contesting the Àtá's autocratic concentration of power.
This chapter sketches Ayede's political structure and history to identify
the formal and informal arenas of effective political action and the conflicts and strategies which such action entails. Drawing on M. G.
Smith's corporation theory and P. C. Lloyd's conflict theory, I argue
that the "functional" regulation of power by authority is an essentially
hermeneutical practice.

POWER AND AUTHORITY

Power and authority constitute the fundamental principles of effective
government—defined as the regulation of public affairs—in San kindreds, in centralized kingdoms, in industrial states, or in any corporation *sui generis* (Smith 1975:29).[1] As analytic concepts, power and

authority define complementary fields of collective action—namely, political action, which seeks to influence the formulation of policy; and administrative action, which orders its implementation. Since political action (politics) is competition for power, expressed through the contraposition of competing groups or persons, it is inherently segmentary. Administrative action (administration), in contrast, is inherently hierarchical, consisting of the authorized processes of organization and management of a given unit. In more intuitive terms, politics mobilizes power competition between equivalent units to influence and determine policy from below, while administration mobilizes conventional rules, laws, and procedures to implement policy inclusively from above.

In his original formulation of this concept of government, M. G. Smith (1956) revealed that segmentary lineage systems, *pace* the received wisdom of Evans-Pritchard and Fortes (1940), derive their characteristic structure from politics and administration rather than from the lineage system itself. Exclusive relations between contraposed lineage segments are political, he argued, whereas the inclusive relations between nested segments belong to administrative hierarchy. By abstracting the principles of government from the lineage system per se, Smith distinguished universal values of power and authority and the structural relations of politics and administration from the particular frameworks in which they occur. Such distinctions form the basis of comparative studies of political variation as well as of diachronic studies of political change (Smith 1960, 1979). Corporations constitute the concrete units of analysis, whether they are simple or complex, aggregate or sole, parts of a political system, or the system itself; hence the structural emphasis in Smith's political anthropology.

In our discussion of Ayede's kingship and government, Smith's concepts of politics, administration, and the corporate group specify the salient units of power competition and highlight micropolitical arenas of action as well. Political networks, alliances, strategies, and "games" formed by leaders and "teams" competing for power do not arise out of a Hobbesian "war of all against all." Rather, they presuppose a political organization which renders them effectual. Even if we egocentrically assume, with Leach (1954), the individual's "innate" desire for power, we should begin not with the individual, but with the object of desire. Power, defined as the capacity for effective action (Smith 1975:175), constitutes the desideratum of political competition and lies at the heart of the political process. Inherently unbounded, unstable and scarce, power must be appropriated, contained, and controlled.

A closer examination of power and authority reveals a dialectic of continuous transformation which underlies competitive politics. Power *sui generis* is inherently anarchic and must be transformed into authority to be effectively controlled:

> Power which is inherently segmentary and conditional, latent as well as manifest, is relativistic in nature and expression, and cannot be centralized. The 'centralization' of power proceeds by its transformation into authority, with a specific administrative hierarchy of its own (ibid., 29).

Like Weber's concept of charisma, power is routinized by an institutional hierarchy which establishes rule-governed constraints on its regulation and control. But if power is transformed by authority, it is never entirely subsumed. A Yoruba king may speak with authority as the "mouthpiece" of his chiefs and subjects, but he can also abuse his power by violating the normative limitations of his office. Power, the capacity for effective action, continuously thwarts the limits of authority. Unlike authority, it lacks prescriptive legitimacy, transcends limitation, and exercises its capacity *ultra vires* to pursue courses and goals "beyond the requirements of rules or in the face of opposition" (ibid., 85), even "despite material and social obstacles" (ibid., 175). Power *sui generis* is thus intrinsically subversive. Powerful Yoruba are often praised as "wicked," "terrible," even cruel to their kin. Portrayed as devious rascals who get what they want, they are admired for their ability to destroy with impunity.

Whereas authority transforms power by regulating its distribution into routinized administration, power, in turn, transforms authority by manipulating, revising, or even breaking and remaking prescribed rules through competitive politics. Corporations not only constitute structural units of comparison and change, but establish dynamic micropolitical arenas of action as well. For the dialectic of power and authority—the continuous interplay of power relations and an authority structure—underlies the regulation of all public affairs:

> Within any corporation, whether this is a lineage, a village, an association or a municipal government, internal and external issues repeatedly arise to which the corpus of agreed rules and precedents are not fully applicable. In these situations, divergent opinions and interests set up cleavages within the plurality over the appropriate course of action. Such conflicts express the exercise of power and are generally resolved by this means. Likewise, competitions for office or movements to

introduce new rules or to modify old procedures and organization, or actions to maintain or change the unit's network of external relations—these are occasions on which public affairs are generally regulated through *contests of power* (ibid., 85, my emphasis).

Embedded in these propositions lies a conflict model of politics based on "contests of power," a model which distinguishes different foci of power competition. First and foremost are issues of public policy which mobilize "cleavages within the plurality." Since competition for power to decide such issues is segmentary and divisive, agreed rules and precedents become objects of negotiation. Politics thereby precipitates modification and revision of public authority structures—their rules, procedures, internal organization, and external articulation. Competitions for office generate similar factions in which powerful rivals can uphold or modify rules of succession and conditions of eligibility and can transform authority by appropriating it. A brief sketch of Ayede's dynastic succession and the major developments during each reign illustrates the frictions and factions of competitive politics within the royal lineage, the capital town, and the kingdom at large.

DYNASTIC SUCCESSION

As we saw in chapter 2, Ayede was founded as a refugee settlement c. 1845 and rapidly developed into a military stronghold under the war chief Eshubiyi. In a calculated series of political maneuvers, Eshubiyi suppressed the ruling dynasty of his Iye followers to crown himself king, the Àtá of Ayede. Eshubiyi held no traditional rights to a crown, but usurped the kingship from the Olú of Iye. To quell opposition from the Iye settlers, he suppressed their civil chiefs and appointed military chiefs among age-sets and non-Iye immigrants to administer his rule. Thus, in centralizing his political power, Eshubiyi transformed Ayede's authority structure into an exceptional military autocracy. To compensate for his nonroyal origins, he introduced two royal òrìṣà cults—Orisha Ojuna from Ikole and Yemoja from Ibadan—which empowered his person and validated his authority.

During Eshubiyi's reign, the kingdom expanded, bringing new immigrant groups into the capital. Ayede's "stranger" quarters swelled with new settlers, intensifying the rift between them and the "indigenes" from Iye. Ayede's six town quarters divided into two "halves," or "sides"—the four Iye quarters, which resented the suppression of their Olú and civil chiefs, and the two stranger quarters, which benefited from it. The contraposed political units in the town capital thus formed into two major factions, reinforced by the reorganization of hunters, diviners, and the age-set system into two corresponding camps under separate leaders. Oral histories relate how the corporation of diviners *(babaláwo)* argued over the division of meat during a meeting to explain why they split into two distinct groups. The stranger diviners allied with the Átá, while the Iye diviners remained loyal to their displaced *Olú.* Both groups of diviners still recognize different leaders *(olórí awo)* and sacrifice separately to Ifa and Osanyin, the gods of divination and of traditional medicine. The division of Ayede's age-sets into two sections was less drastic and complete, owing to the importance of age-sets as administrative structures. Every age-set in Ayede, as in other Ekiti towns, was both segmented by quarter, acting thus in a political capacity in competition for power, and unified for the town at large, administering directives from above. But Ayede's age-sets also formed into two general factions which convened their members on alternating schedules. Today, junior age-sets wrestle and abuse each other during the Oroyeye festival, in which jocular "power competitions" between indigenes and strangers are ritually performed during a moonless night.

After Eshubiyi's death c. 1880, the problem of royal succession persisted for many years. Since Eshubiyi was a self-proclaimed king, he had established a new royal lineage which at that time lacked any significant depth or span. Although he was born into the Odomogun lineage, conflict developed between his lineal and collateral descendants. Genealogies reveal that Eshubiyi had two "brothers" from the same father and different mothers, whose descendants claim to be "branches," or segments, of the royal lineage. Eshubiyi's lineal descendants claim otherwise, however, and restrict the royal lineage to the "Eshubiyi line." As subsequent legal investigations revealed, there is evidence supporting both points of view. Traditions relate how Kushagba, Eshubiyi's senior brother, bore a son named Osinkolu, who became a wealthy farmer and prominent war chief (the Ọtún of Isaoye quarter) and inherited one of Eshubiyi's wives. Amudipe, Eshubiyi's junior brother, took the military title *Alágbayé.* Subsequent succession disputes have involved candidates from these three sections (fig. 3.1).

Ayede historians describe the period from 1880 to 1901 as an interregnum, when the Ọtún Osinkolu (Eshubiyi's fraternal nephew) reigned as a de facto regent. During this time there were several attempts by the Iye people to revive the *Olú* title, but support for a new *Átá* by Isaoye quarter (which wanted a royal lineage) and by the stranger immigrants (who wanted a powerful patron) proved too strong. At one point during the interregnum, the *Balógun Àáfin* mobilized his own standing army to usurp the title for Omole-Akodi quarter, but the conflict was settled by assembled elders, chiefs, and priests

Figure 3.1. Dynastic Succession in Ayede

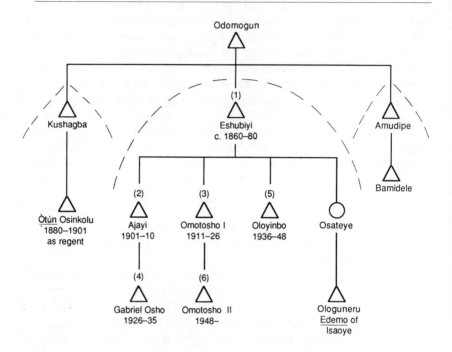

in favor of Osinkolu's continued regency. Why Osinkolu himself never contested for high office is a question which inspires political debate. His descendants today say that he did not want to lose his wealth to the duties of kingship. Members of the Eshubiyi line claim he lacked rights to the Àtá title as a nonlineal descendant.

When Osinkolu died c. 1896, Bamidele, the son of the *Aláqbayé* Amudipe, emerged as an influential figure in Ayede politics and leader of the Kemoke age-set. For reasons never fully disclosed, he declined, like Osinkolu, to contest for the throne. With the support of his age-set and of important members of Odomogun lineage, Bamidele elected Prince Ajayi, one of Eshubiyi's sons, as *Mógàji*, or leader of the Odomogun family, and backed his candidacy for the kingship. Fierce factionalism developed between Ajayi's supporters and those of his rival, Prince Alagbo, breaking into violence and assassination threats. Where Ajayi appealed for the Iye quarters' support, Alagbo cultivated a stranger following. In 1901, in an Odomogun-lineage meeting led by Osateye, a powerful woman and daughter of Eshubiyi, Ajayi was presented to the Ayede kingmakers and quickly installed as the new ruling Àtá. Because of his support from the Iye quarters, he was often referred to as "Oba Iye." His mother came from Offa, near Oyo, and she brought the *òrìṣà* Oshun into the Yemoja cult. The *Àtá* Ajayi therefore consolidated the ritual support of the Yemoja and Orisha Ojuna cults through direct maternal and paternal filiation.

Few internal developments occurred during Ajayi's reign from 1901 to 1911, but the kingdom of Ayede was gradually encapsulated by the wider structures of indirect rule. The *Àtá* visited Lagos in 1903 and again in 1908 in a meeting of Ekiti kings, and he met with the *Ọwá Óbokún*, the *ọba* of Ilesha. He ruled over Ayede kingdom as sole native authority with the backing of the British Crown, preserving the military structure of administration through age-sets that was established by his father, Eshubiyi.

When the *Àtá* Ajayi died in 1911, his junior brother Omotosho Abolokefa was selected immediately to succeed him. Since his mother came from Ikole, the new *Àtá* enjoyed the full support of the Egbe-Oba quarter of Ikole immigrants, as well as renewed ritual support from Ayede's Orisha Ojuna cult. It was during his reign that Egbe-Oba quarter's Oloke cult intensified its links with the cult of Orisha Ojuna and built a special room in the latter's town shrine. Previously linked by affinity to Eshubiyi, the Oloke cult now glorified its newly established maternal link with the ruling king himself, redefining its relationship to Orisha Ojuna as maternal siblings *(ọmọìyá)*.

The outstanding development during Omotosho's reign was the formal establishment, c. 1918, of recognized *ìwàrèfà* chiefs in place of age-set representatives and military-office holders. Accounts vary of what actually happened. Some say that the *Deji* of Akure, leading the annual *pèlúpèlú* conference of Ekiti kings, advised the ruling *Àtá* to install proper chiefs. Others maintain that it was the district officer who issued the directive at a meeting in Oye. In any case, the new order of town chiefs, each presiding over a town quarter and together forming the king's council, did not meet with popular support. First, the original Iye quarters were reranked, with Ejigbo quarter moving from third to first place. Second, none of the chieftaincy titles came from Iye proper; instead, a new line of power brokers was elevated within each quarter:

Title	Quarter	Provenience
1. *Ọbásùn*	Ejigbo	Ora
2. *Ọbadòfin*	Owaiye	Itapa
3. *Ẹdẹ̀mọ*	Isaoye	Ikole (palace chieftaincy)
4. *Aláwẹ̀*	Ilaaro	Ora
5. *Balógun Ààfin*	Omole-Akodi	Ayede
6. *Ọtún*	Egbe-Oba	Ikole (war chieftaincy)

Although Omotosho also resurrected several Iye chieftaincy titles of a lower grade in order to accommodate the Iye people's traditional political claims, these events served to reinforce factionalism between the Iye and stranger sections of the town and to divide Ayede Christians— associated with an emerging elite seeking access to power—from the "pagans," who maintained ritual bases of traditional authority. The new line of civil chiefs lacked traditional support from the disaffected Iye quarters, and the chiefs opted for Christianity to gain from the CMS church the religious authority which they had lost from the quarter cults.

Elders relate how, after Omotosho's death in 1926, for the first time in Ayede's history the entire town mobilized in competition for his successor, with the Christians backing one candidate and the Muslims and "pagans" several others. The selection process nearly provoked an open confrontation between Christians and "pagans." By this time the district officer from Ado-Ekiti supervised the selection, and he allegedly colluded with the Christians to handpick their candidate Orishagbemi, baptized as Gabriel Osho. The four final contestants were Elebute, Orishagbemi, Oloyinbo, and Ologuneru. The D.O. discredited Elebute as a "liar" who claimed to be the son of Eshubiyi but who was actually begot by the late Àtá Ajayi. Oloyinbo was rejected as too old and crafty, while Ologuneru was disqualified as a "pretender," since he traced his relationship to the royal family through maternal, not paternal, filiation. His mother Osateye was the powerful princess who contributed to Ajayi's successful installation, and she now directed her influence to promote her own son. Ologuneru's campaign is important to mention since it shows he lacked sufficient power to modify the patrilineal principle of succession to high office, which was upheld by the district officer and Ayede's Christian faction. We shall see how Ologuneru, although barred from the kingship, emerged as a powerful figure in subsequent struggles for district leadership.

The installation of Gabriel Osho inaugurated an autocratic ruler whose exercise of power eventually violated the limits of his authority. Born of a former wife of Eshubiyi who was inherited by Ajayi, the second Àtá, Gabriel Osho was identified as one of the oldest of Eshubiyi's living kinsmen, possessing the same belligerent personality. Recognized by the British as sole native authority, he reputedly shunned his town chiefs and advisors, and he became the first president of the District Court, a position which provided him with legal mechanisms to further impose his will. Ayede elders relate that town dignitaries who criticized the Àtá Gabriel Osho or committed minor offenses were immediately arrested and criminally charged and had to spend large sums of money (pocketed by the *Àtá*) to redeem their freedom. According to a popular testimony of his "high-handed" manner, Gabriel Osho ordered an evening curfew stipulating that townspeople should not be found outside of their compounds after sundown. Every evening he sent out his palace messengers to arrest "offenders." On one such occasion, a messenger charged some townspeople who were sitting in front of their homes. One man among them replied that they were in front of their homes, not outside on the street. The messenger, knowing that he had the king's authority on his side, struck the man's head with a cudgel, drawing blood. The townspeople reported the event to the *Àtá*, and they demanded that he dismiss the messenger at once. Gabriel Osho refused, and the following day the public convened in the marketplace to voice their complaints.

During this assembly, the *Àtá* was accused of stealing goats for ritual sacrifice. Whether or not he was literally guilty is of little consequence. The accusation itself is a public criticism of antisocial behavior. Goats are owned by individuals and roam freely in Yoruba towns, unattended for days. Anyone who steals such a goat in the town violates basic norms of community trust and sociability. Such an accusation is thus a form of social ostracism; when directed against a king, it signals public disaffection. The Oroyeye cult of Ayede's Owaiye quarter further amplified this accusation in a song of abuse which devotees sang at the palace and throughout the town:

> *Ìkokò t'ó ńkẹran kó adìyẹ,*
> *íníjilẹ̀,*
> *Ọdẹ wọ̀nyí ẹ máa kiyèsí,*
> *Wọ́n ńkó kẹ̀bukẹ̀bu.*

> Spotted Hyena steals goals and chickens,
> it is serious,
> You hunters take notice,
> he [the *Àtá*] takes indiscriminately.

The song, sung in Iye dialect, voices a warning by moral guardians of the community—old women (*yèyé*) past childbearing age whose indictments are ritually elevated beyond reproach.

In 1934 the district officer was summoned from Ado-Ekiti, and he investigated the allegations against Gabriel Osho. The *Àtá* had alienated both Iye and stranger sections of the town. Many stranger families, it is alleged, left Ayede for their towns of origin to escape the king's coercive rule. Elders were annoyed that he invited young children in the CMS school to speak publicly, a prerogative traditionally reserved for members of senior age-sets. But the strongest indictments against Gabriel Osho came from subordinate towns of Ayede District. Chiefs of Omu complained that when an Ayede boy died in their town, the Àtá punished their people by ordering Omu's age-sets to rebuild the Customary Court Hall in Ayede. When Ayede's subordinate towns requested a motor road joining them with the district capital, the Àtá allegedly replied that "vassals ought not to enjoy the privileges of their lords"; recruiting their age-sets, however, he built a motor road from Ayede to Oye. In 1934, Ayede's Yagba towns—Oke-Ako, Irele, and Ipao—formed a Federal Society, joined by Ayede's non-Yagba town of Itapaji, to secede from Ayede District and join other Yagba towns in the Northern Province. In the interests of district unity, the district officer deposed the Àtá Gabriel Osho and established a sessional court at Ipao which increased the legal autonomy and representation of Ayede's subordinate towns. Thus appeased, the district remained intact. Describing the events of Gabriel Osho's downfall, one Ayede chief concluded that "his strength killed him."

The political career of Gabriel Osho illustrates effective sanctions against excessive centralization. Within the town, the public assembled in the marketplace to express their disaffection. The Oroyeye cult added its ritual disapproval. The Àtá had alienated all of his power bases, and when asked by the district officer if he had anything to say in his defense, he allegedly replied, "I cannot fight the whole town." Subordinate towns registered their protest through preliminary motions of secession from the district. They not only formed a Federal Society, but rejected tax-notification slips sent by the Àtá because they no longer recognized his authority. The ultimate mechanism of his deposition—a special tribunal appointed by the British—invoked the same authority which initially granted him extratraditional powers and immunities. In the precolonial kingdom, the authority to depose was vested in town chiefs and priests. To say, however, that Gabriel Osho violated the authority of his office and to chronicle his abuses of power does not by itself explain his deposition. Just as centralized power is transformed by authority, so authority is transformed, revised, and redefined by power holders. In his oríkì, Gabriel Osho is praised for his autocratic behavior:

Ẹkùn á bojú wáí wáí,
Ó mú iná jẹ,
Ó mú oòrùn jẹ.

Leopard who scrutinizes restlessly,
Who eats fire,
Who eats the sun.

In other words, he is one who consumes "hot," dangerous, and unlimited power. Gabriel Osho's very abuses of power became virtues of prodigious strength. Loss of authority, in the last instance, results not in but *from* deposition; it occurs just in case rival factions and contestants for high office attain enough power to displace an errant king.

The key figure who led the rebellion against Gabriel Osho was the same Ologuneru who had contested for the kingship but had had no place in the royal patrilineage. Barred by the patrilineal requirement of succession to high office, he nevertheless sought the de facto powers of the kingship. Ologuneru moved close to Gabriel Osho during his reign by taking a palace title—the Ẹdẹmọ of Isaoye quarter—and he fostered further disaffection among the Àtá's dwindling clients and supporters. The story is that he manipulated a dispute between the king and some families in Isaoye quarter by spreading a rumor that the king had used jùjú to kill one of their titled elders who had collapsed in the palace. After eroding the support of Isaoye quarter, and with the town on his side, Ologuneru took an active role in discrediting the Àtá during the district officer's investigation. In 1935, when the Àtá was exiled, Ologuneru waged a successful campaign to place Oloyinbo, the previous contestant, on the throne. Oloyinbo was then over seventy years old. According to one informant, he was a "spent force who was too old to control or exercise effective control on any problems confronting the town," and he was "alive only in name." With Oloyinbo established as a figurehead, Ologuneru took control of the town. Testimonies describe how he sat daily at the palace gate and handled the complaints that were brought to the Àtá. If a dispute was serious, he would walk into the palace and return with a verdict purported to be the Àtá's. All native authority workers in Ado knew him as the "strong man" of Ayede and as the town's effective leader.

After Oloyinbo's death in 1948, Ologuneru nominated and campaigned for Samson Adedeji Omotosho, the son of Omotosho I, the third Àtá of Ayede. The Kushagba section of the Odomogun lineage nominated Elekenah Ibitokun, while many Ayede Christians recalled Gabriel Osho to reclaim the kingship. In a remarkable display of dissension in the town, each faction performed installation rituals for its candidate, and three "kings" were thus brought to the palace. Ibitokun was disqualified in protracted sittings of the Ekiti kings, who restricted the Àtá title to Eshubiyi's lineal descendants. Ibitokun's backers switched their support to Gabriel Osho, but the reinstallation of a deposed ọba proved too controversial, and in 1949 Ologuneru's candidate was installed as Omotosho II. Again, Ologuneru attempted to rule through a weak Àtá, but he was soon displaced by a more powerful Big Man, the Ọlọ̀là of Ejigbo quarter who has since been accused of controlling Omotosho II. When I left Ayede in December 1984, Omotosho II was still on the throne, having reigned as Àtá for thirty-five years.

The struggles for high office in Ayede's dynastic history illustrate, with paradigmatic simplicity, how segmentary politics and hierarchical administration converge at the center of Yoruba government. The selection or deposition of an ọba involves contests of power between rival factions which extend from within the royal lineage to the limits of the political community. As the unsuccessful campaigns of Ologuneru and Ibitokun reveal, the definition, depth, and span of the royal lineage itself are negotiated through competitive politics, with contesting factions asserting rival genealogies. Beyond the royal lineage itself, town quarters, age-sets, professional associations (hunters, diviners, blacksmiths, traders), indigenes, strangers, and influential clients provide important bases of political support. Thus, with the support of the Kemoke age-set, Bamidele was able to promote Prince Ajayi to the throne. Omotosho I enjoyed the backing of Egbe-Oba quarter because his mother came from Ikole. Gabriel Osho mobilized support from the Christian community, which had emerged as a new political force. His deposition, however, reflects the importance of subordinate towns as power bases which withdrew their support. The installations of Oloyinbo and Omotosho II show how Ologuneru, a Big Man who was barred from the kingship, nonetheless acquired de factor power by manipulating factionalism to control a weak king. In each case, factions, if formed by "teams" of leaders and followers, derive from the dominant corporations within the kingdom as publicly organized, and thus politically effective, interest groups.

There is, of course, more to Yoruba politics than the selection and installation of kings; public affairs are regulated at all levels of government, from the lineage compound to the kingdom or district at large. But competition for high office represents in very clear terms the central preoccupation of Yoruba politics and, more subtly, of Yoruba ritual as well—the delimitation, containment, and control of power by authority, the fusion of the king and the "dangerous" power of his person with the regulative authority of his office. Yoruba kingship, like "divine," or sacred, kingship elsewhere in Africa, literally embodies the apical conjunction of segmentary power relations and a hierarchical authority structure in the fundamentally liminal status of an *ọba*. Part person, he ingests the heart (and other unmentionable parts) of his predecessor to embody his "power"; part office, he exists in perpetuity, with authority, as a corporation sole. At the concrete level of political action, contests for the kingship are politically resolved by the most powerful faction, which installs an incumbent. Like any specific issue of public policy, these contests resolve a political problem (succession) with an administrative solution (investiture). But at a deeper and more abstract level of political organization, the dialectical tension between power and authority, and between their respective modes of political and administrative action, is never resolved, for each continuously conditions and transforms the other. Whereas power appropriates authority by bending, revising, or violating rules, authority regulates and routinizes power by establishing and imposing rules. When the Yoruba greet their *ọba* with the prayer

> *Adé á pẹ́ l'órí,*
> *Bàtà á pẹ́ l'ẹsẹ̀*

> May your (beaded) crown remain long on your head,
> May your (beaded) slippers remain long on your feet

they are wishing him more than a long and happy reign. The greeting constructs an important parallelism between the body of his person (head and feet) and the insignia of his office (crown and slippers), which, metonymically combined, join his power and authority. Implicit, too, is the veiled conjunction that he rule well or suffer deposition.

THE *ỌBA* AND HIS CHIEFS

If the *ọba*'s power is limited by authority, it is the duty of the *ìwàrèfà*—the senior town chiefs—together with senior cult officials and members of the Ogboni secret society, to safeguard the normative limits of high office. These important chiefs, also called *àfọ́bàjẹ́*, or kingmakers, can boycott the palace or depose their king if he overrules their collective will. Even under colonial rule, when the British appropriated the ultimate right to depose Yoruba kings, they acted, as the case of Gabriel Osho reveals, at the prompting of disaffected civil chiefs. These chiefs are thus "kingbreakers" as well as kingmakers; if they "make" the king by investing him with authority, they can equally "break" him by withdrawing their support. The root morphemes of *àfọ́bàjẹ́* signify "breaking," "shattering," and "spoiling" or "rendering useless," as if to derive the kingmakers' supportive functions from their negative and rebellious capabilities.[2] The ọba's authority, in the hands of his chiefs, is in fact predicated on their consensual support and becomes a scarce political resource which they can balance, manipulate, or shatter like a calabash if the ọba becomes too powerful.

The chiefs' management of the ọba's authority is reflected in the ritual domain by the roles of the high priests of the òrìṣà cults, who regulate his relationship with the deities. If the chiefs control their king in secular life, the àwòrò (priests) maintain his privileged place èkejì òrìṣà, or "second to the gods." His sacred power and authority derive from the òrìṣà, whose dictates are beyond criticism and reproach. In this ritual idiom, the ọba's power and authority are combined in the same mystical force (àṣẹ); but they can be distinguished in this force's dual aspects, or valences—which are hot and cool, red and white, dangerous and safe, violent and composed—and they correspond more abstractly to the power of his person and the authority of his office and, ultimately, to the apical conjunction of politics and administration within the kingdom. The priests remind the ọba, as they revitalize his power, that he must rule well or be abandoned by the òrìṣà. Such warnings, however, are never overtly stated, but are critically structured (as we shall see in chapters 4 and 5) by the multiple visions and voices of ritual.

Lloyd's Conflict Model

To develop the thesis that Yoruba òrìṣà worship structures the dialectics of power in the public domain, we can examine the logic of Yoruba politics and the limiting conditions of its practice.

In his pathbreaking article "Conflict Theory and Yoruba Kingdoms," P. C. Lloyd illustrates how chiefs compete singly against each other and collectively against the ọba for the power to influence public policy. Noting that "equilibrium models" of African political systems generally emphasize integration and consensus, Lloyd argues that conflict theory identifies divergent interests and incompatible roles which not only clarify micropolitical processes, but explain structural developments of kingdoms over time, including "radical changes in social structure which are beyond the scope of the equilibrium model" (Lloyd 1968:32). Although he offers his analysis of conflict as a corrective to M. G. Smith's methodology, which, according to Lloyd, stresses "continuity and adaptation" rather than "opposition" between roles, a methodological distinction between approaches would not be absolute. For conflict and integration are not rival perspectives, but apply to complementary principles and processes of government—to the "conflict" of segmentary politics and the "integration" of hierarchical administration. Lloyd (ibid., 33) appears to recognize this complementarity. Since his essay focuses almost exclusively on the distribution of power and explicitly downplays attention to authority, I place his conflict model *within* Smith's framework of government, to specify the distinctively political contests of power and their relation to authority structures in Yoruba kingdoms.

In Lloyd's simplified model of the Ekiti kingdom, lineages form the principal units of political representation, each headed by a chief who, together with other chiefs on the *ọba*'s council, regulates public affairs on behalf of his followers. These public affairs include the resolution of conflicts between individuals and descent groups, the organizing of public activities, and, especially in precolonial times, defense of the community. Policy decisions reached by the chiefs in council are ordained by the *ọba*, who, representing the interests and unity of the kingdom, administers through his chiefs. In keeping with Smith's concept of government, we can say that a chief's power, backed by the support of his descent group, seeks to influence public policy from below, while his authority, which derives from his place on the council, serves to implement public policy from above.

Focusing on politics, and hence on competition for power, Lloyd identifies two structural levels of conflict: (1) conflict among descent groups, in which the *ọba* plays a mediating role; and (2) conflict between the council of chiefs on the one hand and the sacred king on the other (ibid., 34). Conflict among descent groups arises from competition for two related scarce resources—land and political power. As lineages expand and arable farmland becomes scarce, boundary disputes arise and may come before the council of chiefs for adjudication. Whereas the chief of each disputing party tries to resolve the issue in his lineage's favor, the council as a whole seeks a unanimous decision, voiced with the *ọba*'s authority. A chief representing his lineage's interests in land is caught between two sets of opposed obligations. Attempting to settle in his descent group's favor, he may be overruled by the council's support of his rival. A chief's power is thus commensurate to his ability to determine the outcome of such disputes. Each chief therefore seeks to promote his own lineage and maximize his power at the other chiefs' expense. These contests for power between the *iwàrèfà* chiefs are expressed in the negotiation of their ranking on the council. Although the ranking of chiefs represents their order of influence and importance and, by implication, the relative size and significance of their lineages, it can be revised by the *ọba* in certain situations. According to Lloyd (ibid., 40), "a rebellion in which the chiefs are aligned with and against the ọba provides the principal opportunity for enhancing the political power of one's descent group through a reranking of the chieftaincy titles."

The ọba attempts to control his chiefs by manipulating their factionalism to his advantage. When chiefs are divided over public policy, the ọba has a greater voice in determining its outcome; his role as sacred mediator is thus politically more effective. If the chiefs are divided into two rebellious factions, he can take one side and reward one of its chiefs with a promotion in rank, weakening the opposition. In theory, he alone is empowered to install new chiefs or revoke their titles. In fact, however, such decisions require the support of his council. By playing the chiefs against one another, the ọba is more likely to impose his own will. Given his sacred status and the òrìṣà rituals performed on his behalf, his official decisions—those ultimately backed by the council—are *a fortiori* correct and good, and his judgment is deemed infallible. But in fact, two limits constrain the ọba's power. First, by dividing his council he risks fission of the kingdom, for a minority faction, if sufficiently isolated, may emigrate from the town. Second, if the ọba ignores or overrules the will of the chiefs, they can collectively depose him. As the case of Gabriel Osho reveals, these limits are related, for if fission is imminent, the ìwàrèfà can unite to depose their king for the good of the kingdom as a whole. Since the precolonial ọba controlled his army through his chiefs, he could not consolidate his power by force.

Lloyd's model of Yoruba government is of course a reduction to essentials. As subsequent research has revealed, it is the quarter (àdúgbò) and not the lineage which constitutes the principal unit of political representation in the ọba's council of chiefs (cf. J. D. Y. Peel 1979:127, 130–138). Chiefs therefore promote their quarters when deliberating in council and arbitrate disputes between lineages of their quarters without recourse to the ọba. Only when conflicts arise which a chief cannot settle, or which involve members of lineages in different quarters, is a case brought to the palace for binding settlement. In larger quarters one even finds subquarters ruled by junior chiefs who preside with autonomy over the affairs of several lineages. Complex quarters of this type are like kingdoms writ small, in which the quarter chief rules with his elders like a king and can acquire incipient sacred qualities in ritual which may challenge the ọba's authority in the town. Even in simple quarters comprised of several lineages, a chief stands apart from his lineage per se, which, like the others, has its own elder (baálé). Quarters are furthermore stratified by age-sets, which unite lineage elders in a senior grade and younger freeborn males into junior grades. As political units, age-sets articulate with lineages and quarters to promote parochial interests at each level of segmentation. As administrative units, they crosscut political divisions to organize unified action in the town.

The strength of Lloyd's model lies in its identification of generalized conflict among *ìwàrèfà* chiefs and between the chiefs and the *ǫba;* and of the strategies of each in pursuing individual and collective ends. The principles of conflict which Lloyd identifies with such logical economy can be applied, *mutatis mutandis*, to different levels of political segmentation within kingdoms. Within the lineage, household heads compete against each other in disputes mediated by the lineage head *(baálé)*. Like the *ǫba* with his chiefs, the lineage head maximizes his power when members are divided against each other; he is also subject to constraints similar to those on the *ǫba*'s power. Where acute division precipitates lineage fission, collective opposition to a *baálé*'s decision brings the case or issue at hand to a standstill. When such a situation arises, the *baálé* loses control over the case, and it is referred to the chief of the quarter for resolution. The lineage head cannot be deposed like the *ǫba*, but he is, in a sense, temporarily "deposed" from his status when his lineage seeks advice from a higher authority. The same "power game" is played in both simple and complex quarters—and ultimately in the entire town, only with different players and for higher stakes.

The principles of conflict specified by Lloyd are latent, if not manifest, in every Yoruba kingdom. Unlike conflicts over specific policy, which involve negotiated compromises and are resolved by political means, conflicts over the distribution of political power per se are of a type which Middleton (1968:162) calls "normal to the system." They represent *contradictions* in the sociopolitical system which are, in the language of Kant's critical philosophy, necessary conditions of its possibility—that is, transcendental conditions which, I shall argue in chapter 4, are shaped by ritual and knowledge.

BROKERS AND BIG MEN

Within the formal framework of Yoruba government, power is distributed through political titles, which in most cases belong to specific lineages and are ranked and graded in their order of importance in the town. Within the dynamic context of competitive politics, however, this order is renegotiated and revised through contests of power. The reranking of *ìwàrèfà* chiefs is one way discussed by Lloyd. Barber (1981:727) also notes that in Okuku "between 1800 and the present day, the order or rank of the top three senior chiefs has changed at least three times." The perception of rank is itself difficult to pin down. In my interviews with Ayede chiefs on their relative rank, private testimonies often diverged from the official palace version. Referring to Ayede's turbulent past, one educated chief wrote in a legal memo that "to attempt an arrangement of Ayede chiefs even now into order of seniority is to play with fire on a keg of gunpowder." The analogy is apt, suggesting the explosiveness of power competition among chiefs.

Power competition, however, is not limited to formal arenas. Yoruba recognize that de facto power does not necessarily achieve official recognition. As Barber (ibid.) so clearly reveals, many Yoruba "could make a place for themselves which was out of all proportion to their formal position in the chiefly hierarchy." Big Men who rise by their own efforts can play leading roles in local politics without ever obtaining a chieftaincy title. The converse, however, is also true: important titles can hold weak incumbents and can even fall vacant for years. Between these extremes spreads a range of opportunities for powerful men to promote junior, military, or palace titles to senior ìwàrèfà status, to restrict open or rotating titles to a single lineage, or even to establish new titles for themselves. This more fluid and flexible aspect of Yoruba politics both complements and conditions its corporate forms.

Barber relates how, in Okuku during the late nineteenth century, a Big Man named Elemona accumulated wives, farms, followers, and great wealth until he eventually rivaled the ọba himself. During the royal Olokuku festival, he sat on his own throne with his attendants, facing the ọba across the market in an audacious challenge of his authority. When the ọba's drummers sent him a coded warning, "Elemona, go easy, you are not the ọba," his own drummers replied, "The position I hold here is greater than an ọba's" (ibid., n. 8).[3] Ayede Big Men boast of similar, if less ostentatious, exploits. It may be recalled that the town itself was founded by Eshubiyi, a powerful warrior who crowned himself king and ruled primarily through military chiefs. When, c. 1918, the Àtá installed six town chiefs, two of these—the Balógun Àáfin of Omole-Akodi quarter and the Ọ̀tún of Egbe-Oba quarter—represented military titles, while one—the Ẹ̀dẹ̀mọ of Isaoye quarter—rose from a palace chieftaincy title to the senior grade of civil chiefs. In addition, the title of Balógun Èkìtì, earned by a warrior who fought with Eshubiyi, became an important civil title which is often counted among the ìwàrèfa chiefs.

The military pattern of self-aggrandizement was based primarily on looting and slave raiding. As Eshubiyi ravished surrounding towns, his military officers seized booty and slaves; female slaves married into their households or remained as concubines, and males worked on their farms. Military chiefs could thus build up large households, often adopting male slaves, who provided not only labor but also children of their own. Since a man's status was measured by the number of his slaves, wives, and children and by the amount of land he could culti-vate, successful warriors could rise to important positions in the town.[4]

There was more to Big Manship, however, than the accumulation of wealth. A man became big by attracting followers, expanding his household with matrilateral kin and clients who became associated with his lineage as òrẹ̀dẹbí (lit. "friends-become-family"), and by ex-changing his influence for loyalty and support. Friends and relatives of a Big Man would sometimes send a child to live with him, as Barber explains, "to enjoy the benefits of a large and well-to-do household" (1981:728), but also because they believed that the "powers" of bigness would rub off on the child. A man became big by virtue of a variety of agencies and by his own special genius, glorified by his oríkì (praises). Big Men by definition have a good head (orí), or personal destiny (be-stowed by their prenatal spiritual double), which raises their fortunes to uncommon heights. Sometimes bigness is attributed to a special re-lationship with an òrìṣà or to the possession of powerful jùjú medicines. Occasionally, townspeople privately confide that a Big Man is a witch and attribute his success to an association with a coven (egbẹ́). All of these attributions enhance his extraordinary status, but also point to his special vulnerability. For, unlike town chiefs who hold formal au-thority, a Big Man's power is sustained solely by his clients.

If a Big Man overextends his financial obligations, or if powerful rivals draw away clients, he loses his following and hence his bigness. Careers which end in financial ruin are favorite topics of discussion and debate. Usually the Big Man is held responsible for his own demise. Intemperance and greed, according to Ayede testimonies, led Ologuneru, once the powerful de facto king, to a wretched and un-timely death. Ironically, some of the very qualities for which Big Men are praised, which Barber (ibid., 729) describes as "toughness, unas-sailability, intransigence and power—often conceived in terms of the ability to perpetrate outrages with impunity," serve to explain their ruin as well. Loved when they rise and hated when they fall, they are ruthless competitors for public recognition. A Big Man's career is "dan-gerous" in several senses and from several points of view. Big Men *stricto sensu* hold power and influence without formal authority. Their power is in their person, as the terms alágbára (powerful person) and ẹ̀nìyàn ńlá (big person) imply, and it is especially vulnerable to disaffection. Big Men possess powerful *jùjú* medicines with which they protect themselves, influence others, and outmaneuver their rivals. Unlike formal chiefs, they occupy liminal roles on the margins of success and failure. Their vulnerability is, furthermore, proportional to their success. As a Big Man rises, demands on his economic and political resources increase. The more he gains, the more he must give. The greater his power, the greater the jealousy and witchcraft of rivals.

If Big Men pursue dangerous careers, they also bring "danger" to the political community. Their emergence usually precipitates lineage segmentation and fission because they draw followers away from weaker lineage chiefs, often constructing a large household which is identified as the locus of a new line of descent. When Elekenah Ibitokun of Ile-Otun lineage built Ayede's first three-story house c. 1946, a monument to his success as a cocoa farmer, he commanded great respect—and even contested for the throne—but he also caused rebellion and lineage fission, since the elders of Ile-Otun were unable to control him. A Big Man can also threaten the unity of a quarter and even of the town. The powerful S. A. Akerele rose to such prominence as a wealthy, educated Big Man in Ejigbo quarter that he overshadowed Ejigbo's chief, the Ọbásùn, who ranks first on the Àtá's council of chiefs. Akerele emerged as an effective power broker, playing the ọba against his chiefs to secure rewards for his own followers. He also achieved positions of influence and authority in education, the CMS church, credit associations, industry, the courts and party politics after independence. At the same time he developed a formidable reputation as a *jùjú* practitioner and member of the Ogboni society. In 1967 he was installed as the Ọlọ́là of Ejigbo quarter, and he took a place on the ọba's council of chiefs. The title itself reveals its origins, meaning "rich person" or "owner of wealth." Ejigbo quarter consequently divided into two "sides," Oke (upper) and Odo (lower), led by the Ọbásùn and the Ọlọ́là respectively. They agreed "not to fight"—that is, to prevent fission of the quarter, so that Ejigbo quarter would not lose its first rank in the town to Owaiye quarter, which ranks second. Although the Ọbásùn remains the senior chief in Ejigbo, the Ọlọ́là, until recently, controlled a broader range of political resources.

The career of Chief S. A. Akerele is worth outlining in some detail, as it highlights the tactical problems of Big Manship. Akerele described the predicament of Big Manship in terms of traditional medicine: "Anyone who is too powerful or 'big' is accused of having *jùjú* and is brought down with *jùjú*." The statement is intended as a literal truth, but can be read as a general statement about power. For the power which makes a man big can also bring him down.

As a member of the Christian elite, Akerele pursued higher studies at the University of Wales at Cardiff, where he received a degree in education in the early 1950s. He returned to Ayede and became chairman of the Board of Governors of the Ayede Grammar School from 1957 to 1959, and he served as its principal from 1960 to 1972. He was also active in the CMS church, where he held the post of People's Warden from 1960 to 1974. He served twice as an Action Group representative in the Western State House of Assembly. After serving as vice-chairman of the Ayede Progressive Union, he became its president in 1976. His diverse business interests included two successful sawmills which he had established in Ayede. A man of considerable means and influence, he was installed as the Qlólà of Ejigbo quarter by 1967 and occupied a controversial place in the Àtá's council. Although not recognized as a "traditional" chief, he dominated the council and made many enemies.

From 1967 to 1969, Akerele took an active role in a land case between Ayede and Orin-Ido over the possession of land for cash crops. In preparing Ayede's case, he lodged a surveyor and twenty-two laborers in his house for eighteen days. The chiefs met and accused Akerele of usurping the qba's post by lodging official guests in his house, when they should have stayed in the palace. For this he was nicknamed "the Àtá of Ejigbo quarter" and "the second Àtá of Ayede." Although Ayede won the case and the lands, Akerele's prominent role was resented, for he exercised too much independent influence.

Akerele's fall was precipitated by party politics, and it will be discussed with reference to the 1983 election in chapter 8. As leader of the Unity Party of Nigeria (UPN) in Ekiti-North during Shagari's (National Party of Nigeria, or NPN) civilian rule, he conducted a controversial shadow election in 1982 for a UPN representative in Ayede. A few days later, a man from Chief Qbásùn's section of Ejigbo quarter died. The town convened in the marketplace and accused Akerele of killing him with a curse. Akerele was defamed as a wizard, kidnapper, murderer, and cannibal. Ayede youths carried the dead man's corpse to Akerele's courtyard, where they danced around it singing songs of abuse. Events came to a head in August 1983, when Akerele's properties were burned and he fled Ayede for his life. By having decamped to the NPN in January of 1983 and thus joined with President Shagari's ruling party, Akerele had further alienated himself from popular sentiment. The NPN was unpopular in Ondo State, and when the NPN candidate Omoboriowo was declared the winner in the disputed gubernatorial election, riots erupted throughout the state. Many NPN households in Ayede were burned, and Akerele just managed to escape with his family. Many Ayede townspeople today attribute his narrow escape to the powerful *jùjú* which protected him. Stories circulate of human heads buried in his compound, and many medicines were unearthed and taken to the palace for public display. Rioters claimed that his house would not burn until women urinated on his buried medicines.

As we shall see in chapter 8, Chief Akerele's dramatic downfall was complicated by his participation in party politics. His decision to defect to the NPN further isolated him from the *ìwàrèfà* chiefs, who were all UPN supporters. After the Buhari coup of December 31, 1983, when all political parties were dissolved overnight, the *oba* and chiefs met to formally reject Akerele from the council, but no definitive action was taken. Akerele's battle with Ayede moved to the higher courts, where he sought damages for destroyed properties. As many Ayede indigenes point out, Akerele's career is not over. He may rise again and dominate town affairs. Akerele attributes his persecution to the envious positions he has held in Ayede, and he identifies the root cause of the violence against him as a long-standing rivalry between Ejigbo quarter and certain Isaoye chiefs and Big Men, a rivalry which he traces back to Ayede's founding. His critics rebuke him as an arrogant profiteer who built himself up at Ayede's expense, embezzling education and community-development funds and taking NPN bribes.

Even if we disregard the added complications of party politics, Akerele's career painfully illustrates the volatile dimensions of Big Manship. His power and influence threatened the *Àtá* and *ìwàrèfà* chiefs. A well-connected man with friends in high places, he played an effective role as a power broker that disrupted the distribution of power within the king's council. Many of his followers came from Owaiye and other quarters, weakening the bases of their traditional chiefs. He furthermore used strong-arm tactics to place his own candidate into the office of *Balógun Àáfin* c. 1972 after a successor had already been installed, by taking the case to Akure, where he won, and by pressuring the *Àtá* to comply. When the town brought Akerele down during the political riots, it attacked the very symbols of his bigness. His three-story house and two sawmills were reduced to rubble. Many of his followers who remained in Ayede were brought before the Idiya and Ogun shrines in the market and were forced to publicly forswear their loyalty to him. Over forty members of his household fled to Ibadan. When Akerele lost his wealth and followers, he proved to the townspeople how those who want too much end up with nothing. He played a dangerous game of high gains and losses, and he may well have succeeded had the NPN remained in power. Even his most outspoken enemies, however, admire his courage to get as far as he did and escape with his life, feats for which he will be praised if he rises

again. For all Yoruba men are potentially big. The intense individualism in Yoruba society encourages power competition between all men,
without as well as within the formal framework of government.
Through their public records of deeds and misdeeds, Big Men *sui generis* illustrate how political power is available to those who are strong
and bold enough to seize it.

As Akerele's career reveals, the boundary between Big Manship
and formal office is fluid. Powerful Big Men can become chiefs, spend-
ing lavishly on their installation ceremonies to join the *ìwàrèfà* or lower
grades and thereby revise the title system. Yoruba kings are sometimes
accused of selling chieftaincies to Big Men to increase palace revenues.
There is, however, another motive: when a Big Man is incorporated
into formal office, he is constrained by authority and is thus more easily
controlled. His decisions on the ọba's council can be blocked by other
chiefs. Big Men are known to refuse chieftaincy titles, opting for honorary titles without formal constraints. A Big Man *sui generis*, that is, outside of office, is limited only by his own capacities to attract followers
and sustain their support. For in the last instance, his bigness depends
on public recognition as such.

POLITICS AND CRITICAL PRACTICE

The dialectics of power examined in this chapter highlight three areas
of conflict in Yoruba government. The first involves the apical conjunction of segmentary politics and hierarchical administration. It is expressed most clearly in competitions for high office and in the "critical"
distinction between the power of the ọba's person and the authority of
his crown. Another form which this conflict takes is between the ọba
and his chiefs, whose contests for power precipitate fissures and factions within the council and town and can result in deposition of the
king, fission of the kingdom, or the reranking or even revoking of
chieftaincy titles. The political dynamics of Big Manship, however,
involve power outside of formal office, power based on wealth, wives,
large households, followers, and of course material and symbolic capital. Unlike chiefs, who are perceived as guardians of the civil community, Big Men exemplify self-aggrandizement and munificence
through aggressive individualism and private gain. Their flamboyant
personalities and spectacular careers bypass and violate the constraints
of authority to succeed where others fail.

From the more or less "functional" perspective identified in the
Introduction—and here I include Smith and Lloyd, despite their own
theoretical refinements and disclaimers—Yoruba politics generates

conflicts and contradictions which are mediated and regulated by authority structures. These structures are at once corporate and institutional, like a hierarchical chain of executive command, as well as normative and symbolic, like a sacred king who must listen rather carefully to his chiefs. But if authority structures "function" to regulate power in society, they also "signify" to establish a common language for collective action and power competition. To be sure, vulgar functionalists reduce meaning to function by "explaining" its role in "maintaining equilibrium"; myths are charters, rituals generate solidarity, while culture as a whole discourages change. But when, following Smith and Lloyd, we examine the inner relations between power and authority, such dogmatic reductionism begins to fade away. If authority regulates power, power also reproduces, revises, and in revolutionary situations subverts authority structures. It does so by changing the rules of the game—the depth and span of the royal lineage, the prerogatives of high office, the ranking of chiefs, the influence of Big Men—and *can* do so because authority is not simply given or imposed, but is constructed, negotiated, and reconstructed by actors. Myths and rituals can uphold the status quo, but they can also be invoked and performed to oppose it.

It is this dialectical tension in ritual and myth which combines power and authority in interpretive practices. In a crude sense, ritual does mediate the inherent contradictions of Yoruba government to regulate power and "maintain" authority, but such mediation—as Smith and Lloyd point out—does not preclude revision or even radical change. Chapter 1 revealed how Ife-centric rituals and myths sustained a political critique of the Oyo empire. Chapter 2 described how the Àtá Eshubiyi used the Yemoja and Orisha Ojuna cults to build a centralized military autocracy from a resettled mini-state. Chapter 3 has identified arenas of political conflict which are inherently critical of authority structures. As these histories, cases, and contests reveal, rituals have different meanings for rival political actors and constituencies. If official interpretations maintain the status quo, as classic functionalism observes, this is only part of the story, and politically the most superficial. Part 2 of this study, on ritual and knowledge, penetrates beneath the surface of òrìṣà worship to grasp the "deep" (*jinlẹ̀*) interpretations and hidden meanings which harness the power to reproduce *and* restructure the polity.

PLATES 1 AND 2. Beaded *Olókun* crowns of Ayede (*left*) and Iye (*right*). Ayede's *Olókun* crown is carried by one of the *Àtá*'s wives during the King's Sacrifice (pp. 99–104, 119–25). The secluded Iye crown is not officially recognized by Ayede (p. 51).

PLATE 3. Orisha Ojuna priestess and daughter of the king, representing her father in Ayede's Orisha Ojuna and Oloke festivals (p. 58). Her beaded fringe resembles a crown, while her beaded *làbà* panel bears the inscription *Kábíyèsí Àtá Ayédé* ("His Highness, the *Àtá* of Ayede"). The horse-tail flywisk marks the patrimony and continuity of the royal lineage.

PLATE 4. Carrying fire during the Orisha Ojuna festival (p. 59).

PLATE 5. *Yèyéolókun* priestess carrying Yemoja's calabash (pp. 63, 104–14).

Facing page: PLATE 6. The *Ìyá Ṣàngó* priestess's "prediction" (pp. 63, 106, 136–47).

Facing page
(*Top*) PLATE 7. The Ìyàwó Ọ̀ṣun priestess with beaded fringe (pp. 63–64).

(*Bottom*) PLATE 8. The Àtá emerging from a successful divination during the King's Sacrifice (p. 104). His eyes are moist with tears. Note the death-skulls on his crown.

PLATE 9. Yemoja priestesses emerging from the bush into the town. The threshold is marked by raffia palm (p. 105).

PLATES 10 and 11. The *Àtá* embodying the powers of Yemoja's calabash at the palace (pp. 105–6, 134–36).

PLATE 12. *Egúgún* masqueraders of Orisha Iyagba, representing foreign powers from Ipao, one of Ayede's subordinate towns (pp. 156–60). Note the anxious Yemoja priestesses in the background.

PLATE 13. A wife of the *Balógun Àâfin* singing songs of abuse to the *Àtá* and Yemoja priestesses. A potential beaded crown and staff are marked by red climbing vines. indicating the *Balógun Áâfin*'s potential to "climb" toward the kingship (pp. 129–34, 156–60).

PLATE 14. The *Àtá* returning from Orisha Ojuna's town shrine during the cult's annual festival (pp. 56–60). Note the European iconography of this particular crown (cf. Beier 1982:87).

PLATE 15. The *àwòrò* of Orisha Olua in Ayede, receiving devotees of Orisha Ojuna. His leopard skin evokes the former Iye ruling dynasty (pp. 57, 153).

PLATES 16 AND 17. A hotel manager sacrificing a dog to Ogun to protect his new Peugot 504 against thieves. His former car was stolen (see pp. 98–100 on the instrumental logic of ritual sacrifice).

PLATE 18. Orisha Ojuna priestesses concluding their annual festival in front of the king's palace. This final performance dovetails with the Yemoja festival (p. 114).

TWO   RITUAL AND KNOWLEDGE

4

Sacred Kingship and
Female Power

Don't believe the hype.
　—Public Enemy

This chapter and the next focus on the most prominent ritual of kingship in Ayede—the Yemoja festival—and examine the logic of its practice. The analysis which follows discloses a hidden allegory of ritual empowerment which deconstructs and reconstructs "the king's two bodies" (Kantorowicz 1957). Since this "deeper" allegory has profound political implications, my attention to different levels of ritual interpretation shifts away from the "meaning" of ritual symbols as such to highlight their discursive contexts and constraints and to thereby focus on Yoruba interpretations as a form of knowledge, or critical practice. Ritual symbols are of course significant, but what they signify is largely circumscribed by socially recognized claims of restricted access to cosmological knowledge. Yoruba òrìṣà worship is multivalent and polyvocal in both the literal and abstract senses of these terms. As we shall see, the public sees many powers and hears many voices. Public discussion of their deeper meanings, however, is simply out of the question. "Deep" ritual knowledge is dangerous and receives very special attention. It is structured by a closely guarded corpus of religious "secrets" (awo) that are considered powerful and problematic in and of themselves. These secrets are powerful, I shall argue, because they *reflect on* the contradictory conditions of effective government. As Bourdieu (1977:114) has said, "Understanding ritual practice is not a question of decoding the internal logic of a symbolism but of restoring its practical necessity by relating it to the real conditions of its genesis." Following Bourdieu's methodological lead discloses the additional twist that Yoruba cult elders and specialists "understand" ritual practice precisely in this sense, but will not discuss it lightly.

My interpretation of Yoruba ritual practice unfolds in three parts. The first part describes a royal ritual as the Yoruba publicly perform and perceive it—an annual festival for the goddess Yemoja which revitalizes the king. Following the official ideology of ritual representations, our reading at this public level is limited to what public discourse allows. The second part interprets key ritual symbols and segments to grasp their "deep" (jinlẹ̀) and hidden meanings, venturing into a heterodox discourse of paradoxical secrets and subversive themes which reconfigure the king's public identity. Finally, the third part focuses on female power, relating ritual expressions of witchcraft and fertility to hegemonic reproduction in the political domain. I conclude that this critical movement from ritual signifiers to political signifieds *selectively* reproduces the kingship and polity within each òrìṣà cult.

THE YEMOJA FESTIVAL

Yoruba òrìṣà worship is a practical religion (Leach 1968) which "feeds" deities with offerings and sacrifices in return for requested services. Individuals propitiate for personal protection and private gain; a barren woman may pray for children, a hunter may pray for plentiful game, students sometimes offer sacrifices for success on their exams. In like manner, but on a much larger scale, annual òrìṣà festivals (ọdún) propitiate town deities for the public good. In the past, town deities were invoked for protection against slave raids and attacks by neighbors. Today the outside menace may be the federal government, oscillating between civil and military regimes. But if the world beyond is chaotic, unpredictable, uncontrollable, and dangerous, it is also powerful. The principal task of public ritual is to harness the power which rages in the outside world by transporting it from the surrounding bush into the center of the town, where it can purify the community and revitalize the king. Thus contained, controlled, and incorporated into the community, the powers of the outside world—personified by the òrìṣà—replenish the body politic with fertile women, abundant crops, and a strong, healthy king. The king himself in Yoruba cosmology is èkejì òrìṣà, "second to the gods." Although he depends on his chiefs for secular support and advice, his sacred power to rule over others ultimately derives from the òrìṣà.

The "practical" logic of òrìṣà worship rests on a straightforward principle of reciprocal exchange. Propitiation of the deities—by individuals or communities—is strategic action to attain specific ends.

Royal ritual, financed largely by the king, aims first and foremost to please the òrìṣà. When fed with sacrifices, flattered with praise, and glorified by drummers and dancers in commemorative displays, the òrìṣà will protect and revitalize the local community. In return for this investment in public ritual, the king is "invested" with the òrìṣà's power *(àṣẹ),* much like a recharged battery.

This analogy with electricity is illuminating for several reasons. First, it underlies the public attitude toward òrìṣà worship as a flow of power, as something technologically accomplished rather than conceptually interpreted. Ritual paraphernalia such as brass staffs and specialized vessels may be ornamented to please the gods, but their function is practical—they transform, transmit, and store ritual power much as do electric condensers, cables, and batteries. Second, the analogy illuminates the design of such technology. Ritual power, like electricity, is "hot," highly charged, and dangerous.[1] Unbridled, it can kill. It must be contained, limited, and properly regulated to work productively for human society. Finally, ritual power, like electricity, possesses both positive and negative values; the former are associated with water, whiteness, women, fertility, and composure, and the latter with fire, redness, men, death, and transgression. The role of cult priestesses in royal ritual is to carry this power from the bush into the town with just the right balance of force and control. Whereas too much "hot" power can pollute the town and kill the king, too little deprives him of the strength he needs to rule.

Placed within its practical context, Yoruba royal ritual appears both transparent and opaque. Transparently instrumental, it enlists the support of deities to revitalize the king. Rich in iconography, its "icons" are publicly accounted for as instruments of power with no deeper significance. The king's Yemoja festival in the town of Ayede, which I witnessed in two successive years, was thus never overtly interpreted or explained as symbolic activity. Rather, it was experienced—at least by uninitiated spectators free to venture their opinions—as the glorious and dramatic fulfillment of an esoteric technology.

The King's Sacrifice

The Yemoja festival takes place in late August and early September, at the height of the wet season before the annual second harvest of yams and cassava. Its major opening event, called "the king's sacrifice" *(ẹbọ ọba),* occurs on a market day, four days before the festival's climax when priestesses carry the òrìṣà's power from the bush into the town. Ostensibly, the sacrifice effects an instrumental exchange. The *Àtá* of Ayede provides a ram for slaughter in return for the *òrìṣà*'s protection and assistance. Cult priestesses pray to Yemoja on behalf of the *Àtá*; that he will live to see the next festival and continue to rule well; and that his family, chiefs, and town will prosper. The complexity of this important event and the polyvocality of the prayers themselves deserve more detailed description.

The king's sacrifice takes place at the Yemoja cult's bush shrine *(igbó Yemoja)*, where the *òrìṣà* dwells in sacred water *(omi ọṣọọrò)*, unfettered by civic strictures and structures. Unlike the town shrine *(ipara Yemoja)*, which houses the *òrìṣà* in a building much like a palace, with inner chambers and an outer courtyard, the bush shrine consists of two open areas connected by a path. The first area, reached by passing through a raffia-palm *(màrìwò)* gateway which marks the boundary between the town and the bush, opens into a cool glade, shaded by trees, with a walled enclosure which serves as s shrine for sacrificial offerings. Originally made of mud but rebuilt with cement, this enclosure has four walls but no roof; the doorway has no door and is covered instead with raffia palm. At the center of this enclosure, a cement "feeding hole" to Yemoja, her associated deities, and ancestors consists of a raised opening *(ojú orúfú)* which leads into the ground at the base of a large tree. Along the walls of the enclosure, spaces marked by clay pots, rocks, and climbing vines are reserved for sacrifices to the individual *òrìṣà* clustered within the Yemoja cult. These include Orisha Oko, considered in Ayede to be Yemoja's husband among the deities; Shango and Ogun, conceived as Yemoja's sons; and Oshun, the wife of Shango. Just outside the enclosure, a rock represented Eshu's sacrificial shrine. Too "hot" and subversive to be enclosed, Eshu must be propitiated first in every public sacrifice or festival. Eshu is offered red palm oil *(epo pupa)* to "cool" him as it is poured on his rock. He also takes special pounded yam while his cooperation is invoked:[2]

> *Èṣù Láàró,*
> *B'ílé yẹ yẹ yẹ bí ilé ẹiyẹ,*
> *Ènìyàn ń gún'yán,*
> *Wọn ò gejìgbo nílé Látọọpa,*
> *Láàró jé bọ òfin,*
> *Jé'rù ó da,*
> *Ẹ kú ọdún o,*
> *Ẹ mọ̀ kú àṣẹyẹ.*

Eshu Laaro,
One whose houses are here and there like bird nests,

People pounding yam,
They do not pound cooked corn in Latoopa's house,
Laaro please let the sacrifice be acceptable,
Let the offerings find favor,
Greetings for the festival,
Greetings for the festivities.

Since Eshu's power cannot be "housed," it is "here and there," like bird nests in the bush. Eshu is a dangerous deity because he transcends limits and transgresses boundaries. In town he sits at the crossroads. A capricious purveyor of random misfortune, he threatens to sabotage the king's sacrifice to Yemoja and, by implication, the success of the festival and town.

After propitiating Eshu outside the bush shrine, the Ìyá Ṣàngó priestess joins other senior priestesses and cult devotees within its walls to "call" Yemoja in preparation for the king's sacrifice. A complex series of offerings, praises, and prayers ensues, in which priestesses propitiate Yemoja and her cluster of associated deities, each priestess on behalf of the other priestesses and for herself. No unifying voice prevails at this time; rather, a polyvocal text with no leaders or followers invokes Yemoja's presence and secures her assistance. Yemoja herself is praised as *elétí wéyẹwẹ̀yẹ òde ọ̀run*, or "owners of so many ears in the sky," since she alone grasps the totality of voices. Each prayer consists of two basic components; an opening invocation, either a praise *(oríkì)* or a proverb *(òwe)* in parallel construction, and the specific request itself. Both components can be uttered in sequence by one senior priestess, or they can be shared between two priestesses.

After about one hour of personal prayers and offerings by cult members and clients within the bush shrine, the Àtá arrives from the palace with an entourage of Yemoja drummers and palace retainers. These include the king's messenger, several sons (one of whom protects the Àtá's head with a multicolored umbrella of state and another who brings the tethered sacrificial ram), and several of his wives. Although the Àtá himself wears a beaded cap, one of his more junior wives—bearing the Ológun title in the Orisha Iyagba cult, where she represents her late father, the chief Balógun Ààfin—walks before the Àtá with a larger beaded Olokun crown resting on a tray which she carries on her head and steadies with both hands. The king, I was later told, never wears this crown, for it is too powerful and would kill him. The base of the crown is obscured by white cloth, so that the long beaded fringe cannot hang down or be seen. A detachable beaded figure of an ọkín bird (egret), perched atop the crown, is a repository of àṣẹ. It represents royalty, female power, and the guardianship of witchcraft (R. F. Thompson 1976; Beier 1982).

As the Àtá's entourage approaches, heralded by drums, the cult priestesses announce his arrival:

Àtá máa dé, Olú-Odò,
Èrìwọwọlọ́run,
Ìbàbá mi adá bóo ló wẹ̀ jú,
Ó máa dé oo,
[5] Àgbà gbàa gbà tí ó wà nídí Yemọja,
Baba dé,
Àgbà ọkùnrin, àgbà obirin,
Àtá máa dé,
Ó dé mágbò rẹ̀ dé,
[10] Ó mobì ó múyọ̀,
Kí o jẹ́kí aye rẹ̀ dunyọ̀,
Kí ayé rẹ̀ dunyọ̀ láàrin aládé,
Kí ó ṣé òní kí ó tún ṣe ìmọ́dún,
Kíó pọ̀n wá wọ́n,
[15] Kí ó tún pọn àwọn ọmọ rè wọ́n,
Má jẹ́ kí ó jẹ̀bi aládé wọ̀nyí,
Má jẹ́ kí ó jẹ̀bi Ayédé,
Ọmọ jẹ́ kí ó jàre oo,
Yemọja ó máa dọwọ́ rẹ,
[20] Baba ó màà dọwọ́ rẹ,
Yèyé ó màà dọwọ́ rẹ
Kí ó ṣẹ òní kí ó tún ṣe ìmòdún,
Àtá Olú-Odò.

The Àtá is coming, Olu-Odo [King of the River],
Pouring-rain-from-heaven,
My-father-blinking-washing-face-with-medicine,
He is coming, oh,
[5] All elders assembled in Yemọja's place,
Our father [king] is coming,
Male elders, female elders,
The Àtá is coming,
He brought his ram,

[10] He brought kola nut and salt,
    Let his life be full of salt [i.e., sweet],
    Let his life be sweet among the crown-wearers,
    He will do this year and the coming one,
    Let him carry us for a long time,
[15] And also his personal children,
    Don't let him be guilty among the crown-wearers,
    Don't let him be guilty in Ayede,
    Let him be innocent,
    Yemoja, it is left to you,
[20] Father, it is left to you,
    Yeye, it is left to you,
    You should do it today and also next year,
    Àtá Olu-Odo.

The Àtá is praised for providing the sacrifice and thereby fulfilling his ritual obligation to the Yemoja cult in exchange for spiritual protection. The priestesses pray that his life will be "sweet" like salt, particularly among the "crown-wearers"; that he will remain on the throne to do the next year's festival; and that he will enjoy a long reign. I was told that "crown-wearers" (aládé, lit. "crown-owners") refers both to kings and to the senior cult members who safeguard the crown and revitalize its powers. These priestesses, furthermore, possess their own ritual crowns (adé imọlẹ̀)—beaded icons of kingship, which, as we shall see, they balance on their heads during the festival's climax. From this ritual definition of aládé, the injunction "Don't let him be guilty among the crown-wearers" (line 16) registers a warning to the Àtá himself that if guilty in Ayede, he will lose the cult's support. The parallel between cult and town is asserted in the following line, "Don't let him be guilty in Ayede," suggesting how rejection by the cult precipitates rejection by the town chiefs (often referred to collectively as "the town") and ultimately deposition. The prayer's fundamental appeal—"Let him be innocent"—is less for the Àtá's physical or ritual well-being and more in support of his political safety. According to cult ideology, the Àtá's "innocence" is regulated in three ways. It is left to Yemoja (line 19), who can protect him from error if she so pleases; it is left to the Àtá himself (line 20) to respect the values of high office; and finally, it is left to Yeye (line 21), the Yèyéolókun priestess who carries the ritual calabash, to revitalize the king.

The actual killing of the ram is accompanied by a chant called *ègún pípè* for cult ancestors. As the ram's blood flows into Yemoja's deep hole within the shrine and the life ebbs from its body, a priestess sings:

> *Jogun-oṣó ń mò ọń j'ẹran,*
> *Èjẹ ń ṣàn gbuuru o òòò,*
> *Mọ́ ọn mu'tí àìdá-àìro,*
> *Ẹ ṣe Yèyé, l'ófẹ.*
> *Qlárìnóyè ń mu'tí àìdá-àìro,*
> *Ẹ ṣe Yèyé, l'ófẹ . . .*

One who inherits witchcraft/wizardry is eating meat,

[And] blood is flowing profusely,

Keep drinking the [hot] wine not-tapped-not-trickling,

Thank you Mother, rise up without mishap.

Olarinoye is drinking the [hot] wine not-tapped-not-tricking,

Thank you Mother, rise up without mishap . . .

References (after Yemoja) to Ogun-awobi, Omoriyesalu, and other "spiritual names," as well as to the other *òrìṣà* clustered within her cult, invoke the ancestral spirits of great past devotees, who together drink the blood ("hot wine") of the sacrifice. The ram's head is severed and lifted from the ground to the sky three times as the *Àtá* and his attendants nervously look on. A senior priestess then casts kola nut—brought by the king—to "interpret" whether or not Yemoja and *her* spiritual attendants have accepted the sacrifice. When the toss is successful, the devotees shout "Yemoja oo! Omi [Water] oo!."[3] At the first ceremony I attended, the *Àtá* was visibly relieved when I observed this critical moment, for his favor with Yemoja and her associated *òrìṣà* was ritually acknowledged and their support guaranteed for the following year.

The Day of Carrying Water

The denouement of the Yemoja festival, called *ijọ́ ipọnmi*, or the "day of carrying water," occurs on the fourth day after the king's sacrifice, which is also the subsequent market day. Whereas the king proceeded from the palace to Yemoja's bush shrine to offer his sacrificial ram, on this day cult priestesses proceed from the bush shrine through the marketplace to the palace, carrying Yemoja's power into the center of the town. Heralded by *dùndún* drummers and members of the cult, the high priestess of Yemoja, possessed *gùn* (lit. mounted) by the *òrìṣà*, carries a sacred calabash *(igbá Yemọja)* balanced carefully on her head. This calabash contains the concentrated powers *(àṣẹ)* of kingship, conceived as a "hot," explosive, and polluting force which is invoked by esoteric incantations and medicinal preparations and which is regulated by priestesses according to strict ritual procedures. The calabash, I was told, is so "heavy" with power that all the town's hunters together could not lift it. The high priestess is prepared with special *bẹ́rẹ́* and *ofẹ* medicines cut into her scalp to "lighten" the calabash and prevent it from falling. If it does fall or break, common knowledge maintains that the priestess will die and that misfortune will ensue.

Bringing the calabash from the bush shrine to the palace generates tremendous excitement and anxiety. As the welfare of the community is literally balanced on the priestess's head, all measures are taken to ensure her "safe delivery." Cult "messengers" prepare the way by sprinkling salt on the ground to neutralize any bad medicines thrown down by the king's rivals or by any enemies of the town who may wish to make the priestess fall. Water is poured on the priestess's feet to keep them "cool," while talking drums, amidst rhythmic praises, admonish her to "walk cautiously" like any prudent king.[4]

The high priestess, dressed in the white cloth *(aṣọ àlà)* of ritual purity and composure, in effect *becomes* the king. The crowd acclaims her with shouts of "Kábíyèsí!"—an address reserved, in secular time, exclusively for kings. Her potent calabash of power is carried and praised as a crown—*adé imọlẹ̀*, or "crown of the possession priestesses." But Yemoja is an *òrìṣà* of female power. Praised as "owner of the breasts of honey" *ọlọ́mún oyin)* and "owner of innumerable children [sons]" *(ọlọ́mọ̀ ako gbèdọ̀)*, among her many stereotypically feminine appellations, she is generally invoked as a goddess of fertility. Her temperament is calm and collected, expressed by the measured choreographies of her ritual representatives. As the Yemoja priestess approaches the king, she is praised as "walking with self-composed dignity" *(lẹ̀ẹ̀ mì legbẹ̀ẹ̀)*, at once a verbal and visual depiction of authoritative command and control. At no other time during the Yemoja festival is female power so explicitly associated with the kingship.

Carrying the ritual calabash on her head, the *Yèyéolókun* priestess, followed by junior priestesses with smaller vessels of "water" on their heads, visits the graves of former cult members and chiefs as well as major town and market shrines to pay ritual respect *(júbà).*[5] Then she proceeds to the palace. The king, seated in state on the palace veranda and surrounded by elders and family members, awaits the priestesses as his wives and cult members sing his and Yemoja's praises together. The drummers increase their beat and the crowd presses in as the *Yèyéolókun* priestess walks up to the king and turns to the crowd, blocking his view. She turns toward and away from him three times and, with the calabash still on her head, almost obscenely obscures his body and face. The king places his hands upon her and, as his body trembles, absorbs the calabash's power, praying that he will live to witness the next annual ceremony. The king is thus "recharged" with *àṣẹ;* invested with the power of his words to come true, his decisions will be respected and his curses feared.

The *Yèyéolókun* priestess then proceeds to "deliver" the calabash to one of two places: if one year she puts it inside the palace room which houses the king's crowns, the next year she will carry it to the main altar within the Yemoja cult's town shrine. In either case, the priestesses who follow behind her proceed to the cult shrine, where they "drop" their "water" contained in vessels on their heads. Wherever the calabash and water are set down, the *òrìṣà* is said to arrive *(dé).* After the priestesses "put their water down," they emerge from the shrine and dance to seven talking-drum rhythms associated with Yemoja, Orisha Oko, Ogun, Oshun, Shango, Ibeji (the deity of twins), and the Ogboni cult. After the final rhythm, the Shango priestess ascends the *odó* of Shango, an inverted mortar (used for pounding yam) set in cement and inscribed with Shango's *oríkì*—"the king didn't hang" *(ọba kò só).* As she "climbs" *(gùn)* the pedestal, she is in turn "mounted" *(gùn)* by Shango, who speaks through her to the assembled public, prescribing collective sacrifices to avert imminent misfortune. After this "prediction," as it is colloquially called, the public festival is officially concluded.

ANTINOMIES OF KINGSHIP

The "technological" interpretation of the Yemoja festival is official political ideology. It not only is proudly proclaimed—during the festival and in subsequent reflection—but also, quite literally, invests the king with power. Revitalized by *àṣẹ,* the king, through his words, can effectively influence the future—both positively, in decisions which determine public policy, and negatively, in curses *(èpè)* which destroy his detractors (Lloyd 1968:47). Since the public observes that the king is thus empowered, his sovereignty is effectively reestablished. It is no wonder that functionalist interpretations of royal African ritual dwell on the maintenance of political authority, since that is what the official ideology of these rituals proclaims. But herein lies an interpretive limit. The ethnographically recorded *opacity* of ritual symbols, reflecting public proscriptions *against* interpretation, privileges official discourse at the expense of exegesis. In such cases, functionalists turn to function because meaning is out of bounds.

The symbolic exegesis of òrìṣà-cult ritual is publicly prohibited because it belongs to a corpus of esoteric secrets which provide access to ritual power itself. The cults ensure that such knowledge remains scarce. When a devotee joins an òrìṣà cult, undergoing expensive initiation and prolonged seclusion, he or she buys into a highly restricted ritual resource and swears a blood oath (ìmulè) not to reveal cult secrets. Within the cults, knowledge is differentially distributed according to seniority.[6] Elders and high-office holders possess "deep" knowledge to which junior members and new recruits (adóṣù) are gradually exposed. As an uninitiated anthropologist seeking to penetrate the "unspeakable," I was allowed to witness, photograph, and record public rituals, but was denied "deep" explanations of ritual symbols and forms. Gradually, after honorary initiations into several cults, I was brought into restricted sacrificial groves and could ask more penetrating questions without causing offense. My inquisitive presence, however, was always dangerous to the cults, since the more I learned, the more I could expose and undo. This threat extended to the deities themselves. On many occasions when I pressed devotees for information, they explained that if they revealed cult secrets, the òrìṣà would lose its power.

Such statements appear to frustrate an ethnographic understanding of Yoruba ritual, but actually they contribute to it. The logic of secrecy entails a double compact—one among cult members to keep their power among themselves, the other with the òrìṣà, to keep its power alive. Ritual power is thus enclosed in a "watertight" system of discursive restrictions. The power of the cult is actually referred to as water, contained in the calabash and ritual vessels balanced on the priestesses' heads. It is water drawn from the grove where the deity dwells, in deep pools of hidden mysteries where only initiates can visit and officiate. Like cult secrets, this water must never leak, spill, or flow forth. Since ritual symbols *deflect* "deep" interpretation, they signify, in their very opacity, the hidden conditions and contents of their efficacy. Here it is tempting to dismiss cult symbols and secrets as vehicles of deliberate mystification. Perhaps cult knowledge has no other content than the manufactured illusion that it actually exists. The proscriptive principle that the more you know, the less you can tell would insulate this complicity from public exposure. Indeed, a senior cult member is described as someone who has eyes but no mouth, who sees the truth but cannot talk.

The possibility that ritual vessels are semantically empty is intriguing but inaccurate. Cult members do divulge esoteric knowledge, circuitously, in fragments, under exceptional conditions of friendship and trust. The process is one of gradual introduction and partial revelation. Late at night I was told "deep" secrets in anxious whispers behind closed shutters and doors—not to keep others from hearing, for people were sleeping and well out of earshot, but to keep the òrìṣà from hearing. What I learned of the forbidden discourse was that ritual symbols are neither arbitrary nor meaningless, but are icons and indices of political power. It is not power commonly understood as political authority, but power *ultra vires* and structurally opposed to authority—that is, power which dismantles, deposes, kills the king, and consumes his flesh and blood.

We can focus on what is clearly a key and complex symbol in Odun Yemoja—the cult's calabash *(igbá)* of power. If, according to my argument, discussion of ritual symbols is inversely related to their significance and "depth" as cult secrets, then *igbá Yemoja* is of paramount importance. Several weeks after witnessing the Yemoja festival for the first time, while drinking palm wine in the high priestess's parlor, I boasted that before leaving Nigeria I would learn the true contents of the calabash. My friends were appalled, and the priestess was visibly upset. Mere mention of the calabash was bad enough; to assert my intention of knowing its secrets was tantamount to treason. Only after two weeks of begging the priestess not to be annoyed, that I was practicing my Yoruba and did not know what I was saying, did I regain her confidence. What I learned much later illuminated her reaction, for the "decorations" on the calabash signify its subversive contents.

With its lower half wrapped in white cloth, the calabash exhibits several icons of kingship. A beaded *abèbè* fan, an insignia of the kingship, "decorates" the calabash with a design—the "face," "eyes" *(ojú)*, and "head" *(orí)* of the òrìṣà—similar to one which appears on the king's beaded crown. The fan protrudes above wrapped velvet, expensive *àrán* velvet used for the king's royal robes. The red beaded fringe over the high priestess's forehead completes the imagery of a beaded crown, carried by a female king in the ritual domain. The calabash-crown and the king's beaded crown are both called Olokun, the generic òrìṣà of the sea and deep waters. But there is a marked difference. Only the calabash displays red parrot feathers *(ìkó odídé)*, "crowning" the calabash in bundles of three.

The calabash is thus ritually packed to bring power to the king and the community. We can "unpack" its principal icons to disclose the subversive power embedded within it:

The Abèbè fan. Generally held in the right hand, the *abèbè* signifies chieftaincies of various grades. A *beaded* fan, however, connotes kingship. Decorated with the "face" of the òrìṣà and carried in the calabash, it identifies the Yemoja priestess as a female ritual king. A verbal pun deepens this association. *Abẹ̀bẹ̀* also means "petitioner," or "person who pleads for the granting of a favor" (from *a* [agent] + *bẹ̀* [begs or requests] + *ẹ̀bẹ̀* [a request]); or it can stand as a sentence meaning "we request" (*a* [we] *bẹ̀bẹ̀* [petition, request]). The Yemoja priestess thus symbolically petitions the king on behalf of the cult and, by extension, the town at large to give—as we shall see—of himself. The fan also "cools" his power, as suggested by the incantation

Bí oòrù bá mú,
Abẹ̀bẹ̀ l'á fìí bẹ̀ ẹ.

When heat strikes,
We use the fan to beg ["cool"] it.[7]

The Àrán cloth. The cloth of kingship "wraps" and "encloses" the king's person. Yemoja herself is praised as someone who "takes two *àrán* cloths and two chieftaincy titles" (*èjì àrán atéjì oyè gbée*), meaning that she is *more* powerful than the king, but also that in addition to her own cloth and chieftaincy titles, she can take those of the king. This is reinforced by a parallel invocation to Yemoja, "Don't eat the owner [i.e., the person inside] of the cloth" (*má jẹléwù*); it refers at once to cult members and pregnant women (that they deliver their spiritual water or children safely), but also to the king (that he not be "eaten," i.e., consumed by witches or deposed by his chiefs).

The Ìkó Odídẹ (red parrot feathers). These feathers are worn by individual priestesses in their hair, either singly or in hairpieces of three—the number of the secret Ogboni society, which can order the king's (or anybody else's) death.[8] Crowning the calabash, they display the collective power of the cult. These feathers serve as signs of witchcraft and public disaffection. If a king loses favor with his *ìwàrèfà* chiefs (and this implies rejection by the Ogboni society), they will present him with *ìkó odídẹ* inside a calabash.[9] When the king opens the calabash and sees the red feathers, he knows he must commit suicide (since it is sacrilege to kill a sacred king, he must kill himself). The Ogboni cult would then prepare his corpse.[10]

Yemoja's calabash (igbá Yemoja). The calabash is wrapped in the white cloth of ritual composure because its contents are so "hot" that the calabash must be "cooled." According to official ideology, if the calabash falls or breaks, social upheaval will ensue. Successful ritual negates this proposition. If the calabash remains whole and is safely "delivered" to the king, social upheaval will *not* follow. The calabash thus represents a whole, healthy town, fragile but powerful, and regulated by the cult. Since the calabash contains *àṣẹ*—the essence of kingship and the power to influence the future—it also contains the "future" in the symbol of the womb, as that which perpetuates lineages, dynasties, and towns. Yemoja is the paradigmatic goddess of fertility. Her calabash contains the power of successful delivery, allaying the deadly appetites of witches who consume fetuses during nocturnal feasts. Yoruba sculpture often depicts women presenting calabashes that are carved as extensions of their healthy, pregnant wombs (Pemberton and Fagg 1982:99, 100, 119). And in markets, calabashes and enamel trays are used interchangeably to standardize measures of value and exchange. These trays are used as "calabashes" in rituals as well, where they become icons of female mediation and mercantile profit. Finally, in some myths, the base and lid of the calabash represent earth and sky (G. A. Ojo 1966b:196).

Veiled references to the vulnerability of the crown which can fall, the king who can be deposed, the town which can break or split, the cosmos which can rage; to the womb which can create, resist, or destroy new life; and to the female who "owns" the earth, rules the marketplace, procreates as mother, and devours as witch—all paradoxically conceal and reveal the contradictions or antinomies of Yoruba kingship. A king is deposed when his rule is too powerful, when he transcends or violates the limitations of his office. His chiefs, however, have appetites of their own, seeking power to appropriate the kingship for themselves or to break away and found independent kingdoms. The destructive forces of male power competition—the forces which precipitate deposition and fission and thus structurally establish the real limits of sovereignty—are transposed, by the calabash, into cosmological idioms of fertility and female control. The fundamental paradox contained in the calabash is that the very qualities of power *sui generis*—which the king receives from the *òrìṣà* and metonymically embodies—make him strong by killing and consuming him. The king is "petitioned" by the Yemoja cult to submit to a mode of Promethean dying. If he refuses, he will be deposed. His compliance reestablishes his sovereignty in order to regenerate the fertility of women and land and promote peace and prosperity in the town.

Of course I was never told this in so many words. But the evidence for this "deeper" interpretation follows from a hidden substitution. Recall the preliminary king's sacrifice which opens the festival and enlists

Yemoja's support. The king provides a ram which is sacrificed in the bush shrine. As in many African rituals where the sacrificial victim represents the sacrificer, the ram "stands in" for the king himself. Recall the incantation, "One who inherits witchcraft/wizardry [i.e., Yemoja] is eating meat, [and] blood is flowing profusely." And recall the ram's severed head, lifted three times from the ground to the sky in front of the king and his beaded crown. The king is praised for bringing his ram because by the paradoxical rule of a cosmological secret, he offers *himself* to the *òrìṣà* in return for the power to rule over others. Perhaps this is what the senior cult members see but cannot say.

WITCHCRAFT, FERTILITY, AND FEMALE POWER

Thus far I have discussed female power in stereotypes, as manifest in the goddess Yemoja and embodied by her priestesses. Yemoja is beautiful. She is praised as the "ocean of all women"; her flowing waters cure barren women by incarnating fecundity. In the explicit discourse of official ideology, female power is openly acclaimed as antithesis and antidote to the destructive power of men. Whereas men are "hot," volatile, violent, and tough, ritually represented by staccato drum rhythms and wide, stamping choreographies, women are "cool," subdued, peaceful, and soft, seducing men with slower motions. These gender stereotypes have a ritual design. During the king's sacrifice to enlist the goddess's support, a prayer for a successful festival invokes female power to regulate the violence of men:

Ọdún dé lóni oo,
K'ọdún nìyí yábo,
Abo lálà bò mo,
Abo ni tura,
Abo ni rọra,
K'ọdún wa má y'áko,
Ako ló ni lílè.

Our festival has arrived today,
May this festival turn out to be female in nature,
It is in femaleness that peace is buried,
It is the female that comforts,
It is the female that soothes,
May our festival not turn out to be male,
For it is in the male that toughness lies.

The official meaning of this prayer is clear. Without the "cooling" influence of women in ritual, male power competition will blow the kingdom apart. The sexual, political, and aesthetic dimensions of this statement relate successful insemination and childbirth to the welfare and stability of the king and his kingdom. For it is in the soft and comforting female that male "toughness" is buried and "soothed," that male desire is satisfied and converted into new life. This logic of sexual reproduction is ritually extended to the king and his kingdom on the climactic day of carrying water. The delivery of the calabash from the bush to the palace is, like insemination, a deep implantation of external power and, like childbirth, a delivery of new life. When I first heard a Yemoja priestess pray for a woman's safe childbirth—"May she carry it [the fetus] safely and put it down"—I assumed it was simply a prayer for a private client. I recorded the very same phrase, however, in a prayer for the Yemoja priestess, that she carry *the calabash* safely and put it down. The same prayer in such different contexts suggests a parallel between successful childbirth and the ritual revitalization of the king.[11] Consistent with our deeper interpretation of this ritual is that if Yemoja and her priestesses consume and kill the king, it is with their calabash—both womb and crown—that he is born and crowned again.

The king's revitalization, then, entails ritual death and rebirth. The king is secretly consumed by priestesses, only to be reproduced with greater power. It is as if the paradoxical moment of succession to high office—"the king is dead, long live the king" (or, more concisely, ọba kò só, "the king didn't hang")—is mimetically anticipated and thereby postponed. Successful ritual avoids death and deposition; it "guarantees" the king at least another year in office. But the ritual reproduction of the king, like sexual reproduction, is always vulnerable to affliction. A woman may be barren or can lose her child in delivery. The Yemoja-cult calabash, like a womb, can break. Or the goddess herself, like a fickle or displeased woman, may withhold her procreative powers altogether. The female power of Yemoja, of her priestesses, and of Yoruba women in general has two antithetical values, or sides. The official ideology of seductive beauty and fertility upholds the virtues of sexual reproduction; hidden witchcraft, however, explains death, disease, and infertility.

Since witchcraft, like fertility, is latent, if not active, at different times of a woman's life, it can be allayed but never fully eliminated or destroyed. One of the ostensible goals of òrìṣà worship is to promote female fertility by placating witches with song, dance, prayer, and special sacrifices (Drewal and Drewal 1983). Witchcraft works against fertility by interfering with sexual reproduction in several ways. I was told that women who sleep in unnatural positions—with the top of their heads on the ground or their anuses exposed and lifted high— transform their "hearts" (*ọkàn*) into deadly night birds which torment and eat their enemies. These birds can consume the fetus of a pregnant woman or obstruct the expulsion of the child from the womb. Prince (1961:798) reports that a Yoruba witch can "borrow" a man's penis to have sex with his wife or another woman, causing impotence in the man and barrenness in the woman. Even small girls can practice witch- craft. A story circulated about a young girl in Ayede who could destroy a child in her mother's womb simply by defecating. The girl's excre- ment would turn into the witchcraft spirit, climb into her mother's womb through the vagina, and there consume the fetus.[12]

The word *àjẹ́* (witch) denotes the woman who consumes life and blocks the flow of reproductive fluids. Since the utterance of this term is considered dangerous, witches are more casually referred to as *ìyá wa*, or "our mothers." Another term for witch, *alábara méjì*, translates literally as "one who has two bodies," i.e., the woman's corporeal body and that of the nocturnal bird of death. Witches control the flow of menstrual blood. As saboteurs of pregnant women, witches can sub- vert women's reproductive roles. Yoruba witchcraft, in this restricted sense, is the *inverse* of fertility and successful delivery. But if witchcraft and fertility constitute irreducible antinomies of female power, these not only refer to sexual reproduction but extend to the ritual reproduc- tion of the king and his polity as well.[13]

From the more inclusive perspective of hegemonic reproduction through cosmological renewal, the dual components of female power acquire a much richer, "deeper," and self-reflexive meaning. If the "fer- tility" of priestesses reproduces the official hierarchy of the king ruling through his chiefs, their "witchcraft" devours and dismantles this hier- archy. Yemoja's status as a fertility goddess is compounded and con- founded by her status as a witch. In addition to her seductive appella- tions, she is praised as "mother of witches" and "inheritor of witchcraft." It is the witchcraft of Yemoja's calabash which devours and *deposes* the king, for as Prince (ibid., 796) documents in his psychologi- cal research on Yoruba witchcraft and schizophrenia, "the red tail- feather of the parrot is used as a sign of witchcraft power, and may be placed in the calabash . . . containing witchcraft power." Thus Yemoja's calabash of ritual power is also a repository of witchcraft, symbolized by the same red parrot feathers which the chiefs send to depose their king. According to Ifa divination poetry, Yemoja's power is "a bird contained in a covered calabash" and is named "calabash- power: to kill and eat people" (Gleason 1973:137, 133).

Yemoja's calabash contains antithetical powers. As a delicate womb, it contains witchcraft and fertility; as a female crown, it deposes and regenerates the king; as a unified town, it contains the contested violence of deposition and fission; as cosmos, it contains earth and sky. The official discourse seems to openly acknowledge (1) that the calabash empowers the king; (2) that female power "cools" and "softens" men; (3) that the festival promotes fertility and suppresses witchcraft; and (4) that it sanctifies and fortifies political hierarchy and safeguards against subversion. It is here, however, that official interpretations stop and that the esoteric logic of ritual empowerment entails its more disturbing story. The Yemoja festival promotes fertility and political hierarchy by deposing the king and feeding him to the witches. The secret icons of the calabash—the red parrot feathers which demand the king's suicide and signify witches who "kill and eat people"—combine with outward manifestations of fertility and authority which regenerate the king and put him back on the throne. When the king receives Yemoja's calabash, he embodies the paradoxical condition of his own reproduction—the hidden power to break the rules and structures which establish his authority.

●●

To isolate the Yemoja festival from Ayede's ritual calendar is to remove it from its practical context and fullest narrative frame. Orisha Ojuna's festival dovetails into Yemoja's, which intersects one day ahead to "fight" with Orisha Iyagba (see chapter 6). Each has sacrifices and a day of carrying water, and each is an episode of a larger story. Orisha Ojuna brings the king's body from Ikole and glorifies Eshubiyi's consolidation of power; Yemoja carries his crown from Ibadan and glorifies Oyo; Orisha Iyagba represents the powerful *Balógun* from Alu who "meets" Eshubiyi in the market and, after some very tense moments, recognizes the king. The priestesses of different cults thus perform together, in a composite narrative that recalls Ayede's founding and includes its original and immigrant groups. The recollection is of course revisionary and need not be faithful to a single set of facts, since each cult reflects on its own conditions, reproduces its own power, and has its own version of the truth. But it does represent common themes and centers—expressed in different ways and approached from different pathways—which keep the social order going provided nobody reveals too much.

Unless one is highly placed, one cannot know when the cycle will begin; the high priests and priestesses set dates and schedules which articulate with seasonal, agricultural, market, lunar, menstrual, even molting cycles which mark the passage and repetition of time. There is sometimes conflict over these dates, as when two subquarters in the neighboring kingdom of Ishan contested the mode of reckoning for their Epa festival—by the moon or by market days—indicating incipient fission of the quarter. Moreover, as with the ranking of chiefs, which the calendar "officially" recapitulates, it is difficult to find agreement on the precise opening and closing festivals in the cycle. Is it the Àtá's New Yam festival, or Owaiye's Olua, or Egbe-Oba's Oloke, or Ejigbo's Orisha Oniyi? I have heard yes and no for each, but the calendar should not be discussed. When I asked the àwòrò of Olua how he determined the appropriate time for his festival, he replied with silence. One of his sons exclaimed, "Look at Baba who is sitting down here, he already knows the next date, but he will never reveal it to us ahead of time!"[14]

In addition, there are distinct calendars for quarters, subquarters, lineages, and even households which possess variable degrees of autonomy, and this variation appears directly related to the centralization of power. In centralized Ayede, one official calendar of performances unites the major cults and dominates the others, while in the decentralized village clusters, such as neighboring Ishan and Itaji, the cycles of each quarter predominate over the whole. One obvious sign of autonomy is a negation, an avoidance of the king (and his market) which shows uneasy respect, since by ritually avoiding the king, the chief of a quarter assumes kingly dimensions. Such quarters are often referred to as "towns" and can establish their own markets and break away. Sacred time itself is thus contested. To commit a ritual calendar to paper may represent "function," "behavior," and official ideology (and what Bourdieu [1977:97–109] calls a synoptic illusion), but it misses the complications underneath, the "possession" of time by different groups and deities. Devotees of Yemoja praise her for owning the day:

Jogún Ọṣó ló lọjọ́ òní,
Ọ̀jọ́ òní ò nira rẹ.

Inheritor of wizardry [Yemoja's praise name] owns today,
Today does not own itself.

And the same attribution of "ownership," logically closed by its negative complement, belongs to every other òrìṣà with ritual power. Discussion about time is thus restricted by secrecy to protect different calendars and their critical agendas. For whatever their place in the official cycle and its ritualized narrative, all cults reproduce their own king in their own way, during their own time.

In its most general contours, Yoruba *òrìṣà* worship signifies on multiple levels according to an *indigenous* hermeneutics of power. The official ideology of ritual representations may not say very much, but this interpretive silence is an essential part of the ethnographic record. Silence indicates not the ignorance of blind tradition or limited thought, but the understanding that when knowledge *is* power, it must be differentially distributed in the public domain. The "deeper," paradoxical interpretations of Yoruba ritual revise and subvert official ideologies not through faulty logic or a perverse sense of play, but because they grasp power *ultra vires*, opposed to authority, traducing its structures and rules. In Ayede's Yemoja festival, the king is "killed" in order to survive. His official charters are "falsified" by esoteric genealogies and counterclaims. His singular sovereignty fractures into multiple identities. As a ruler, he belongs to every town cult and chief. As a man, he embodies the female power of witchcraft and fertility. As an institution, sacred and perpetual, he belongs to the past, present, and future.[15] As an incumbent, he is eminently selectable and substitutable. The following chapter will deepen this analysis by examining the linguistic dimensions of these powerful themes.

5

The Language of Àṣẹ

The rhythm is the rebel.
—Public Enemy

The study of language in Yoruba religion, particularly ritual texts in their performance contexts, is at once the most profound and most difficult stage of entry into Yoruba culture.[1] It is profound because the Yoruba conceive of their religious discourse as such: ritual language is "deep" (*jinlẹ̀*) and stylized, and it possesses *àṣẹ*—the capacity to invoke powers, appropriate fundamental essences, and influence the future. Rich in metaphor and poetic devices, it expresses fundamental ideas of ritual power which are highly valued and closely guarded. Because of restrictions imposed by *òrìṣà* cults, ritual-language texts are difficult to record. Many are performed only once a year, and some only once in a lifetime.[2] To sing or perform them at other times is infelicitous. Even during public performances, permission to record these texts can be difficult to obtain. One must bring offerings and undergo many "initiations" to gain access and trust.

In addition to these practical problems of restricted access, the texts themselves are difficult to understand. Stylized speech modes with parochial allusions, archaic words, veiled references, and subtle ambiguities pose interpretive difficulties even for indigenous linguists. Adequate readings of Yoruba ritual-language texts—which include praises (*oríkì*), prayers (*àdúrà*), songs (*orin*), incantations (*ofọ̀*), and talking-drum texts (*èdè ìlù*) among their many possible styles, or genres—require specialized cosmological knowledge. Such readings must also be context-specific, relating the internal properties of ritual texts to their external contexts of reference and reverence. Yoruba ritual language, like Yoruba "art", is in motion (cf. R. F. Thompson 1974). It builds images, sets moods, and merges subjects and objects, nouns and verbs; it implores and commands, upholds and subverts, repeats and recalls, possesses and repossesses, with many voices, on multiple levels, even in different dialects. That the same is true of "black" textuality more generally is argued in chapter 9. The more immediate goal of this chapter, however, is philological and descriptive—to establish key texts in a preliminary form and to identify their critical strategies and diacritical features.

Ritual-language texts are of course verbal, oral, "talking" texts (cf. Gates 1988:127–69). They are spoken, sung, chanted, incanted, even danced in "dialogue" with talking drums. As such, they resist graphemic reduction and challenge conventional paradigms of textuality (Barber 1984). Attempts to classify Yoruba oral literature into canonical categories are highly problematical (Olatunji 1982). Formal categories based on stylistic criteria are always mixed in practice—praises can include proverbs and incantations, while incantations may "quote" extensively from Ifa (see, for example, Adeniji 1980). Pragmatic categories based on the identities of speakers (e.g., hunters, wives, cult members, herbalists, diviners), type of event (ritual, naming ceremony, funeral, diagnosis), or, more specifically, the character of the speech act (honoring, cursing, praying, predicting, protecting) are equally fuzzy in that no one text conforms to a single type. Using Yoruba labels does not solve the problem. One finds *ọfọ̀* in *oríkì*, *oríkì* in *ijálá*, and instances of each in different chanting modes *(pípè)*. As Barber (1984:510–11) explains:

> Yoruba oral literature in general appears like a vast stock of
> verbal materials—themes, formulas, stories, poetic idioms—
> which can float through the permeable boundaries of all the
> genres and be incorporated into them to fulfill different
> functions. Genres freely incorporate parts of other genres, with
> much sharing and borrowing of material.

Barber resolves the problem of classification by defining ritual texts as paradigmatically intertextual. Lacking unity, closure, and "sole authority," Yoruba oral literature professes a style of deconstruction, Barber argues, that is more critical—as practice—than its Eurocentric forms.

This type of intertextuality is important to bear in mind because it illuminates ritual-language use as signifying practice, relating "meaning" to "doing" in the intentional and rhetorical senses of these terms. Again, the reading of discursive structures—intertextual, polyvocal, intentionally transparent, and metaphysically opaque—is foregrounded by public strictures *against* interpretation. Meanings voiced in ritual texts cannot be discussed in "ordinary" language—definitely not in public, and only uneasily in private. As with the official ideology of Yemoja's calabash (examined in chapter 4), ritual language is publicly accounted for in strategic and instrumental terms. Thus I was freely told what the priestesses were doing when an òrìṣà was called, praised, or glorified by song, or when a devotee was praying for assistance—even when the Shango priestess "predicted" for the community and prescribed collective sacrifices. But the language itself remained a closed book. Textual fragments which possess power, or àṣẹ, are clearly rich in metaphor and allusion, but the metaphors and allusions—as in most poetry—are sensed and intimated rather than formally explicated. Like the deeper meanings of ritual symbols, the language of àṣẹ undermines the fundamental differences—linguistic and hegemonic—which it outwardly reproduces.

Perhaps the best way to discuss ritual language is by letting it speak for itself, as it were, through transcriptions, translations, and enough explication to highlight the most basic critical strategies. Rather than abstract, classify, and canonize specific genres, I shall represent key texts as they were performed and recorded during the Yemoja festival sketched in the previous chapter.

FIGURES OF THE DEEP

Returning to the king's sacrifice in Yemoja's grove (chapter 4), we can "reread" this "critical" event by attending more closely to its language. In our first reading we noted the èégún pípè chant which accompanied the killing of the ram. The chant calls Yemoja and the powerful spirits of her past devotees to feed on the sacrifice and enter the town. Just as the sacrifice is shared with Yemoja's ancestral spirits, so the text is shared among assembled devotees, whose responses are indented from the leading text:

> Jogun-oṣó ń mò ọ́ń j'ẹran,
> Èjẹ̀ ń ṣàn gbuuru o òòò,
> Mọ́ ọn mu'tí àìdá-àìro,
> Ẹ ṣe Yèyé, l'ófẹ.
> [5] Ọlárìnóyè ń mu'tí àìdá-àìro,
>   Ẹ ṣe Yèyé lófẹ.
> 'Móríyesálú ń mu'tí àìdá-àìro,
>   Ẹ ṣe Yèyé lófẹ.
> Ògún-àwòbí ń mu'tí àìdá-àìro,

[10]   Ẹ ṣe Yèyé lófẹ.
Ó ń mu'tí àìdá-àìro,
     Ẹ ṣe Yèyé lófẹ.
     [Ẹ pe Ògún.]
Ó ń jẹran
Èjẹ̀ ń ṣàn gbuuru o.
[15]   Ẹyọ̀'gún ṣèṣè!
Ògún-àwòbí ń jẹran
Èjẹ̀ ń ṣàn gbuuru ooo.
Èrò odò!
     Ó ń jẹran
[20]   Èjẹ̀ ń ṣàn gbuuru ooo eee.
Ajagun ń jẹran bọ̀ lódò Òòṣà-Oko,
Ògún-àwòbí ń jẹran
Èjẹ̀ ń ṣàn gbuuru ooo eee!
Ẹ yògún ṣèṣè!
[25] Ògún-àwòbí ń forí odì yílẹ̀ kiri.
Èrò odò!
     Ó ń forí odì yílẹ̀ gbiri . . .
Mo sàjà sọ́mọ rẹ lọ́rùn gbọngan ooo,
Èrò odò!
[30]   O bé ẹ lórí ọmọ-òfegééé,
     Ládéjọlúmọ̀, ayaba Òòṣà-Oko,
     Mo sàjà sọ́mọ rẹ lọ́rùn gbọngan ooo eee.
Agbe ń dún "pogún-pogún,"
     Ẹyògún ṣèṣè!
[35] Àlùkó ń dún "pọgbọ̀n-pọgbọ̀n" oo,
Ohùn àlùkó ń' mo gbọ́,
N ò gbóhùn agbe o;
Èrò odòòòò!
     Agbe ń dún "pogún-pogún,"
     Ládéjọlúmọ̀, ayaba Òòṣà-Oko,
     Àlùkó ń dún pọgbọ̀n-pọgbọ̀n oo,
     Ohùn àlùkó ń' mo gbọ́,
     N ò gbóhùn agbeee ooo eee.
     Ẹ yògún ṣèṣè!

[1]   One who inherits witchcraft/wizardry is eating meat,
      [And] blood is flowing profusely,
      Keep drinking the [hot] wine not-tapped-not-trickling,
      Thank you mother, rise up without mishap.
[5]   Olarinoye is drinking the [hot] wine not-tapped-not-
            trickling,
            Thank you Mother, rise up without mishap.
      Moriyesalu is drinking the [hot] wine not-tapped-not-
            trickling,
            Thank you Mother, rise up without mishap.
      Ogun-awobi is drinking the [hot] wine not-tapped-not-
            trickling,
[10]   Thank you Mother, rise up without mishap.
      He is drinking the [hot] wine not-tapped-not-trickling,
            Thank you Mother, rise up without mishap.
      [At this point a priestess instructs the chanter, "Call on
            Ogun."]
      He is eating meat
      [And] blood is flowing profusely.
[15]   Hail Ogun!
      Ogun-awobi is eating meat
      [And] blood is flowing profusely
      Pilgrims of the river [I call you]!
            He is eating meat
[20]   [And] blood is flowing profusely.
      Man of War is eating meat [and going] toward Orisha Oko,
      Ogun-awobi is eating meat
      [And] blood is flowing profusely!
      Hail Ogun!
[21] Ogun-awobi is dragging the enemy's head on the ground.
      Pilgrims of the river!
            He is dragging the enemy's head on the ground.
      I strap the sacred rattle around his child's neck,
      Pilgrims of the river!
[30]   It has been skillfully decapitated,
            [Hear] Ladejolumo, queen of Orisha Oko,

> I strap the sacred rattle around his child's neck.
> The blue touraco utters the call *"pogún-pogún,"*
> Hail Ogun!
[35] The [red] woodcock utters the call *"pọgbọ̀n-pọgbọ̀n,"*
> I can only hear the voice of the [red] woodcock,
> I cannot hear the voice of the blue touraco;
> Pilgrims of the river!
> The blue touraco utters the call *"pogún-pogún,"*
[40] Ladejolumo, queen of Orisha Oko,
> The [red] woodcock utters the call *"pọgbọ̀n-pọgbọ̀n,"*
> I can only hear the voice of the [red] woodcock,
> I cannot hear the voice of the blue touraco.
> Hail Ogun!

Even a literal reading of this text is difficult, since the narrative has no single theme, but combines cryptic segments and blocks—what Barber (1984:507) calls "a clustering of units"—to achieve "a thematic drift." The obvious theme is provided by the sacrificial context. Yemoja is "eating meat" of the ram and drinking its blood. The blood does not "trickle," but "flows profusely," like the unbridled spiritual water of the *òrìṣà*'s power. It is not "tapped," like palm wine, since tapping is gradual and does not kill the tree—rather, it gushes, giving life by taking it. Neither is the blood "cool," like the sweet and white palm wine; it is likened to *ọtí*, the "hot," potent, and intoxicating alcohol of locally distilled gin (*àgogoro*) and imported European spirits. The sacrificial blood and the language of invocation are charged with *àṣẹ* to transmit new life and to influence the future. The "Mother" is thanked and implored to "rise up," without falling or mishap, to ensure the successful "delivery" of power in the town. The "chorus" reiterates the thanks (lines 6, 8, 10, 12) to amplify their efficacy and to voice the devotees' collective concern. But the appeal is not to the goddess Yemoja alone. After line 12, a priestess instructs the chanter to "call" Ogun, the violent god of war and of iron locally identified as one of Yemoja's sons. Thus in line 13, the pronoun shifts to Ogun "eating meat" and drinking blood, a shift reiterated by the chorus and referring the same textual unit to a different deity (lines 13–14, 19–20).

After this shift, the language "deepens" and becomes "spiritually heavy," indicated by the increasing opacity of its figures (and by prosodic features such as the intensified elongation of final vowels). Lines 21 and 25 gloss hidden histories and narratives which must remain unexplicated. Ogun chews meat in the direction of Orisha Oko to imply an aggressive campaign of bloody carnage which threatens that òrìṣà who, in the cult's ritual genealogy, represents Ogun's father. As Ogun's mother (Yemoja) is "satisfied," his father (Orisha Oko) is "killed" and his head dragged on the ground (line 25). This dangerous (and clearly Oedipal) interpretation recodes its sacrificial context. The ram's head is in fact "dragged" on the ground while Ayede's king—the "father" of the kingdom—is ritually "killed" and awaits his fate by divination.

"Deep" speech is further marked by its multifunctional morphology. In line 28, strapping the sacred rattle around his child's neck connects àjà with òrun to invoke (with minor tonal play) Àjàlóòrun, a creator deity whose very name offers protection (àjàlóòrun á gbà ọọ, "may you remain safe and sound!"). But more profoundly, Ajaloorun erases cosmological difference through a chain of identities which trace back to Ife origins. In Abraham's *Dictionary of Modern Yoruba* (1962), he is also Aramfe, the pre-Shango (and hence pre-Oyo) thunder god who subsumes the rival creators Oduduwa and Obatala by personifying both. But if difference is inwardly undermined, it is outwardly reproduced. The morpheme àjà ("rattle") also recalls Shango, literally with his ṣẹ́rẹ́ rattle which—as àjà—announces his arrival. Shango, like the Àtá of Ayede, is here morphologically deposed and resurrected by a regressive chain of primordial powers. Both parallel dramas are embodied by the ram, which, the chorus proclaims, "has been skillfully decapitated" (line 30) to protect "his" children.

To judge such readings right or wrong misconceives the hermeneutics of ritual speech. Subversive interpretations are neither truth-functionally verifiable nor intersubjectively redeemable; rather, they are rhetorically coherent as critical practice. Complex, contracted, and overcoded signifiers allow contestable signifieds and multiple meanings. The texts themselves have many voices and many languages, and they support many interpretations. In line 33 and 35, the language of birds (witches) makes devastating sense out of non-sense. The blue touraco *(agbe)*, which always appears in parallel construction with the red woodcock *(àlùkó)* is quoted as calling *"pogún-pogún."* I was told that this simply represents the bird's call. The same applied to the woodcock's *"pogbòn-pogbòn."* But within this parallel frame, the "nonsense" syllables invoke a fearful asymmetry. Whereas *pogún* contracts *pa ogún*, or "kills in twenties," *pogbón* contracts *pa ọgbòn*, or "kills in thirties"—a reading which gains coherence from the cultural association of the "cool" blue touraco with positive sanctions and the "hot" red woodcock with punitive sanctions. The priestess does not hear the voice of positive sanctions (lines 36–37); only death "by thirties" is audible. The chorus reiterates that the cult will show no mercy. It will eat meat, drink blood, skillfully decapitate, and kill in thirties to replenish the cosmos and empower the king.

Within this critical babble of tongues, perhaps the most powerful voice of all emerges from the possibility of silence. During the *èqún pípè* chant, the *Iyálòde* priestess divines with kola nuts to establish the acceptability of the sacrifice. Beneath the *èqún pípè*, in hushed tones, another chorus responds to the toss:

[1]   *Bá áà wí wí wí,*
      Bá a láà fohùn-ún fò o,
      Òwíwí eye oko
      Ni yíó gba tàwa wí.

[5]   *Bá a láà wí wí wí,*
      Bá a láà fohùn-ún fò o,
      Òwíwí eye oko
      Òun ní 'ó gba tèmi wí.

[1]   Even if we say nothing,
      Even if we decide to utter nothing,
      Owl, bird of the farm
      Shall utter words on our behalf.

[5]   Even if we decide to say nothing,
      Even if we decide to utter nothing,
      Owl, bird of the farm
      Shall utter words on my behalf.

The text epitomizes the complex interplay between meaning and sound in powerful incantations *(ofò)*. The active verb "to utter" or "to speak" *(wí)* activates the utterance (line 1) in two repetitions *(wí wí)* which intensify its efficacy. But what is "said" is nothing, what is decided is the absence of speech. Active speech departs from the priestesses, who become speechless, and relocates within the owl *(òwíwí)*, where, transmuted from verb to noun, speech to speaking subject, it says the unspeakable. The forbidden subtext—what cannot be said—is that the divination may disclose Yemoja's rejection of the king. If this happens, the priestesses remain silent. It is the owl who "embodies" their speech, that nocturnal bird of witchcraft which "drops on its prey" suddenly, without warning (Abraham 1962:495). "Speech" is repeated in line 1, is nominalized in line 3, and says what it cannot say in line 4, to construct a powerful incantation which then repeats itself (lines 5–8). The "movement" of the text—morphological, syntactic, semantic, thematic, even the movement between the spoken and the unspoken—empowers the king by "deconstructing" his sovereignty.

Next the priestesses turn their text into a variety of "call" and "response," appealing for the king's spiritual protection yet refiguring his fate:

> Ẹ mọ́ jẹ́ẹ́ ó bàjẹ́ o,
>> Báun layé ń ṣe.
> Yíyí layé ń yí,
>> Bìrí lọkọ̀ ń dà.

> Let it not be spoiled,
>> That is how life is done.
> Life turns characteristically,
>> [Just as] the boat suddenly capsizes.

Although the priestesses pray that the king's life not be spoiled, the same "life" turns (*yí*), tropologically, to capsize the very structure which supports it. The simultaneous negation and affirmation of the king is evoked by the polyvocality of *dà*. In addition to meaning "capsize," as an intransitive verb it can refer to flowing or pouring, as the blood of sacrifice flows; or to favorable divination, as in *obì yìí dà*, "the kolas used in divination gave a favorable omen" (ibid., 120). And as a transitive verb it "divines" in one of the *Àtá*'s ritual praises—*adífágbadé*, or "one who performs divination and receives a crown."[3] Thus, again, the king is deposed, resurrected, and ritually recrowned by divinatory sacrifice and the hidden significations of speech.

IDENTITIES AND ATTRIBUTES

Four days after the king's sacrifice, as the Yemoja cult carries its calabash to the palace, royal wives and priestesses honor the *òrìṣà* and glorify the king by filling the air with *oríkì*. This stylized panegyric is at once the most basic and the most complex form of Yoruba oratory, building images, reputations, and cryptic narratives from strings, or chains, or attributive epithets. Again, Barber (1984:503), the outstanding scholar of *oríkì*, explains:

> Sometimes translated 'praise poetry', *oríkì* are actually
> equivalent to names—names which can indicate undesirable
> qualities as well as desirable and which are seen as being in

some way the key to a subject's essential nature. By uttering a subject's *oríkì*, one is calling upon or unlocking hidden powers; the activity of naming is thought of as being effectual. Human subjects react to the utterance of their *oríkì* with deep gratification and an enhancement of their aura which is sometimes actually visible in their physical behavior. Spiritual beings are invoked and empowered by the utterance of their *oríkì*. Animals, plants, and all kinds of inanimate objects possess *oríkì* too; but the most developed and most frequently performed are those of people, *orílè* ('clans') and *òrìṣà* ('gods').

As Barber points out, the general idea of a complex appellation, whether it addresses an inanimate, animate, or spiritual subject, is that it invokes, "unlocks," and appropriates the special power or quality of what it re-presents. As such, *oríkì* occupy an important place in the language of *àṣẹ*, a language which captures essences and influences events. An *oríkì* exercises a command over its subject. In secular life, a person praised must "dash" the chanter (or drummer) with money or risk loss of reputation, status, and the very "qualities" of praise (cf. M. G. Smith 1957). In ritual, the obligations are more complex and serious, invoking gods and enhancing kings to secure their beneficence and support.

On the climactic day of carrying water, praises of the king and of the goddess Yemoja weave a complex intertext of identities and differences which both fuse and distinguish their exalted subjects. Palace wives and priestesses emerge from the bush shrine, through a raffia-palm gate, "out" into the town, where, as official testimony explains, they "pay homage" to the king and cult. A royal wife chants:

Wá fẹ́'re pàdé gbogbo wa.
Olójú ma-wò-mí.
Abojú ro bí ẹfun.
Abìpá tayọ aṣọ.

Come and blow the wind of fortune for all of us.

He whose eyes are fearful.

He whose eyes are harsh as lime.

He whose swollen testicles protrude from the cloth.

As Barber mentioned, *oríkì* names can represent undesirable qualities which attest to the subject's outrageousness and unlock its power. In this case, the king's power is invoked to bring fortune. His eyes are "fearful"; they burn like "lime," because his powerful vision perceives beneath the surfaces of things to grasp inner states and, in Paul de Man's self-incriminating phrase, "the secrets of interior life" (Derrida 1988:629). The protruding "swollen testicles" hyperbolically indicate sexual potency but also disease and grotesque abnormality. Indeed, the king is a monster, with abnormal "powers" which can regenerate but also spoil the order of things. A group of wives picks up the chant:

> A-gbọ́ná-bí-agbada-epo.
> Àjàlá mọ̀ ti gun kákà o!
> Ó-datí-bí-ẹni-da'mi.
> Ó-dàgọ̀rọ̀-bí-ẹni-dàran-òyìnbó.
> [5] Ọkọ dúdú,
> Ọkọ pupa,
> Ọkọ èyí rògbọ̀dọ̀ tí ń tayọ̀ lójà.

> He-who-is-hot-like-the-frying-pot.
> Ajala has been possessed by the spirits!
> He-who-pours-[drinks]-the-[hot]-wine-like-water.
> He-who-pours-[drinks]-the-date-palm-like-European-
>   liquids.
> [5] Husband of the dark ones,
> Husband of the light ones,
> Husband of the fat one who sells salt in the market.

The units of praise contract phrases and entire sentences into descriptive names and predicates that are saturated with meanings. The interpretation of these overcoded glosses is not meant to be easy, but sustains different levels of knowledge and access. Barber (1984:505) accounts for the complexity of *oríkì* by identifying their pragmatic conditions and referential strategies:

> The units of *oríkì* are separate not only because they were
> separately composed to refer to unrelated events but also
> because each unit may make a different *kind* of reference. Since
> *oríkì* are characteristically cryptic and obscure, the hearer, to
> understand them needs to know the separate background story
> of each one. But hearers also need to know *how* the words refer
> to this background—directly, ironically, as history or as parable.

In addition to referring in more than one way, the *oríkì* chanted during the Yemoja festival can refer to more than one addressee, redefining their subjects as complex discursive objects. In the Àtá's oríkì chanted by his wives, qualities of kingship appear clear and direct. The king is "hot" like the frying pot, possessed by spirits which empower his person. Ajala is an oríkì name referring to one who fights, a characterization which refers historically to Ayede's founding warrior-king and which works parabolically to express indomitable rule. Lines 3 and 4 describe the king as a great drinker, while 5 and 6 praise his appetites for women of all shades. In line 7, the Àtá has a special wife, "the fat one who sells salt in the market"—referring to the goddess Yemoja and, more abstractly, to Olokun, goddess of the "deep," owner of beaded crowns, and locus of ritual power itself.

Already we see hyperbole, history, and parable at work. But the entire oratorical picture is elevated to new heights as a Yemoja priestess continues to chant, repeating much of the text but changing its referent:

> Omi-gbùú.
> Òjò-gbùú.
> Ọkọ-dúdú,
> Ọkọ-pupa,
> [5] Ọkọ-èyí-rò- gbọdò-tí-ń-tayò-lójà,
> Aláya-láà-kẹnkẹ . . .

> The-deep-splashing-water.
> The deep-splashing-rain.
> Husband-of-the-dark-ones,
> Husband-of-the-light-ones,
> [5] Husband-of-the-fat-one-who-sells-salt-in-the-market,
> One-who-has-wives-with-many-white-clothes . . .

In this oríkì, sung by a priestess, it is not the "hot" male power of the king but the "cool" female power of Yemoja which is invoked in the first two lines. Like the king, she is "husband" of the light and dark ones, not in the literal or jural sense, but ritually, since all priestesses are "wives" of their òrìṣà and wear their hair in the irun àgògo style of brides. In ritual, Yemoja is also "husband" to Olokun, with whom she reposes in the deep. And like the king, whose wives are assembled in the white cloth of ritual purity, the "wives" of Yemoja assemble in white to invoke her powers with flattering praise. The text continues with deep mythic allusions. Her concatenated names include:

> Alélódò-bí-òsùmàrè
> She-who-rises-in-the-river-like-a-rainbow

Aládàá-òyìnbó
She-who-has-the-European-cutlass

Agbọmọ-obìrìn-wẹ̀lẹ̀wẹ̀lẹ̀
The-active-midwife-of-children

Adífá-gbadé
One-who-performs-divination-and-receives-a-crown

Aríkú-sọ̀rọ̀-láàjìn
One-who-talks-about-death-at-night

Olówó-orí-àwa
Owner-of-our-bridewealth (lit. "money of our heads")

Omi, Èjì-àrán
Water, [owner of] Two-velvets

Omi, Aríbú-ṣọlá
Water, One-who-makes-the-deep-a-place-of-honor

Ògbóná-bí-i-ṣẹ́kẹ́ṣẹkẹ̀
One-who-is-hot-like-the-chain

Ayẹ̀rañ-wò-bí-Olódùmarè
One-who-looks-into-the-future-like-Olodumare [God]

Abiyamọ-afìdí-ṣojú-ọ̀nà
One-whose-vagina-is-the-road-of-passage

Abiyamọ-abìrìn-wẹ́lẹ́wẹ́lẹ́
Nursing-mother-of-gentle-strides

Each cryptic gloss has many meanings, secrets, and even addressees. But the basic strategy highlighted here is how the same textual units and blocks, sung by different groups of women and addressing different figures, fuse the identities of gods and kings into
powerful discursive subjects and objects. When the wives of the king
and the "wives" of the cult praise their respective "husbands" with the
same *oríkì* names, the very essences of the *Àtá* and the goddess Yemoja
converge.

While the king's wives praise their husband as a goddess and the
cult's priestesses praise their goddess as a husband, a third voice enters
the epideictic arena to recast the *difference* between deity and king.
Priestesses of the *Balógun Ààfin*'s Orisha Iyagba cult join the procession

when it arrives at the palace, greeting their "mother" and "father" separately:

> Yèyé tèmi mọ̀ yà o!
> Mọ́ mọ̀ jẹ́ n ṣàṣì-ṣe!
> Iyemọja má yà ooo!
> Mọ́ mọ̀ jẹ́ n ṣàṣì-ṣe.
> [5]   Òrìṣà ìyá o,
> Mọ́ mọ̀ jẹ́ n ṣàṣì-ṣe.
> Inú mí mọ̀ dùn,
> Mo ní Yèyé ń'lé ooo.
>   Inú mí mọ̀ dùn,
> [10]   Mo ní Yèyé ń'lé ooo.

> My own Mother, do stop over!
> Let me not do it the wrong way!
> Yemoja, please stop over!
> Let me not do it the wrong way.
> [5]   Orisha, the Mother,
> Let me not do it the wrong way.
> I am so happy,
> I have the Mother at home.
>   I am so happy,
> [10]   I have the Mother at home.

The priestesses of the Orisha Iyagba cult are "happy" to find their "mother" Yemoja at home, to find she has arrived safely at the palace after her dangerous journey through the town. They are similarly "happy" to find their "Father" at home, seated on his throne at the palace:

> Inú mi dùn,
> Mo rí bàbá ń'lé o.
>   Inú mí dùn,
>   Mo rí bàbá ń'lé o.

> I am so happy,
> I found the Father at home.
>   I am so happy,
>   I found the Father at home.

After greeting them thus separately, the priestesses bring their greetings together, preserving the *difference* of their addressees:

Inú wa dùn,
A rí Yèyé ń'lé.
Inú wa dùn,
A rí bàbá ń'lé.

We are so happy,
We found the Mother at home.
We are so happy,
We found the Father at home.

After this chant, the drum rhythm changes to signal a new text. Deep "play" centers on the duality of subjects and objects:

Eré d'èjì,
Eré d'èjì,
   Eré d'èjì.
Eré ọlá o,
   Eré d'èjì.
Eré owó o,
   Eré d'èjì.

Fortune becomes two,
Fortune becomes two,
   Fortune becomes two.
Fortune of wealth,
   Fortune becomes two.
Fortune of money,
   Fortune becomes two.

On the surface of this text, double fortune refers to the positive attributes of Yemoja and the *Àtá* of Ayede, who "become two" after being praised as one. But the double subjects of the praise—the goddess and the king—cover the less obvious "doubling" of *eré* (good luck, fortune): it can also mean "play," as in festival play or ritual performance. In this deeper sense, then, "fortune" becomes two when the festival itself is shared by two cults. The arrival of Yemoja at the palace, heralded by the arrival of Orisha Iyagba, divides both "fortune" and "festival" into two and proceeds to break sovereignty itself into two parts. Facing the king, priestesses of Orisha Iyagba sing:

> A mọ̀ mójú bọba wa,
>> Orubú lóyè.
> A mọ̀ mójú bọba wa,
>> Orubú lóyèeee.
> Orí-adé o e.
>> Orubú lóyè.
> Orí-adé o e.
>> Orubú lóyè.

We meet our king face to face,
> He that gorgeously sits on the throne.
We meet our king face to face,
> He that gorgeously sits on the throne.
The-head-that-wears-the-crown.
> He that gorgeously sits on the throne.
The-head-that-wears-the-crown.
> He that gorgeously sits on the throne.

Sung in the cult's Iyagba dialect to register northeast provenience, ritual possession, and significant contrast to Yemoja's Ibadan dialect, the song distinguishes the king's powerful person, which the cult addresses "face to face," from formal office—where he sits enthroned and crowned. The song is implicitly confrontational, since the singers represent Ayede's Yagba "strangers" within the capital and throughout the kingdom. An ironic voice lurks beneath the text's surface, indicating an unstated preference for a rival, Yagba king. This irony advances with the text, undermining its face-value message of support and protection as the strangers of Ayede pray for their king. The Yagba priestesses continue:

> Orí á gbé á lékè,
> Orí á gbé á lékè,
> Orí á gbé á lékè aṣebi,
> Aṣeni-bá-'ni-dá'rò.
> [5] Orí á gbé ọ lékè,
> Orí á gbé ọ lékè,
> Orí á gbé ọ lékè aṣebi,

Aṣeni-bá-'ni-dá'rò.
Oyè mi.
[10] *Oyè mi.*

We will outlive,
We will outlive,
We will outlive the evildoer,
One-who-pretends-to-be-friendly-but-doing-one-evil.
[5] You will outlive,
You will outlive,
You will outlive the evildoer,
One-who-pretends-to-be-friendly-but-doing-one-evil.
My king.
[10] My king.

But subversive implications abound. Pronominal ambiguity of the collective "we" may or may not include the king. The town may outlive evildoers, or more exclusively, Ayede strangers and followers of Orisha Iyagba may be the ones to outlive their evildoers. The evildoer's epithet (lines 4 and 8) may double as a name for the king, implicating the Àtá as a ruler who pretends to help Ayede's strangers but actually does evil by excluding them from the crown. The ambiguous connection between lines 8 and 9 reinforces the association between evildoer and king, sustaining both possibilities—continuity or contrast.

A literal reading of what is idiomatically protective suggests further evil intentions. Lines 1–4 signify outliving or surviving one's enemies, but translate literally as "the head will carry us to the top," implying that the collective destiny (*orí*) of the Yagba strangers is to achieve the kingship for themselves. Although the Àtá is similarly addressed (lines 5–8), the former signification is never fully erased; it reemerges with the ambiguity of "*Oyè mi*" (lines 9 and 10), which officially refers to the king but literally means "my title," "my chieftaincy," or "my official position," thus invoking the strangers' *Balógun* as possible addressee and rival king. As if responding to this forbidden claim, the wives of the king praise the Àtá's privileged status:

Àrìrà ò ṣe é f'ara,
  Àrìrà ò ṣe é f'ara wé.
Àrìrà ò ṣe é f'ara,
  Àrìrà ò ṣe é f'ara wé.

[5]   *Ọba wa Ewégbèmí o.*
      Àrìrà o!
      Orí mi ò gbé e,
         Àyà mi ò gbé e.
      Ọrọ̀ àrìrà ṣoro ó dá.
[10]   *Orí mi ò gbé e.*
      Ọrò Àwòyó ṣoro ó dá,
         Orí mi ò gbé e.

      Lightning cannot be,
         Lightning cannot be imitated.
      Lightning cannot be,
         Lightning cannot be imitated.
[5]   Our king, Ewegbemi o [he-who-finds-favor-with-herbs].
         Lightning!
      My head cannot carry it,
         My chest cannot carry it.
      It is a big deal to get into trouble with lightning.
[10]   My head cannot carry it.
      It is a big deal to get into trouble with Awoyo,
         My head cannot carry it.

Lightning is the quintessential power of kings; personified by Shango, it strikes, kills, burns, explodes. Since lightning *is* the king, it cannot be imitated by the Orisha Iyagba cult and their *Balógun*. In line 5, the *Àtá*'s wives praise their king with Shango's *oríkì* (Ewegbemi); in line 6, he becomes lightning. If the priestesses of Orisha Iyagba insinuated that their head would carry them to the top, the king's wives remind them that their "head cannot carry it" (lines 7, 10, 12), where "it" signifies the weight of kingship both as Yemoja's calabash and as the king's beaded crown. Lines 9 and 11 drive the message home: if Yagba strangers aspire toward the kingship, they will find themselves in serious trouble with the god of the king (Shango) and the goddess of his crown (Yemoja).

This exchange reveals how different oratorical voices perform different rhetorical functions. Whereas the Iyagba priestesses "deconstruct" the king, Yemoja priestesses and royal wives put him back together again, praising him as a composite of "hot" and "cool" powers. As Yemoja's calabash reaches the *Àtá*, at the very moment of

actual contact, the cult priestesses sing a powerful praise which reconstitutes both king and *òrìṣà* in a compact, fused, discursive object:

> *Olówó orí mi ooo!*
> *Ọọfẹ òòòò!*
> *Ọọfẹẹẹẹẹ!*
> *Ooolúayéééé!*
> [5] *Iiikúúú!*
> *Ó-jí-ooo!*
> *Ẹẹkùn ọbà'rìsà!*
> *A-tọ́ba-tẹ́lẹ̀*
> *A-lọmọ-loye!*
> [10] *Aré'ó-ròpó-òyìnbó!*
> *Ọ̀sà-kí-ń-lù-bókun-jó!*
> *Onikejìó-jénìkejì-sinmi!*
> *Agburujugbu-eju-'gbọ̀n-ọ́n!*
> *Àrìmọ̀-mọ̀-gbọ́n-a-gbọ́n-ọn-lórí-ara-rẹ̀!*

> One who owns the "dowry" of my head!
> Rise without mishap [falling]!
> Rise without mishap [falling]!
> Owner of the world [cosmos]!
> [5] Death!
> One-who-electrifies!
> Leopard, One-who-comes-into-contact-with-the-gods!
> One-who-equaled-kingship-before [becoming-a-king]!
> One-who-owns-children-as-much-as-official-titles!
> [10] One-who-has-money-to-buy-the-European-staff!
> The-lagoon-that-beats-the-drum-for-the-sea-to-dance!
> The-one-that-gives-the-other-comfort!
> The-violent-one-in-the-outside!
> The-flash-of-light-that-flashes-over-his-own-head!

The text verbalizes the passage of powers from Yemoja's calabash
to the king. Each praise name applies equally to the *Àtá* and the *òrìṣà* as
the two transcend their differences. Both own the "destinies" of their
"wives," both must rise without falling, both embody the cosmos, both
can kill and electrify (*jí*).[4] Line 7 presents a masterpiece of *àṣẹ*, a linguistic fusion of king and deity which is semantically, syntactically, and

morphologically coordinated. The leopard represents the king's powerful person, one whose contact with the gods involves physical contact with Yemoja's calabash. This is suggested by the syntactic sequence of the name itself: *o* (agent) + *ba* (to come into contact with) + *òrìṣà* (gods), which morphologically re-parses as *ọba* (king) + *òrìṣà* (god or gods). Even their lexical identities contract! The king receives Yemoja's *oríkì* because he embodies her fundamental essences and refracted manifestations: titles, children, wealth, the complementary powers of calm lagoon and stormy sea, the cool water of the deep and the violent flash of the "spirit." As the king is revitalized by the priestesses' calabash, he assimilates their powers and objectifies their speech.

THE GRAMMAR OF POSSESSION

After the king receives Yemoja's calabash, the priestesses proceed to their town shrine *(ipara Yemoja)*, where they "put their water down." This event marks the final passage of ritual power from bush to town. As the priestesses enter the shrine, bending down to clear the doorway, their "calabashes" of "water" brush against raffia palm which hangs from the lintel, representing the final threshold and last potential barrier to "safe delivery." The passage echoes a myth of deposition, in which a king entered Orunmila's house without permission and knocked off his crown as he passed through the door. The *Àtá* of Ayede must remain at the palace, for he is temporarily displaced by a more powerful "king." When the priestesses reemerge into the public courtyard in front of their shrine, drums "count" the rhythms of their associated *òrìṣà* while hunters fire their guns. The atmosphere is more jovial and relaxed, since the critical passage of power is over; but a final "visitation" and "annunciation" soon take place. After the *Yèyéolókun* priestess comes out and dances to her subdued rhythm, the Shango priestess mounts her pedestal—an inverted mortar *(odò)* set with cowries in cement—to deliver Shango's "prediction" for the town.

The "prediction" does not really predict, but prescribes collective sacrifice on behalf of the town inclusively. Shango foresees imminent dangers and calls for immediate sacrifices to reestablish security and peace. The text is deceptively simple; its "basic" message is dialogically structured by possession, prayer, and specific prescriptions involving a multiplicity of discursive identities. As the *Ìyá Ṣàngó* priestess "mounts" *(gùn)* her mortar, she is in turn "possessed" *(gùn)* by Shango and thereby receives the spiritual power of kingship. Her first words redefine her status as a passive agent in ritual affairs; her ritual power

(*àṣẹ*) does not belong to her, but passes through her on behalf of those
who possess her:

> *Wọ́n rán mi wá,*
> *N ò rán'ra mi,*
> *Àṣẹ d'ọwọ́ ẹni tó rán mi wá.*
> > *Wọ́n rán mi wá,*
[5] > *N ò rán'ra mi,*
> > *Àṣẹ d'ọwọ́ ẹni tó rán mi wá.*

> I was only sent here,
> I did not send myself,
> Power belongs to those who sent me.
> > I was only sent here,
[5] > I did not send myself,
> > Power belongs to those who sent me.

The three-line text is repeated by surrounding priestesses, devotees, and spectators, who amplify the message and collectivize its
theme, so that the entire crowd—as singular voice and personal
pronoun—becomes "possessed" by *àṣẹ*. The priestess continues:

> *Ẹ ṣe é,*
> *Mo rú'bà,*
> *Mo rú'bà o.*
[10] > *Ìyá mi òṣòròǹgà,*
> *Mo rú'bà o.*
> *Ẹrugàgà,*
> *Mọ́ mò jà o.*
> *Ẹrugàgà,*
[15] *Mọ́ mò jà.*
> > *Ẹrugàgà,*
> > *Mọ́ mò jà o.*
> > *Ẹrugàgà,*
> > *Mọ́ mò jà o.*

> Thank you,
> I do pay homage,
> I do pay homage.

[10]   My mother *òṣòròǹgà* [witches],
         I do pay homage [to you].
         You of the highest order,
         Please do not fight [with me].
         You of the highest order,
         Please do not fight [with me].
[15]   You of the highest order,
         Please do not fight [with me].
         You of the highest order,
         Please do not fight [with me].

Pronominal shifting reframes the communicative context. The thanks of line 7 may refer to "those" who sent the priestess, to the chorus of priestesses, or to both. Similarly, the Shango priestess pays homage, but to whom? Presumably to Shango, but the chorus redirects its homage to personify the witches. Whereas the Shango priestess begs Shango not to fight with her (lines 12–15), the chorus reiterates her text in what may be read as a parallel appeal to the witches. The ambiguity is apposite, since the referent of "the highest order" is characteristically contested in ritual discourse, and in either case the text refers obliquely to the king—that he not "fight" with his people by opposing his chiefs. As the Shango priestess shouts a forceful greeting, the chorus responds with the appropriate address for a king:

[20]   *Ẹ kúúú ooooooo!*
             Kábíyèsí!
         Ẹ kú ooooooo!
             Kábíyèsí!
         Ẹ kú ooooooo!
[25]   *Kábíyèsí!*
         Olo'ó wa ẹ kú oooo!
             Kábíyèsí!
         olo'ó wa ẹ kú oooo!
             Kábíyèsí!

[20]   Greetings [to you]!
             Your Highness!
         Greetings [to you]!
             Your Highness!
         Greetings [to you]!

[25]   Your Highness!
   Our Lord, greetings!
    Your Highness!
   Our Lord, greetings!
    Your Highness!

A man suddenly shouted one of Shango's "deep" *oríkì:*

[30] *A-gbe-baálé-g'orí-ọdán!*

[30] One-who-scared-the-family-head-to-hide-on-top-of-
   the-*ọdán*-tree!

Whatever its specific mythical allusion, the *oríkì* describes an outrageous figure whose domineering will frightened the official family head into hiding high up in a tree. The figure is of course Shango, who, invoked by his praise, possesses the Shango priestess in a shift of dialects and pronouns:

  O Ṣeun.
  Ṣé mo bá yín pẹ̀lú ìrọ̀rùn?
   Àlàáfíà n'aṅ wà!
  Ṣé mo bá yín pẹ̀lú ìrọ̀rùn?
[35] *Àlàáfíà n'aṅ wà!*
   Kábíyèsí!
   Kábíyèsí baba!
   Kábíyèsí 'lẹ̀!

  Thank you.
  Do I meet you in perfect peace?
   It is well with us!
  Do I meet you in perfect peace?
   It is well with us!
   Your Highness!
   Your Highness, our Father!
   Highness, Owner of the land!

The "Thank you" of line 31 contrasts significantly with that of line 7, in that the former represents Ibadan and Oyo dialect while the latter is dialectally unmarked. The addresser is now Shango, speaking through his priestess—the "I" refers to the deity himself. But still, Shango must be prodded with speech; the same devotee who chanted Shango's *oríkì* (line 30) now chants a metapragmatic incantation:

Mọ́-ọn-wí-mọ́-ọn-wí ní í ṣohùn ẹnu rẹ,
[40] Mọ́-ọn-rò-mọ́-ọn-rò ní í ṣorógùn ọkà.

Say-on-say-on acts the utterance of your voice,
Stir-on-stir-on acts the stirring stick of *ọkà* pudding.

As a type of praise name, the incantation nominalizes Shango's speech as subject and activates it as verb to mobilize its power *(àṣẹ)*, broadening its range by analogy to the stirring of *ọkà (àmàlà)*, one of Shango's favorite foods (yam flour). The "stirring" of *ọkà* is also potentially dangerous, since reducing *ọkà*'s first-syllable mid tone to a low tone yields the "stirrings of death" *(òkà ikú)*. Shango's replay plays on the morphology of the *orógùn* (stirring stick), incorporated within an injunction against calamitous fighting (lines 41 and 43) as he prays for Ayede's welfare:

Gbogbo yín ẹ̀ mọ̀ ní r'ógun-ùn!
Àṣẹẹẹẹ!
Pínrínpínrínpínrín, mọ̀ ní í rógun-ùn!
Àṣẹẹẹẹ!
[45] Níníníní, ìbànújẹ́ ò ní wò'lú yín!
Àṣẹẹẹẹ!
Kè ní sákì!
Ṣíṣẹ-ṣíṣẹnitìlákọ̀ṣẹ!
Ìdágìrì ò ní wọlú yín,
[50] Àṣẹẹẹẹ!
Gbogbo obìrin ìlú,
Gbogbo ọkùnrin ìlú,
Gbogbo obìrin ìlú,
Onílé òun àlejò,
[55] Kí òde yín kó dẹ̀rò!
Àṣẹẹẹẹ!
Eè ní rú'bi iniraà.
Àṣẹẹẹẹ!
Ẹni Èṣù ń ṣe kò mọ̀ ní sá yáa yín.
[60] Àṣẹ!

> May you [all] not experience calamitous fighting!
>> Let it be!
> [Sound of fighting], may you not experience calamities at
> all!
>> Let it be!
[45] [Sound of sadness], may sadness not enter your town!
>> Let it be!
>> It shall be so [may it not misfire]!
>> Irrevocability is the nature of *Ìkákòṣẹ!*
> May tremor [pandemonium] not enter your town!
[50] Let it be!
> All women of the town,
> All men of the town,
> All women of the town,
> Citizens [indigenes] and strangers,
[55] May all your outings [outside] be in peace!
>> Let it be!
> May you not experience the misfortune of pain.
>> Let it be!
> May one disillusioned by Eshu not pursue you.
[60] Let it be!

Shango's prayers are transparent and direct. Aside from pho-naesthetic reduplication (lines 43 and 45), there is nothing to distinguish them from typical prayer. The town is protected against fighting and sadness, chaos and enmity, while its principal social categories—men and women, indigenes and strangers—are unified by collective sacrifice. Shango "speaks" in a clear Oyo dialect. The public responds the way one does to any prayer, by invoking the very power *(Àṣẹ)* which makes it efficacious—hence "let it be," or "it will come to pass." Line 48 is a "deep" response, particularly rich in *àṣẹ* since the reduplication of "coming to pass"—the morpheme *ṣẹ* in *ṣíṣẹ-ṣíṣẹ*—is objectified by the small *ìlákòṣẹ* snail, which is itself associated with the realization of wishes (Abraham 1962:302). Prayer is transparent because it upholds official hierarchy and promotes prosperity and peace. The only difference with Shango's prayer is in the speech act itself. Most ritual prayers to an *òrìṣà* are uttered by a priest or priestess on behalf of a client. Here the speech situation is reversed; the Shango priestess remains a mediator, but it is the *òrìṣà* Shango who prays for the public.

The town must perform sacrifices to ensure the efficacy of Shango's speech. In the third part of the text, following the possession and prayers, the Shango priestess becomes "herself" again to narrate the prescriptions. By doing what Shango says they must do, the public ensures that his words come to pass. The very performance of public sacrifice translates his directives into immediate actions, uniting the town as one body. As the priestess shifts from "I" to "he," the dialect returns to that of Ayede:

> *Ó ní kí ẹ dákun,*
>
> *Kí ẹ wá elékúté,*
>
> *Kí ẹ máa sọ òrí sí i.*
>
> *Ó ní kí gbogbo yín mị mọ ti ẹnìkan sọ̀tọ̀.*
>
> [65] *Kí ẹ mọ́ ọn dá a jọ síbi kan.*
>
> *Kí ẹ wá ìgbín,*
>
> > *Ìgbìn-ín?*
>
> *Ó ní gbogbo yín pátápátá nínú ìlú àtàlejò, atonílé,*
>
> *Kí ẹnikankan mọ́ mọ̀ sọ pé kò kàn 'un-ùn!*
>
> [70] *Kábíyèsí!*
>
> *Kí ẹ mọ́ sì jáfíra!*
>
> > *Kábíyèsí!*
>
> *Kí ẹ mọ́ sì jáfíra!*
>
> > *Kábíyèsí!*
>
> [75] *Yín yín yín yín, ń'gbà ẹ bá ti ṣe é,*
>
> *Yín ẹ wá gìrìpá òbúko,*
>
> *Níbí Èṣù bá wà kí an mọ́-ọn fi bọ́ ọ́.*
>
> *Íí "atúgun,"*
>
> *Íí kéẹ bá ti fẹ́ fi bọ́ k'án í "atúgun,"*
>
> [80] *Íí gbogbo yán 'an'ún yígbà-yígbà-yígbà kò ní dé'lùú yín.*
>
> > *Àṣẹẹẹẹ!*
>
> > *Kábíyèsí!*
>
> *Í ẹ mọ́ an ṣégun,*
>
> *Í kéẹ mọ́ jáfíra.*
>
> [85] *Kábíyèsí!*
>
> *Í ẹ mọ̀ mọ̀ fi ṣié o.*
>
> > *Aà! A á ṣe é ni o!*
>
> *Í ẹ dákun, ẹ mọ́mọ̀ p'ó pọ̀ ń'lẹ̀ẹ̀.*
>
> *Í èyí ǹ bá ti ń sọ ìí,*

[90] *Kí ẹ mọ́ ọn ṣé kíákíákíá!*
        Kábíyèsí!
            Ọ̀runkúfùú!
    Í "nígbà tí mo wọ̀ ní Alátàá,"
    Íí "Ǹjẹ́ mi ò sọ pé mo mú'yọ̀ wá fún yín?"
[95]   *Kábíyèsí!*
    Íí bí añ lọ́ ọ mọ́ ín lọ́wọ́,
    Lọ́ọ o mọ́ ín lọ́wọ́ ẹ́ẹ́ pínyọ̀ọ yín!
        Kábíyèsí,
            Àṣẹẹẹẹ!
[100] *Íí ẹ́ẹ́ pín'yọ̀ yín.*
        Àṣẹ!
    Í iyọ̀ léé ṣe ti yín.
        Àṣẹ!
    Í kẹ́e dákun, íí kẹ́ ẹ dákun . . .
[105] *Kí ni mo sọ?*
        Àgbọ́yé!
            Àgbọ́yè!
    Íí onílé, í àlejò, í ọkùnrin, í obìrin,
    Ẹ mọ́ sọ pé kò kàn yín.
[110] *Í kí ẹ múra, kí ẹ ṣe é.*
    Í kí ẹ ṣe é kíákíákíá.
    Ó ní kí ẹ bá ṣé é kíákíá,
    Kí gbogbo yín sọ pé t'Ayédé sàn.
        T'Ayédé sàn oooo!
[115]   *Kábíyèsí!*
    Ó ní e ò ni rógun àdájà.
        Àṣẹ!
    Í kí ẹ yárayárayára kíákíákíá!
    Í kí ẹ ṣe é o!
[120] *Ní ọmọdé ní agbàààà!*
    Ní ọkùnrin ní obìrin!
        Kábíyèsí!
    Ní kí ẹ mọ̀ ṣe éè!
    Ní kí ẹ mọ̀ ṣe éè!
[125] *Ní kí ẹ ó mọ̀ ṣe éè!*

Mo mò sọò!
Èyí tí mo rí,
Mo mò sọ óò!
   Kábíyèsí!
[130] *Í àmọ́ ìbànújẹ́ è ní wọ̀'gboro yín.*
   Àṣẹ!
Í àmọ́ ìbànújẹ́ è ní wọ̀'gboro yín.
   Àṣẹ!
Wọn ò ní t'ẹ̀jẹ̀ sílẹ ń'bẹ̀!
[135]   *Áàṣẹẹẹẹ!*
Ẹ dákun o, kí ẹ yára.

He said please,
You should look for *elékúté* [type of rat],
You should add shea butter to it.
He also said you should all work together, not individually.
[65] Pour everything in one place.
You should also find a snail,
   A snail?
He said all of you in the town, indigenes or strangers,
Nobody should be unconcerned!
[70]   Your Highness!
You should not tarry!
   Your Highness!
You should not tarry!
   Your Highness!
[75] He said, he said, he said, he said, after doing that,
He said you should look for a huge he-goat,
Wherever Eshu resposes [i.e., at the crossroads], offer it to
   him.
He said "He-who-shatters-the-battle,"
He said as you sacrifice say "He-who-shatters-the-battle,"
[80] He said [if you do this] all present violence will not enter
   the town.
   Let it be!
   Your Highness! [thank you]

He said you shall be victorious,
He said you should not tarry.
[85]   Your Highness! [we shall not]
He said you must not toy with it [the prescription].
      No way! It must be done!
He said please don't consider it too much to offer.
He said that as soon as I say it,
[90] You should get it done instantaneously!
      Your Highness!
      Heavenly storm!
He said, "When I descended at the palace of the *Àtá*,"
He said, "Did I not tell you that I brought you salt?"
[95]   Your Highness! [yes]
He said no matter the struggle against you,
You shall surely share your salt!
      Kábíyèsí! [thank you]
      May it be so!
[100] He said you shall surely share your salt.
      So let it be!
He said your portion shall be salty.
      So let it be!
He said you please, he said you should please . . .
[105] What did I say?
      Listening to understand!
      Listening to survive!
He said be you an indigene, stranger, man or woman,
You dare not feel unconcerned.
[110] He said you should get up and do it.
He said you should do it immediately.
He said if you all do it immediately,
You should say [know that] it is well with the town of
    Ayede.
      It is well with the town of Ayede!
[115]   Kábíyèsí! [long may you live]
He said may you not experience a civil war.
      So let it be!

He said you should act immediately with alacrity!

He said you should do it!

[120] Both children and elders!

Both men and women!

Your Highness! [accepted]

He said you should do it!

He said you should do it!

[125] He said you will do it!

I have spoken!

This which I have seen,

I have spoken [reported].

Your Highness! [thank you]

[130] He said [if you do it correctly] the wave of sadness will not enter your town.

So let it be!

The wave of sadness will not enter your town.

So let it be!

There shall be no bloodshed there!

[135]   So let it be!

Please do act immediately.

I have reproduced the text at length because it establishes a complex discourse of ritual closure. On the surface, it appears almost ordinary, lacking the layered images and ambiguities of deeper invocations and incantations. Shango's message is really quite clear. A sacrifice of rat, shea butter, and snail must be collectively offered "in one place" (one of the market shrines) without delay, followed by a large he-goat, which must be presented at the town's different crossroads. As Eshu—trickster of the crossroads—is appeased, the officiants must utter "Atúgun," signifying one who unties or undoes the battle. The sacrifice concludes a "chain" of verbal command which originates with Shango, who broadcasts through his priestess, and continues with the people of Ayede, who carry his words into further actions and utterances to satisfy deities and determine the future. The utterance of "Atúgun" is powerful because it possesses the accumulated àṣẹ of Shango's speech, which is quoted and reported by the priestess; registered and repeated (e.g., lines 113–114) by the public; and ultimately repossessed by the deities themselves when they "eat" their sacrifices. Immediate and collective response to Shango's demands ensures cooperation, unity, and spiritual protection against impending violence, civil war, and the wave of sadness in the town.

Syntactic repetition and lexical reduplication stress the urgency of Shango's message and function rhetorically to *reduce* ambiguity. Indeed, conditions in the town in 1983 required urgent solutions—for the gubernatorial elections that year in Ondo State (which we shall examine more fully in chapter 9) fomented "civil war" in Ayede and many other communities. Thus "victorious" (line 83) and "struggle" (line 96) refer quite immediately to the UPN's fight against NPN electoral rigging; the "violence" (line 80) and "sadness" (line 130) which must not enter the town are not the work of unknown powers, but refer more concretely to the mobile police and the Nigerian army. These references are not explicitly verbalized, but constitute the context and subtext of particular events which Shango's discourse seeks to stabilize and control. The contingencies of power competitions are regulated by ritual and linguistic necessity. Times may change, but each year Shango possesses his priestess to prescribe collective sacrifices which redress the imbalance of powers.

In this broader ritual context, the grammar of possession indicates cosmological repossession. When Shango descends, he displaces the Àtá of Ayede, who is temporarily "exiled" in the palace—which (as Alátàá in line 93) morphologically "owns" or "possesses" him. Not only pronouns and dialects, but even sovereignty shifts to register "possession" of the people by the deified Oyo king. Shango's directives are beyond dispute. His subjects can only respond by affirming. Response is in fact limited to repetition (lines 67 and 114), ritual assent ("Àṣẹ"), passive obedience (lines 106–7), and royal address ("Kábíyèsí!"). Thereafter the public must respond with a sacrifice at the crossroads, a standard means of appeasing Eshu but also an echo of the dismemberment and burial of a dead king. When a king dies, specific body parts are buried at the crossroads and corners of the town.[5] The sacrifice of the he-goat—in Girard's (1977) terms, the objectification and displacement of collective violence by a scapegoat—indeed "shatters" or "undoes" violence in the town. By sacrificing the "old" king—dismantling his surrogate into political pieces, which are buried at the very crossings of chiefly jurisdictions—the whole body politic transcends the violence of its parts to repossess Shango, the original king who did not die.

●●

The interpretation of Yoruba texts reveals a remarkable array of critical concepts and strategies which reflect on the power of language itself.

Ritual discourse possesses àṣẹ—the capacity to invoke powers, appropriate essences, and determine events through complex significations. In incantations, deep "forbidden" meanings depart from "official" surface readings to subvert the dominant political and linguistic structures of authority and to achieve effective results. In oríkì, nominalizing claims and counterclaims deconstruct and reconstruct the king's identities and attributes to empower his person and reproduce his exalted status. Possessed speech speaks in shifting dialects and registers to dispossess the dying king and repossess his undying powers. But the language of àṣẹ, like ritual power generally, is ultimately predicated on secrecy and silence. Hidden powers can be linguistically unlocked but never openly articulated, for reasons which the public must uncritically accept. It is only the most forbidden and dangerous discourses which self-consciously reduce the king's authority to contested identities, to hidden substitutions, and to the empty plenitude of ritual vessels and reduplicated syllables.

There is, of course, a danger of going too far. It is one thing to "deconstruct" the language of àṣẹ in a privileged exercise of demystification (or as some no doubt feel, remystification) and quite another to argue—as I have ventured to do in this chapter—that Yoruba ritual discourse *is* a deconstructive practice. Anthropologists are experts at reading passing trends into "exotic" cultures—cybernetics, computer programs, and three-valued logics have been found among !Kung "bushmen," Australian aborigines, and Evans-Pritchard's Azande. Do we now find deconstruction among the Yoruba? Clearly one can only consider such a question with humor and irony and with respect for the other. The high priests and priestesses of Eurocentric critical theory and those of Yoruba òrìṣà worship speak very different natural and specialized languages. They come from different intellectual traditions, educational systems, and positions of access to global economies and resources. To erase *these* differences would be anthropologically obscene. Relating Yoruba ritual language to the restricted conditions of its production and interpretation, however, does reveal an indigenous hermeneutics which "deconstructs" to empower but which also (unlike so much of our own critical theory) recovers, engages, and—when necessary—changes the world.

6

Interpreting the Pantheon

rom a logical point of view, cosmology is prior to social action as the condition of its possibility. It is for MacGaffey (1986:3) a prerequisite to social life in that "all communities implicitly accept a cosmology, a certain concept of the universe and the place of man within it" which provides "the ultimate conditions of action." The key phrase here is "implicitly accept," for a cosmology is rarely recognized by its adherents; rather, it is routinely embodied as "common sense." As such, it is like the grammar of a language—presupposed by its speakers but explicated by few. If Yoruba cosmology is unconsciously internalized, however, it is also self-consciously restricted, safeguarding an interpretive space for political maneuvering. The more fundamental the categories of agency and power, the "deeper" the secrets of their esoteric signs. For this reason, Yoruba cosmology cannot be elicited and documented according to formal "discovery procedures." It eludes the conventions of ordinary language and direct observation to establish the "transcendental" conditions—expressed as silences and gaps—of ritual experience and forbidden knowledge. The most basic questions about òrìṣà worship are therefore among the most difficult to answer. This chapter examines how the òrìṣà are conceptualized and how they are organized within indeterminate pantheons.

The characterizations which follow, still partial and hypothetical, attempt to synthesize different scholarly views. My own abstraction of cosmological "schema" relates the conceptual framework of ritual renewal to the dialectics of power in Yoruba kingdoms.

IDENTITIES AND DIFFERENCES

As a "spiritual being," an òrìṣà is notoriously difficult to define. Partly this is due to the pact of secrecy (ìmulè) with the earth which all initiates swear, proscribing them from openly divulging what they know and preventing non-initiates from finding out. The uninitiated public, in effect, *cannot* know very much about the òrìṣà; hence, definitions and explanations should be difficult to establish and confirm. Different definitions, furthermore, reveal contradictory attributes. In 1938, William Bascom (1944:21) deliberated with Yoruba priests and diviners for nine months to work out a cultural definition:

> An orisha is a person who lived on earth when it was created, and from whom present day folk are descended. When these orishas disappeared or 'turned to stone', their children began to sacrifice to them and to continue whatever ceremonies they themselves had performed when they were on earth. This worship was passed on from one generation to the next, and today an individual considers the orisha whom he worships to be an ancestor from whom he descended.

This definition isolates the "ancestor" component of the òrìṣà concept, but it must be heavily qualified. The Yoruba do not practice ancestor worship in the canonical ways of the Tallensi (Fortes 1945) or Lodagaa (Goody 1962). As Bascom notes, devotees of the same òrìṣà can marry one another, whereas descendants of a common ancestor cannot. And given Bascom's distinction between "single-sib" and "multi-sib" cults, it is clear that, unlike classic ancestor cults in Africa, òrìṣà cults employ nongenealogical as well as genealogical principles of recruitment.

More recently, Horton (1983:60–64) has drawn a sharp distinction between ancestors (àgbànlá) and òrìṣà, focusing his attention on the "double aspect" of the òrìṣà as "part nature spirit" and "part deified hero."[1] Observing that most òrìṣà are associated with natural landmarks—streams, rocks, groves—which represent "forces of nature," as well as with "great men or women of earlier times" who represent "forces of society," Horton (ibid., 63) devises a psychohistorical explanation by which nature spirits gradually merge with the memory of outstanding devotees:

> Now it seems likely that, as the memory of an association between an outstanding individual and an *orisa* passes into tradition, the distinction between the two will become blurred, and that the traits of the human partner will merge with those of the *orisa*. In this way, an *orisa* that started its career as a 'force of

nature', pure and simple, will come to acquire a strong overlay of deified human individuality.

The cultural-hero aspect of the *òrìṣà* is further illustrated by its mode of deification. Whereas ancestors die, *òrìṣà* "disappear" by turning into stone, vanishing, entering the earth, or ascending directly into the sky. They do not "die" as mortals do, but "depart" *(kúró)* from the beings on earth *(ará ayé)* to become beings of heaven *(ará òrun)*.

Between these two views, Barber (1981) holds something of a middle course. An *òrìṣà*, she maintains, is a person who is deified after "departing" from the earth and is worshipped by followers who may or may not be conceived as descendants. Neither ancestors (which are more typically represented by *egúngún* masquerades) nor nature spirits *(iwin)* (which refer more to ghosts, demons, and shades of the bush), the *òrìṣà* represent the spiritual equivalents of Big Men (and women) in Yoruba society. This would identify them, in Horton's scheme, exclusively with cultural heroes, and it explains how different *òrìṣà*, like Big Men, can rise and fall.

To be sure, the identity of an *òrìṣà* is more than the sum of its properties; it rests partly on the *òrìṣà*'s place and function in the grand scheme of things. As the myriad myths and traditions relate, the *òrìṣà* are variously conceived as "ministers" (Idowu 1962:57–106), "chiefs," even "refractions" (Beier 1980:xi) of a High God (Olodumare), who intercede on behalf of their devotees and suppliants. In creation myths, at least some *òrìṣà*, such as Obatala and Oduduwa, clearly predate the origin of humans, while others, such as Ogun and Shango, become *òrìṣà* after "departing" from human society. When I asked one senior *babaláwo* to explain this difference, he replied:

> All *òrìṣà* were human beings before, but as they were popular and strong, they became *òrìṣà* after departing from the beings on earth *(ará ayé)*. Before human beings were created there were *òrìṣà* but they had no names. Only after they come to earth and depart do they get names.

This statement supports Barber's conviction that the *òrìṣà* are modeled on Big Manship—"popular and strong" individuals become *òrìṣà*—but it adds an interesting theory of names. The *òrìṣà* already exist in heaven *(òrun)* as empty schemata or nameless forms, similar to the prenatal destinies *(orí,* "head") chosen by all individuals before their birth into the world (cf. Abiodun 1987:257). About this the *babaláwo* would say no more. The place of the *òrìṣà* is thus fixed in heaven; its content is determined by achievements on earth. The power of the *òrìṣà* relates at once to its abstract status as a form in heaven and to the empirical achievements of bigness and strength on earth.

Viewed as a schema with variable content, the identity of an òrìṣà possesses *all* of the properties mentioned above. Part ancestor, part Big Man or cultural hero, and part nature spirit as well, an òrìṣà constitutes what philosophers of language call a *cluster concept* (Putnam 1971:111). The meaning of a cluster concept is given by a cluster of attributes of which only some, not all, need to be shared by the members of its class.[2] From this perspective, Bascom, Horton, and Barber are correct in what they include but incorrect in what they exclude from their definitions. If one òrìṣà possesses more of the ancestral properties and less of the Big Man (cultural-hero) or nature-spirit properties, while another òrìṣà is characterized just the other way (as more of a Big Man or nature spirit and less of an ancestor), neither ceases to be an òrìṣà. Rather, each òrìṣà emphasizes different properties. The flexibility of the òrìṣà as a cluster concept is not arbitrary but systematic. The emphasis on different properties corresponds to different positions within the cult system and to different aspects of the ritual process.

The history and politics of ritual in Ayede revealed three basic types of òrìṣà cults based on the lineage, the quarter *(àdúgbò)*, and the town as a whole—that is, on the three basic levels of political segmentation. In minor lineage cults, members worship what is clearly defined as their common ancestor. Those who are not members of the lineage are excluded. Lineage cults do not possess a bush shrine, but perform their sacrifices in the *baálé*'s compound in a simple exchange of food, libation, and blood for mystical assistance. There is no harnessing of power from the bush, and no ritual calabash of *àṣẹ*. As cluster concepts, the òrìṣà of this cult type emphasize ancestral properties at the expense of Big Man or nature-spirit properties.

The òrìṣà of quarter cults transcend the limitations of ancestors proper because their devotees include members of different lineages. They also wield a different kind of power. Modelled more on Big Men with followers from different lineages, their power, like that attributed to Big Men and cultural heroes, comes from outside the social order. Whereas Big Men rise with special destinies (*orí*), assisted by medicines, witches, large households, and clients, the power of quarter-based òrìṣà themselves comes from the bush. The ritual technology of these cults includes vessels and icons which contain and transport ritual power from sacred groves and ponds to houses and shrines within the town. The "double aspect" of the òrìṣà which Horton identifies as part nature spirit (forces of nature) and part cultural hero (forces of society) corresponds here to the two fundamental values of ritual power:

the "hot," red, male, and violent power of the bush, associated with subversion, death, and deposition; and the "cool," white, placating power of women, associated with peace, fertility, and civic authority within the community. What Horton attributes to human memory— the association, over time, of an outstanding individual with a nature spirit until the two merge into a single entity—relates, in my interpretation, to power and authority in Yoruba government. Reduced to essentials, power is to the forces of nature (in the bush) as authority is to the forces of society (in the town). An *òrìṣà* combines both, not as a historical residue, but as an object of mediation which revitalizes the kingdom with power from the bush.

Royal cults are like quarter cults, but they focus on the king rather than on his chiefs. One might reason that the *òrìṣà* of royal cults are least like ancestors and most like cultural heroes, or Big Men, and nature spirits because they harness powers of the bush on behalf of the most inclusive political unit, the kingdom as a whole. This may be the case, but the ancestral component of a royal *òrìṣà* is never entirely eliminated. All *òrìṣà* cults, including royal cults, are *vested* in specific lineages or lineage clusters, in which succession to senior cult offices follows what Scheffler (1966) calls descent-phrased rules. The senior titles of Ayede's Yemoja cult, for example, are restricted to the Eshubiyi line. In other Oyo and Egbado towns, however, the Yemoja cult is vested in nonroyal lineages and therefore is not royal.

Thus far we have considered the *òrìṣà*'s variable attributes in relation to different cult types and ritual procedures. The *òrìṣà* as a cluster concept, however, articulates not only different levels of political segmentation, but the processes of segmentation, fission, and fusion as well. An *òrìṣà* cult can start out in a given community as mainly ancestral and develop into a royal cult. When Eshubiyi brought Orisha Ojuna to Ayede, for example, it was no more than a family cult which had been brought to Iye from Ikole by Eshubiyi's natural father. In Ayede, however, it rose with Eshubiyi to become a major royal institution. The spectacular rise of Orisha Ojuna is paralleled by the spectacular decline of Olua in Ayede. Before Ayede was founded, the *Olú* of Iye owned the royal cult of Olua, the largest and most powerful cult in the town. After Eshubiyi usurped the kingship from the *Olú* dynasty and suppressed the Iye civil chiefs, the cult of Olua dwindled to a lineage cult worshipped by Ilisa lineage in Owaiye quarter. The *àwòrò* of the Olua cult still retains a leopard skin and certain privileges vis-à-vis the *Àtá* which commemorate the cult's former status. But the cult has lost its bush shrine and calabash of power—these it now shares with the *Àtá*'s Orisha Ojuna cult, which affiliated Olua with its central town shrine (fig. 2.3). If the form or schema of an òrìṣà endures over time, its content changes, emphasizing different attributes according to the changing relative status and position of its cult.

PANTHEONS IN THEORY

As a cluster concept, the generic properties of an òrìṣà—as ancestor, Big Man (cultural hero), and nature spirit—define members of a poly-thetic class, treating each member as a discrete spiritual being. But in addition to generic properties, the òrìṣà possess specific attributes, elaborated in their oríkì (lit. *attributive* poetry), such as Yemoja's graceful neck and honey breasts or Shango's fiery eyes and thunder celts. These attributes define the identity of individual òrìṣà and distinguish them from each other. Distinctions between òrìṣà and, more abstractly, between the one and the many, however, are relative rather than abso-lute. The "identity-in-difference" of all òrìṣà is explained in myths about Orishanla, which, if we switch philosophical registers, amounts to a remarkable master-slave dialectic (Idowu 1962:59–60; Beier 1980:6–7). In these traditions, Orisha, as the primordial òrìṣà was called, owned a slave who decided to kill his master. The slave rolled a large boulder onto Orisha, who was crushed into hundreds of pieces which scattered all over the world. Orunmila tried to save Orisha by collecting the pieces in a calabash, which he deposited at Ife and named Orishanla, or "the Great Orisha." The scattered pieces which he failed to collect became the different òrìṣà found throughout Yorubaland.[3]

One of the claims which this myth supports is that "Orishanla is the most important and senior" of all òrìṣà (Beier 1980:7) in what schol-ars have described as a hierarchical pantheon of deities. But pantheon models seem to assume that discrete òrìṣà occupy fixed positions in an enduring heavenly theocracy.[4] Viewed as such, the Yoruba "pan-theon" appears contradictory and illogical. Relations between the òrìṣà are equivocal at best. The apical status of Orishanla is hotly contested by variant traditions which attribute to Oduduwa the role of para-mount òrìṣà, creator of the world, and progenitor of the Yoruba people. In some traditions, Orishanla, also called Obatala, is Oduduwa's junior brother. In others, Oduduwa is Obatala's wife (Daramola and Jeje 1967:42–49). Not only the identity but also the gender of the senior òrìṣà is open to debate. The same applies to imputed relations of con-sanguinity and affinity.

My point here is not to assemble variant traditions of the para-mount òrìṣà, which are legion, but to draw attention to the flexibility of the pantheon, if indeed one exists. As with the concept of the òrìṣà itself, I prefer to conceive of the Yoruba pantheon as a set of more abstract relations between schemata (similar to Bourdieu's [1977:96–158] concept of a generative scheme), the content of which varies—both within and between regions and kingdoms—but the matrix of which endures. The cosmological message of the Orisha myth is not that Orishanla, Obatala, or any other substitutable òrìṣà reigns over the others, but that all òrìṣà can be deposed and displaced, deconstructed and reconstructed, because they are all cut from the primordial calabash. Certain qualitative and quantitative consequences follow from this "identity-in-difference."

First, despite their diacritical differences—whether they are "hot" or "cool," male or female, Pan-Yoruba or purely parochial—all òrìṣà with organized cults assist and empower followers in exchange for their devotion. Second, if the òrìṣà are one, they are also infinitely many. The odù of Ifa speak of "one thousand seven hundred òrìṣà" (èrúnlọjọ òrìṣà) and "four hundred and one divinities" (ọkàn-lé-ńirínwó imọlè) (Idowu 1962:67) not as precise inventories but as figures of infinite differentiation. Each òrìṣà has many praises, names, and manifestations. Barber (1981:736) identifies the devotee's individualism as the social basis of these fluid designations:

> The Yoruba gods are at once fragmented and fused. They are fragmented because of the intense personal nature of the òrìṣà-devotee relationship, which makes each devotee desire her own version of the òrìṣà imprinted with her own personality and identity. They are fused because, underlying their differences of character and ambience, all the òrìṣà share the same qualities and do the same things for their devotees.

Barber's explanation can be extended to the polity. Her association of the òrìṣà with the dynamics of Big Manship captures the relations of mutual dependence which characterize òrìṣà worship, and it accounts for the devotee's freedom to leave one deity for another. But the relationship is primarily egocentric. "The core of the religion," she maintains, "lies not in the public framework but in the personal bond between each devotee and the spiritual being which she serves" (ibid., 730–31). A more inclusive explanation, however, relates private to public domains. The fragmentation and fusion of the òrìṣà—what McKenzie (1976:197–198) calls theistic particularity (*Götterspaltung*) and theistic reunification (*Göttervereinigung*)—relate not only to the individual's appropriation of spiritual beings, but to groups which break and merge, grow and decline, succeed and fail in their efforts to accumulate power. The apparent inconsistency of the Yoruba pantheon—the flexibility and indeterminacy of its centering and decentering deities—supports shifting political relations and expresses rival political claims.

Properly conceived, the Yoruba pantheon exists as a practical calculus of differential, substitutable, and integral relations which can be variously interpreted according to changing contexts and situations. Every kingdom adheres to the same schematism but applies it differently, positioning its own òrìṣà in relation to its dominant cults and corresponding bases of political power. Not only do different Yoruba kingdoms provide alternative pantheons based on the corporate configurations of their dominant cults; more importantly, pantheons vary *within* kingdoms as well. In Ayede, Yemoja and Orisha Ojuna are equally paramount because they belong to the Àtá and subsume subordinate òrìṣà within their cults (see chapter 2). Orisha Iyagba, according to palace testimonies, occupies a subordinate place because it is owned by a chief. But Orisha Iyagba cult members tell a different story. In the Yagba town of Alu, their cult is royal, and it predates the rise of Eshubiyi in Ayede. One of their subversive cult secrets is that Orisha Iyagba is really the senior cult in Ayede. The àwòrò of Olua similarly indicated the true paramountcy of his òrìṣà in the spiritual scheme of things, a cult secret which members of Yemoja and Orisha Ojuna are not privileged to know. Each òrìṣà cult organizes the pantheon around its own central deity. Such dissension does not undermine the pantheon model, but subjects its interpretation—the placing of different òrìṣà in relative positions—to the critical claims and counterclaims of cosmological renewal.

PANTHEONS IN PRACTICE

Again we can see how the "functional" regulation of power by authority is equally a question of interpretation. Here we can focus on the nonroyal cult of Orisha Iyagba, which ritually objectifies the aspiring king in every civil chief. If, from the official point of view, Orisha Iyagba joins the Yemoja festival in the spirit of friendship and cooperation, from the more critical perspective of Ayede's Yagba strangers and subordinate towns, their participation resembles more an attack.

On the same day that the Yemoja cult carries its water, a procession of Orisha Iyagba priestesses enters the ritual arena, singing rival songs and praises to different tunes and drums. As both cults converge in the marketplace, a violent confrontation mimetically occurs between the head of the Orisha Iyagba "warriors" and the Yemoja priestesses with their sacred calabash. The Orisha Iyagba "warrior" priestesses—ritual representatives of the Balógun Ààfin's standing army of the past—

brandish brass cutlasses *(àgàdà)* at the approaching Yemoja priestesses. This action represents a double threat. As a literal act, it can sabotage the Yemoja festival itself by smashing the sacred calabash and releasing its *àṣẹ*. The cutting blades of the warrior cutlasses emphasize the frailty of the "calabash crown" and its vulnerability to attack. As representatives of the *Balógun Ààfin's* power and authority, however, the Orisha Iyagba "warriors" convey the deeper and more subversive threat of civil revolt. For the *Balógun Ààfin*—chief of the Omole-Akodi quarter of Iyagba immigrants in Ayede—can rise up, with sufficient backing, to usurp the kingship from the *Àtá's* ruling dynasty. The force of this threat extends beyond Ayede town to the kingdom at large, for the *Balógun Ààfin* could mobilize additional support from the Yagba towns of Irele, Oke-Ako, and Ipao. Such support is ritually represented by the presence of Orisha Iyagba cult officers from these towns. Included among those who confront Yemoja's calabash are Ẹkùn (Leopard) and the Èyémọlẹ̀, both from Ipao. Although they bear no weapons, they represent, in their complementary roles, the "hot" power and "cool" authority of their Yagba chief as a potential king.

If civil chiefs can symbolically "fight" with the king, they also come dangerously close to becoming "kings" of their quarters. The Orisha Iyagba festival, like the royal cults of Yemoja and Orisha Ojuna, transports a sacred calabash with "water" from its bush shrine to the palace to revitalize the *Àtá* and the *Balógun Ààfin* on alternate years. Whereas the leader of the *ọlóòtun* carries the cult's calabash, priestesses behind her carry their water individually, in bottles containing water and leaves from the bush. Each bottle "contains" the power of an *òrìṣà* in the cult. Partially decorated with white cowries and red coral beads, they represent potential beaded crowns. While the *Àtá* sits in state, the priestesses enter into his chamber of crowns and deliver their water from their heads. When the cult calabash is put down, the drummers praise Orisha Iyagba. As individual bottles are put down, the drummers beat praises of the specific *òrìṣà* clustered within the cult. The priestesses execute specific choreographies associated with each *òrìṣà* and its drum rhythm. If these rhythms and dance steps are properly performed, the *òrìṣà* will "arrive" and will cooperate with the king. The powers of the cult thereby enter the palace.

Thus witnessed and described, the Orisha Iyagba cult resembles royal cults by regulating ritual power on behalf of the *Àtá*. Potential conflict between the *Balógun Ààfin* and the *Àtá* is ritually expressed in a staged confrontation, but it is also ritually resolved at the palace. To appreciate the ritual representation of the *Balógun Ààfin* as a potential king, however, one must observe at least two annual festivals in succession, for the festival follows an alternating routine. If one year the cult carries its power to the palace, the next year it avoids the palace and proceeds directly to its town shrine, where the *Balógun Àáfin* receives the procession. The town shrine symbolically becomes his palace, the calabash of *àṣẹ* represents his crown. Orisha Iyagba mobilizes Ayede strangers from Iyagba into a distinct, momentarily autonomous corporation, a kingdom within a kingdom. The arrival of *Ẹkùn* from Ipao represents an external source of power which serves the *Balógun Àáfin*, just as Yemoja's Shango priestess serves the *Àtá*. And like Shango, the leopard represents the unbridled power of kings. *Ẹkùn* is performed by a man in violent possession who behaves like a wild animal. He snorts, growls, and dashes back and forth, rolling in mud, appearing on rooftops and in trees, and terrorizing spectators by waving his red cloth indiscriminately—a release of unbridled power which townspeople equate with madness *(ìwèrè)*.[5] Like a possessed Shango devotee, *Ẹkùn* rips off the head of a chicken with his teeth and drinks its blood directly from the neck before staggering into the cult shrine to regain his senses. It is thus the *Balógun Àáfin*'s town shrine which ultimately contains and controls *Ẹkùn*'s power. The *Èyémọlẹ̀*, the "cool" priestess of ritual composure, remains seated in state with assembled cult members. Her coral beads and horsetail fly whisk represent the authority of her office within the cult and of the *Balógun Àáfin*'s "kingship" within Ayede at large.

The Orisha Iyagba cult poses an indirect threat to the ruling *Àtá*. By strengthening its civil chief, the cult empowers him like a king. One day after the priestesses deliver their water to the cult shrine, they dance to the marketplace to more playful rhythms of the cult's *ìkòkò, ibèmbé*, and *agèrè* drums. Whereas the ritual transport of water to the cult's town shrine separated the Yagba cult and its chief from Ayede, the dancing in the market on the following day marks their ritual reintegration with the town. The female "warriors" *júbà* (ritually salute and pay respect) in front of the shrines in the market—the shrine of Eshubiyi, the Idiya shrine where he founded the town, the Esi-Onigogo mound which protects the town and market, and the Ogun shrine which represents the *Àtá*'s forefathers.[6] At each of these sacred locations, the "warriors" sprinkle salt to make the town "sweet" and to pay their ritual respects. In this context, Abraham's translation of *ijúbà* takes on a special significance; what is normally glossed as paying ritual respect he calls "swearing fealty" and "acknowledging overlordship" (Abraham 1962:354). The *Balógun Àáfin*'s ritual representatives reaffirm their loyalty to the *Àtá* of Ayede.

The iconography of Orisha Iyagba's warrior priestesses emphasizes the separation and reintegration of the cult within the town. In addition to cutlasses, they brandish iron spears which are ritually invested with the power of the cult.[7] These spears serve as instruments of death which can be sent at night to enemies of the cult and town to kill them as they sleep. Nobody, I was told, is immune from these spears, not even the king himself. The "warriors" are also considered to be dangerous during the festival, for if their spears strike any part of a person's body, it is said that the person will die. It is not the spears themselves, however, which indicate deeper political motives; it is how they are symbolically marked. Before the ọlọ́ọtun priestesses carry their water, the Orisha Iyagba warriors decorate their spears with raffia-palm fronds *(màrìwò)*, known also as the "cloth" of Ogun. Since Ogun is the òrìṣà of iron and war, who in myth kills indiscriminately, the palm fronds associate the power of the spears with Ogun's military might. The palm fronds themselves, furthermore, resemble swords and spears. While their flat sides are smooth, their sharp edges can cut. Spears marked with palm fronds are thus doubly dangerous and poised to kill. The day after the ọlọ́ọtun deliver their water, the palm fronds are removed from the ritual spears and are replaced by strips of white cloth. It is with spears cloaked in the color of official hierarchy that the "warriors" of Orisha Iyagba "swear fealty" to the Àtá's ritual representatives. After the spears are "cooled" with sacred water and white cloth, the threat of insurrection is over. As the Yagba priestesses conclude:

> Jàre ká re'lé oooo!
> Ó yá káa lọ!
> Gbe'ra ń lẹo!
> Ọmọ erin oooo!

> Please let us go home!
> It's time to go!
> Rise up!
> Offspring of the Elephant!

But if the cult exhorts its chief to "rise up," the Yemoja priestesses warn him not to rise too high:

> Oníwèrè wo'jú Olókun,
> Kó má gun'gi aláta,
> Oníwèrè wo'jú Olókun,
> Kó má gun'gi olóyin.

Let madness watch Olokun's eyes,
  He shouldn't climb the hot-pepper tree,
Let madness watch Olokun's eyes,
  He shouldn't climb the honeybee tree.

With characteristic linguistic economy, the Yemoja priestesses warn the Iyagba cult to reduce its power to sane proportions, for it will suffer the sting of bees and of hot pepper if it rises too high and challenges the crown (Olokun). The "hot-pepper tree" (igi aláta) doubles as the "tree of the Àtá"; it signifies the singular stature of kingship and, more concretely, Ayede's Ìdìyá shrine, which marks the tree where Eshubiyi founded and centered his kingdom.

I have described the Orisha Iyagba festival in some detail because its very performance interprets Ayede's pantheon in terms which rival the pantheon of the palace and promote the Balógun. The deeper meaning of this ritual cannot be openly discussed because the power of its cult—as far as its members are concerned—would subsume Yemoja, Orisha Ojuna, even the Àtá himself. In ritual, the Balógun is empowered like a king. The town becomes his cosmos, with non-Yagba "strangers" housed in Ayede's different cults. His priestesses fight for him as hunters and warriors, reproduce for him as daughters and wives, and bring him the calabash of a potential crown like any royal cult. Orisha Iyagba's relationship to the goddess Yemoja, like that of the Balógun to the Àtá and of the Yagba strangers to the Iye indigenes, is uneasy, contested, volatile. The priestesses of both cults can dance and play like friends or plot and fight like enemies. Although they cooperate on the surface of events, their interests and ambitions are continually at odds. Deadly spears and witches attack cult enemies at night. Not even the king is immune or safe. As Orisha Iyagba openly and outwardly supports the king, inwardly and secretly its devotees turn northeast to honor rival gods and kings.

●●

In functional terms, the Orisha Iyagba festival is a classic ritual of rebellion. Armed insurrection is mimetically expressed to safeguard the king against actual attack. The subversive aspects of òrìṣà worship identified thus far, signifying deposition, fission, rebellion, and rival kingship, represent ruptures of the sociopolitical order which well-performed rituals safeguard against. Subversion in ritual, then, appears virtual and potential—in Langer's (1953:188) terms, a "non-actual semblance" of the real thing. Well-performed ritual, moreover, negates the real thing.

The virtual rebellion of Orisha Iyagba "warriors" against the Yemoja cult and the incumbent *Àtá* strengthens Ayede's king and kingdom in both functional and publicly praiseworthy terms. It is only when the town is "fighting" with the king—when the civil chiefs object strongly to his decisions—that the *òrìṣà* cults boycott the palace and withdraw their ritual support.[8]

Again, I would stress that this "functional" interpretation is not wrong but shallow, since it represents the official—and hence uncritical—vision of events. The "revitalizing," "integrative," "stabilizing" virtues of *òrìṣà* worship and its ritualized rebellions appear not only in anthropology textbooks but also in palace propaganda. What is missed in such instrumental readings is the deeper critique— of hegemony, oppression, exclusion, and appropriation, as well as of the official pantheon which encapsulates the kingdom. Rival pantheons organize more critical discourses, which are lost on the insensitive or uninitiated public. They decenter official ideology by reorganizing the cosmos. They establish their own truth conditions within the confines of their cults to subvert and revise, in the most powerful terms, the official hierarchy and vision of the world which they outwardly confirm. The following two chapters examine the power of this revisionary principle as citizens of Ayede bring the church, state, and nation within the town's local cosmological command.

THREE   HEGEMONY AND RESISTANCE

7

The Genius of "Paganism"

ince, as I have thus far argued, political relations in Yoruba kingdoms are critically structured, reproduced, and revised by ritual,
it is hardly surprising that Christianity and colonial rule were dialectically shaped by òrìṣà worship. That the immediate impact on òrìṣà
worship was negative is clear: the imperial power and authority of the
British Crown was sanctioned by the white man's religion, which
preached "enlightenment," "civilization," and "salvation" in missionary rhetoric and promised attractive opportunities for willing climbers
and converts. Islamic conversion in the nineteenth century, propaga-
ted by Fulani jihad and hegemonic claims in the north, had already
provided religious alternatives to òrìṣà worship among the Ekiti
Yoruba, but in this region Islam was rarely associated with the power
and authority of Yoruba kings (Mason 1970). Under the British, however, Christianity was the religion of the divisional officer, the provin-
cial resident—in short, of the entire hegemonic framework of colonial
rule. If under colonialism, as Akintoye (1970:258) argues, "the powers
of the ọba were vastly increased vis-à-vis their chiefs, subordinate villages and other traditional institutions," such change was "ration-
alized" by British models of politics and religion.

While Christianity imposed salvation from above to liberate the
damned, the "heathens" and "pagans" (as they were negatively
named) resisted from below. The immediate struggle was over political
resources, which the British successfully appropriated. There is no
question that òrìṣà cults lost prestige, followers, and jural authority to

growing numbers of Christian converts. But they also expanded their critical horizons to embrace the wider structures and contradictions of indirect rule. Despite zealous campaigns against traditional religion waged by missionaries and prophets of the emerging Christian elite, and to some degree because of them, òrìṣà cults have survived and developed *contra* changing patterns of stratification and oppression. The genius of "paganism" (Augé 1982) lies within its oppositional logic, one which confronts and appropriates the outside world to control it from within its kingdoms and cults.

POLITICS AND STRATIFICATION

At the turn of the twentieth century, British rule over Ekitiland transformed political relations between and within kingdoms, established new legal and fiscal institutions, and promoted the growth and development of Christianity, all within the framework of "native" administration. In 1899, Ekiti and Ilesha formed the Northeastern District of the Lagos Protectorate. In 1913 Ekiti constituted a division based in Ado, and two years later combined with the Owo and Ondo divisions to form Ondo Province with headquarters at Akure. Each kingdom within the Ekiti Division became a district with its ọba as sole native authority; and in 1920, the year direct taxation was introduced, the Ekitiparapo Council was reorganized with only the Ekiti ọba as members. In 1915 the first customary courts were introduced, and by 1930 there was a native authority court for each district (ibid., 258–59). The British desire to consolidate Ekiti kingdoms into a single administrative unit modeled after the northern emirates was resisted by the Ekiti themselves, who preferred the more localized autonomy of their precolonial polities.

Political change in colonial Ekitiland contributed to the complex differentiation of Yoruba society into more specialized institutions, statuses, and roles. The establishment of native courts, district treasuries, and local police, within the new conciliar framework of the native authority, narrowed the jurisdictions of traditional chiefs and created new opportunities for a rising literate and largely Christian elite (Ajayi 1965). At the same time, the powers of the ọba increased. Ekiti kingdoms in the nineteenth century were loose federations of autonomous towns which received military protection from a metropolitan center in return for what was mainly symbolic tribute and the sporadic provision of warriors and labor organized into age-sets. The dominions of such federated kingdoms were often in flux, with subordinate towns breaking away to assert their independence or to ally with more powerful kings. British rule, at least from 1900 to 1948, redefined Ekiti kingdoms into more rigid administrative units which restricted the autonomy of subordinate towns. After his 1899–1900 tour of Ekitiland, the first traveling commissioner, Major W. R. Reeve-Tucker, reported, "I have called in all the tributary villages to the capitals of the several Ekiti kingdoms and have placed the Bales securely under their kings. The Bales who were endeavouring to make themselves independent, a lingering remnant of their old wars and disputes, I have effectively placed under their proper kings" (in Weir 1934:34). To maintain the augmented authority of kings, the British overruled traditional mechanisms of deposition which were formerly controlled by chiefs and priests. Only the British could suspend, depose, or exile an errant king.

The structural changes precipitated by British rule affected civil chiefs and cult priests alike. In the political and ritual domains, their powers were diminished; within the emerging stratification system, their social status dropped. Prior to the establishment of native courts, chiefs and priests exercised considerable jural authority. Secular offenses were resolved by lineage heads within their compounds, by subchiefs within their subquarters, and by town chiefs within their quarters; and they were referred to the ọba in council when they involved members of different quarters. At each level of politico-jural segmentation, the titled head was advised by elders, including high priests and other ritual-office holders. A substantial part of a chief's income derived from "gifts" provided by litigants to sway his judgment and from fines paid by the guilty party. Much of this income was redistributed by chiefs to maintain clients and fulfill expectations of chiefly generosity. The introduction of native courts centralized the structural bases of litigation within kingdoms defined as districts. All secular crimes were referred to the ọba, who sat as president with his quarter chiefs and baálẹ̀ from subordinate towns. Minor chiefs—the àgbà ílú, or town elders—lost their voice in legal affairs, while quarter chiefs, baálẹ̀, and even kings lost their customary "revenues," receiving fixed salaries from the divisional office and allocating legal fines for sitting fees and for the maintenance of the courts instead.

Traditional politico-jural authority did not erode entirely. The native courts administered an alien law (codified as "custom") which many people bypassed by bringing matrimonial and land disputes to chiefs and baálẹ̀ for a more traditional settlement, a practice which continues today. But such an option, discouraged by the British, was only an alternative in a rapidly changing system of political and jural relations. Many minor chieftaincy titles became vacant during indirect rule and remain so today. The usual explanation is "because of poverty," which if interpreted sociopolitically means that minor chiefs no longer commanded the political influence and resources to attract followers and redistribute gifts. Other factors, such as out-migration of menial and clerical workers to the cities and the rise of a literate, educated elite of civil servants, detracted from the traditional labor pool which minor chiefs once controlled, further contributing to their poverty. One such chief voiced a common complaint: "Who is left to work on my farm? My children have traveled and bring me nothing." As chiefs lost control over political and economic resources, they also lost respect. There is a resentment among such chiefs of the "insults" and "abuse" which they suffer, particularly from the young. Another chief described how only elders greet him with traditional respect, saying "ẹ bọ àǝfín" ("greetings to the palace," North Ekiti dialect) while prostrating to the ground; whereas young men ridicule him as a useless government worker with no salary to be proud of.

Such erosion of traditional respect concerned not chiefs alone, but titled elders of the town and gerontocratic authority in general. Age-set stratification in the precolonial polity prescribed a "chain of command" in the exercise of political policy and military decisions. After the *Pax Britannica*, the growth of Christian missions and schools, and the rise of a literate, English-speaking elite, elders and chiefs lost leverage in local politics, relying more and more upon younger, literate "sons of the soil" to voice complaints and apply pressure on the district officer. The reorganization of the Ekiti district councils in 1951 to include elected members serving three-year terms, in proportion to the number of taxpayers in each quarter and subordinate town, represents the emergence of this younger voice into a more "rational' system of local government, in which two principles of social stratification— gerontocracy and educational literacy—were often at odds.

Òrìṣà cults suffered from similar limitations. With the backing of the district officer, who was represented in the religious sphere by the Church Missionary Society based in London, the ọba could transcend the traditional sanctions of his chiefs and priests. If a king could now rule without the support of his chiefs, he was also, ideologically, less dependent upon the òrìṣà. In the precolonial polity, a cult could withdraw its support of the king by refusing to perform its annual ceremony in public. It would perform private, "remedial" rituals in the bush to ensure the safety of its members, but the king was made vulnerable to mystical misfortune. The CMS church, associated with indirect rule, provided counterclaims against "pagan" sanctions, although the latter were never taken lightly by Yoruba leaders.

Such limitations on the powers of priests, who as àwòrò are conceived as "chiefs" and "kings" in the ritual domain, combined with a decline in their cult memberships as the Christian church won more and more converts. The momentum gained in Christian conversion was intimately linked with the politics of indirect rule. As J. F. Ade Ajayi points out in his seminal *Christian Missions in Nigeria* (1965:xiii), "the missionaries were able to exploit the prestige and the power of the white man already won by the colonial soldiers and administrators. It was then that . . . the fabric of the old society began to give way and people flocked to the missions." The impact of Christian conversion on òrìṣà-cult memberships is difficult to determine in any statistical sense because the "pagan" figures were never recorded. Not all Yoruba were initiated into cults in precolonial society; many simply consulted the òrìṣà for ritual assistance. At this more popular level of ritual participation, Christianity and òrìṣà worship are by no means mutually exclusive. Christians still "beg" the deities for help and attend the annual ceremonies. They must leave the church, however, to take a title in a cult. That the memberships of cults as ritual corporations have dwindled in response to massive Christian recruitment in this century is undeniable. That Christianity displaced òrìṣà worship, however, is simply untrue.Within Ekiti kingdoms, communities, and even individuals, both religions coexist.

In addition to the loss of cult members to Christianity, òrìṣà-cult officers experienced the same erosion of jural authority as civil chiefs. In precolonial Ayede, for example, after the Àtá Eshubiyi's death, two strong chiefs, the Ọ̀tún Osinkolu of Isaoye quarter and the Balógun Àáfin of Omole-Akodi quarter, competed for high office. Each had standing armies, and each belonged to a different òrìṣà cult; Osinkolu was a member of Orisha Ojuna, while the Balógun Àáfin had consolidated Orisha Iyagba into a major town cult. In the absence of an installed king to mediate their dispute (Osinkolu was de facto regent), the Oloke priest, wearing the white cloth of ritual composure, stepped in with his devotees to stop the conflict. Since the Oloke cult came from Ikole to Egbe-Oba quarter in Ayede, it possessed a relatively neutral political voice. After British intervention, however, such jural functions were appropriated by the district officer.

Christian dogma also undermined the jural powers of Ayede's bull-roarer cult of Babatigbo. In minor family and matrimonial disputes, the compound head could take the case to Babatigbo, a male cult and oracle of the earth, where the litigants confessed to a concealed idol who talked from behind a cloth. Since lying to a deity meant instant misfortune, such oracles would bring out the truth. Once guilt was determined, cult members flogged the offender until his body was marked and scarred. At times the assaulted would run away into the bush to escape, only to suffer further humiliation if caught. Cult members danced around such a "second offender" while he dug the ground until his fingers were bloody and torn. After that, he would lead the cult through the town, singing:

Ó fó un kè gbà o, óní tó mú ni gbà, mo re o kọ́,
A wí ṣẹ́ ni ńkè gbà o.[1]

They warned me before but I took no heed,
This is the punishment that will make one obey.

Not all òrìṣà cults administered such punishments—only those male cults such as Aku, Oro, and Egungun, which were associated with the bull-roarer in the bush. With the ascendancy of native authority courts and Christian concepts of retribution, such cults lost their official sanctions and controls, although they went underground and continued to operate.

Given such fundamental changes in local government and social stratification, perhaps the questions to be raised are less how and why òrìṣà cults declined and more how and why they have persisted to the present day. To be sure, òrìṣà-cult offices are now generally associated with low social status. Priests and priestesses tend to be illiterate; the men are often farmers, hunters, herbalists, night watchmen, and craftsmen; and the women are usually petty traders in local markets. Christians and Muslims often use the English term "pagan" with low-status connotations when referring to traditional cult members. But even the most urbane and educated Yoruba respect, even fear, the ritual powers of the cults, and they consult the olórìṣà (cult-title holders) when modern medicine and prayers to the Christian or Muslim God fail. Kings and town chiefs continue to attend and help finance the public cult festivals despite the admonitions of the Bible or the Koran, for such ritual duties belong to their public responsibilities.

Some high-office holders resent these ritual obligations, but they nonetheless comply. I attended an egúngún festival in Ikun, a North Ekiti town near the Kwara State border, where the ọba read a newspaper while masqueraders danced before him. His message was quite clear—as an educated Christian and university graduate, he preferred modernity to "pagan" ceremonies, but he would perform the ritual duties of his office. Even Christians can be "called" to òrìṣà cults against their will. The àwòrò of Orisha Oniyi, the cult of Ejigbo quarter in Ayede, remains a member of the CMS church, perhaps the most conservative denomination in Nigeria today. He was "forced" by Ifa divination to succeed his father to cult office, though he maintained that he would rather stick exclusively to Christianity. This is the only example that I found of an *òrìṣà*-cult priest *(àwòrò)* who remained a churchgoing Christian; but many traditional herbalists, diviners, and drummers boast membership in Christian churches. This is especially true in Ayede's subordinate town of Omu, which one townsman described as "90 percent Catholic and 100 percent pagan."

The persistence of *òrìṣà* worship in the face of such dramatic change follows a pattern of structural opposition to shifting fields of political power. Ayede's *òrìṣà* cults became important channels of protest against the changing order of things. This in fact makes traditional sense, since critique is built into the logic of *òrìṣà* worship and should be located within the structural conflicts and contradictions which generate ritual power. To understand the dynamism of the traditional ritual system and what has undoubtedly been a reduction to essentials, we can document its articulation with changing levels of conflict and contradiction within local and national arenas. *Òrìṣà* cults were not displaced by new religious ideologies, nor did they persist because "culture dies hard." Rather, they realigned with changing sociopolitical cleavages under indirect rule.

RELIGIOUS STRIFE

Dissension between "pagans" and Christians in Ayede stemmed from the association of the CMS with British power and authority. Local traditions relate how the son of the war chief *Balógun Èkìtì* (not to be confused with the *Balógun Àáfin*) brought one white man—the Reverend Harding—to Ayede in 1911, to establish a CMS headquarters of the Ekiti Division. This missionary, the elders maintain, came from London and belonged to the British royal family, a belief which served as a religious charter of colonial rule. Members of the Yemoja and Orisha Ojuna cults went to the ruling *Àtá* of Ayede and the town elders to protest this intrusion of an alien religion. The missionary, they said, was a slave dealer who would "disassociate their posterity from their gods and later sell them into slavery" (Chief S. A. Akerele, personal communication). Rejected by the town, the Reverend Harding relocated in Ado-Ekiti, where he established the Emmanuel Vicarage. Although a small CMS church remained in Ayede, its founder, David Ajayi, was banished with his wife and children to neighboring Ishan, where he settled and remained for many years. The rejection of the Reverend Harding is referred to as *"Ayédé kọ iyọ̀,"* literally "Ayede rejects salt," but figuratively, for Christians, "Ayede rejects goodness" or "Ayede rejects God."

Despite "pagan" opposition, the CMS church continued to grow, and in 1920 religious conflict developed into a crisis. Oral traditions relate how, during the Olua cult festival, the *àwòrò* of Orisha Ojuna was sitting in front of the town shrine and demanded that all townspeople come and greet him. One boy from David Ajayi's house came out but refused to stop at the shrine. The "pagans" declared that the *imọlẹ̀*—in this context, devotees possessed by the *òrìṣà*—would kill him. The boy fell ill and died, and the Ayede Christians accused the "pagans" of murder. In a variant tradition, the *àwòrò* of Orisha Ojuna touched the boy's head with a ritual staff, causing him to die. The case was taken to the district officer, who advocated religious tolerance and friendly relations between "pagans" and Christians. The Christians interpreted his response as a victory, for their accusation against the "pagans" was never revoked or proved false. To annoy the "pagans," they danced in unison, singing:

Gbegberegbe, mò jẹ bún o,
wọ́n ní mo bú ni gbegberegbe.

I am justified,
they said I did not abuse anybody.[2]

The "pagans" responded by combining forces with *òrìṣà*-cult devotees from Omu and processing together through Ayede. Ayede Christians responded:

A gbé Ẹ̀ṣù na lẹ̀ yòngí fọ́.

We knock the "devil" ruefully down.

They also climbed trees and cut off branches, which they placed in bundles in front of the senior devotees' houses, singing:

A gbé Omù lu lẹ̀,
àkéké fọ́.

We knock Omu people down,
the calabash [scorpion] breaks.

The ritual calabash—the focus of the cult's power—is referred to as a scorpion *(àkéké)*, implying, in this Christian insult against the Orisha Ojuna cult, that the "poisonous" power of the "pagans" was shattered by the church.

Christianity continued to grow in Ayede, backed by British rule and local civil chiefs. In 1926 Ayede installed Orishagbemi as the fourth ruling *Àtá;* he became the first Christian king and was known by his baptismal name, Gabriel Osho. Although his overweening political ambitions culminated in his deposition, Gabriel Osho is still remembered as a progressive Christian leader. He promoted education in the CMS school and punished idle children for not attending school or not working on their family farms. Many of Ayede's civil servants emerged from this era of education, and Christianity became the religion of the educated elite. The promotion of Christianity, however, generated opposition from Ayede "pagans." To regain their support, the *Àtá* Gabriel Osho rebuilt the town shrine of the Orisha Ojuna cult and took a more active role in its annual ritual. This annoyed Ayede Christians, who blame his ultimate downfall on his association with the cult. After he was deposed in 1934, members of Ayede's Patriotic Society (forerunner of the Ayede Progressive Union)—formed by wealthy elites who left Ayede to live in Lagos—petitioned the district officer to reinstall their errant king; but the townspeople were against him, and the D.O. turned a deaf ear.

The reign of the *Àtá* Gabriel Osho represents an important period of structural change in Ayede, during which the CMS church channeled centralized political power to a rising literate elite. As Christianity provided access to new centers and sources of power and wealth, it bypassed, displaced, and dispossessed the "pagan" elders. The church developed into a prestigious social club, internally organized into male and female age-sets with their own church "chiefs." Not all members were educated, but wealthier farmers engaged in tobacco and cocoa farming enhanced their social status by joining the church and taking one of its titles. As the church profited from the wealth of its members, and as they in turn were visibly prosperous, the Christian God appeared beneficent indeed, promising material gains in this world as well as salvation in the next.

The growing participation of the educated elite in district politics precipitated the reorganization of district councils in 1952 to include younger, literate members and broadened the horizons of the political and religious community. In 1955, Ayede's Christian elite formed the Ayede Progressive Union (APU) at the Action Group Secretariat in Ibadan. The APU Christians allied with the rising Action Group political party under Obafemi Awolowo—then premier of the Yoruba Western Region—in order to secure government grants that matched locally generated donations for self-help projects. Some of Ayede's town chiefs, already "progressive" Christians, traveled to Ibadan for the first APU meetings; others sent their personal representatives. Mr.

Longe of Odoalu quarter—a literate civil servant but not a traditional chief—was voted the Union's president and rose to the position of permanent secretary of Nigeria's Western Region under Obafemi Awolowo. Longe thus became a highly placed power broker mediating between Ayede town and the Nigerian federation through the APU and advocating progress in Action Group politics, Christianity, and education. The APU's first government grant established the Ayede Grammar School, which represented the goals and accomplishments of the Christian elite and provided attractive opportunities for the young.

After independence in 1960, Ayede Christians became champions of the "new" Nigeria. A government clinic with trained doctors and nurses—established in Ayede through Longe's influence with Awolowo—discouraged traditional healing by jùjú herbalists. The APU's monthly newsletter, published in English, reported on Ayede's progress, discussed Action Group politics, and in one issue (1962) urged Ayede citizens to abandon expensive rainmaking ceremonies because they were clearly unscientific. Not all Christians, however, adhered to such views, and a proliferation of independent churches led by Christian prophets in Ayede (Celestial Church of Christ, Christ Apostolic Church, Holy Apostolic Church, The Gospel Church, Cherubim and Seraphim, and The Church of the Lord, Aladura, to name the most prominent) provided Christian alternatives to the Anglican CMS that were more compatible with traditional religious beliefs. A satisfactory analysis of these different churches in Ayede alone would require more detailed research. Basic memberships and patterns of recruitment, however, indicate what can be posed here as a hypothesis: that the independent churches articulate less with local political cleavages and more with the emergence of "middle-range" social strata comprised of semiskilled and semiliterate traders, workers, and craftsmen and growing numbers of resident immigrants (cf. J. D. Y. Peel 1968).

COMMUNITY AND COSMOS

To return to our initial question: Why, in the face of such dramatic change, did the òrìṣà cults continue to develop, reduced as they were to essentials? The answer emerges from the character of change and the logic of ritual renewal. The initial Christian challenge to òrìṣà worship, a challenge which developed into a violent confrontation in Ayede, was intensified by the reorganization of kingdoms into native authorities with district councils. The increased powers of kings and the rationalization of local administration were local consequences of a more general process—the amalgamation and incorporation of autonomous polities into a British colony. Indirect rule reproduced the basic form of Ekiti kingdoms even if it transformed the content of traditional offices and councils. Two levels of government—one indigenous and local, the other alien and national—although integrated, remained distinct, defining their political horizons in different religious idioms. Ayede's colonial experience clearly illustrates how Christianity introduced the colonial state into the Yoruba town, rewarding its most ambitious and capable converts with positions of power and access to government resources and grants. But a complementary conversion was also occurring, less visible to outside observers but equally profound—namely, the cosmological *appropriation* of the state *by* the town.

According to the logic of ritual renewal, òrìṣà cults bring the raging powers of the bush and beyond into the very centers of the kingdom—the marketplace, cult shrines, and the king's person, palace, and crowns. On the critical day of carrying water, the boundary between bush and town is marked by gateways of raffia palm which represent liminal thresholds of passage. The passage from bush to town, however, is more metaphysical than physical; it crosses the most fundamental boundaries of space, life, and experience. Even as a literary topos in Yoruba novels, the bush is the place of ghosts, demons, monsters, even inverted societies which only the most powerful hunters and heroes can survive.[3] It is also the habitat of dangerous animals and special plants used by herbalists to make jùjú medicines. In ritual, the bush shrine is off-limits to the uninvited and uninitiated. It is the domain of powers which dwell in ponds, streams, hills, and trees, but which roam freely and capriciously. The bush is wild, dangerous, uncultivated—it intrudes upon farms and has to be cut back. In a deeper sense it represents the void, the unknown, the other side of social life—bad death, estrangement, unbounded space, unpredictability, chaos. The ritual passage from bush to town is clearly transformative. It invokes, contains, and controls the other side of social life by bringing it into society, carefully, following strict procedures. "Hot" power is carried, cooled, and incorporated into the body politic for private gain and public good. At the same time, however, a deeper transformation occurs in which the local community encapsulates the cosmos.

In this respect, every òrìṣà represents the primordial Orisha who was shattered and disseminated throughout the world. Every cult houses a piece of the whole and reconstitutes that whole in its calabash of power—icon of the womb, the head, the crown, the town; of wealth, witchcraft, the earth and the heavens. The ritual procession revitalizes the community by recreating the world, by retracing the

Figure 7.1. Popular Depiction of a Capricious Bush Spirit (ẹbọraa)
From Ogindele (1961:13)

town's steps back to Ife, where Yoruba kings and *òrìṣà* cults originated. The town itself becomes a cosmographic map of Yorubaland, its four corners marking the limits of expanding frontiers, its cults representing its immigrant groups, speaking their dialects, and reconstituting the "exemplary center" of ancient Ife (cf. Geertz 1980:11–18). In the precolonial era, each kingdom and community recreated the world on its own terms, with its own centers, kings, and horizons. If Old Oyo tried to displace Ife-centric origins, these were ritually resurrected by its vassal kingdoms. If Ayede suppressed the Iye ruling dynasty, its Olua cult could reassert its royal claims in ritual. Even Ayede's royal cults of Orisha Ojuna and Yemoja invest the king with rival histories and regional identifies, while Orisha Iyagba confronts him with Yagba traditions. In every kingdom, such cosmological transpositions allowed political quarters (*àdúgbò*) and subordinate towns to assert themselves as centers of *their* universes of discourse.

In the context of Christianity and colonial rule, the totalizing transpositions of *òrìṣà* worship appropriated church and state, together with more familiar forms of uncultivated chaos, within the metaphysical horizons of the cults. White missionaries, district officers, and their African employees, clients, and followers may have entered the Yoruba universe of power relations, but they certainly did not displace it. Because they opposed and oppressed the "pagans" from above, with administrative structures which reached back to London, *òrìṣà* worship turned upward and outward, projecting ritual idioms of the local community upon the surrounding and impending national frame. Within this indigenous interpretation of the state, the work of the cults became more vital, not less. If the missionaries and colonial administrators were dangerous forces to reckon with, all the more reason to regulate their powers by traditional, time-honored, ritual means to work for, not against, the welfare of the local community.[4]

In this light, the local contributions of church and colony can be seen as "pagan" victories engineered by the cults, which transformed externally imposed repressive measures into community initiatives and concrete gains. Nor were such visions restricted to self-proclaimed cult members, since ritual renewal is a collective concern which embraces the entire community. In many of the sacrificial prayers and "predictions" which I recorded, Christians, Muslims, political parties, and—after the Buhari coup—the Nigerian military entered the universe of ritual discourse and took its prescriptions seriously. The following chapter examines what happened when local leaders of Shagari's National Party of Nigeria did not listen closely enough.

8

The 1983 Elections

O n 16 August 1983, towns throughout Nigeria's Ondo State erupted into violence. The ostensible cause was popular reaction against rigged gubernatorial elections which favored a National Party of Nigeria (NPN) candidate in an overwhelmingly Unity Party of Nigeria (UPN) state. It is easy to dismiss the violence in Ondo (and in Oyo State, too) as the protest of a frustrated plebiscite—as indeed it was. But Western accounts of "the breakdown of democracy" in Africa, which are so often associated with primordialism, "tribalism," and class conflict in plural societies, seldom grasp the logic of the breakdown itself.[1] From the external perspectives of national integration and voting behavior, the popular violence of mobs and crowds is characterized as affective, politically immature, "irrational" action in contrast to the "rational" norms of institutionalized democracy.[2]

What I hope to reveal in this chapter is the often-neglected view from below: how popular protest in Ondo State—seen from *within* one local community—became a sanctified struggle against the nation at large.[3] This more internal, phenomenological perspective highlights the *rationality* of Yoruba protest—the symbolic construction of its microcosmic idioms and the instrumental logic of its destructive acts—within a more indigenous understanding of politics and power.

One of the concrete questions this analysis addresses is why so many Yoruba in Ondo State turned against kinsmen, age-mates, associates, and friends when the enemy was a corrupt federal government. The answer, I argue, involves the transposition of different political

horizons, of the more abstract, remote national state into the more concrete, immediate parochial town. If the former, however, was condensed into the latter, where it was regulated and controlled by ritual
idioms, the town simultaneously became larger than life, a symbolic
terrain in which local acts of violence would purify the nation of NPN
corruption.

Before the breakdown of democracy in the Second Nigerian Republic, local, state, and national politics were integrated in a series of
widening horizons which sustained a myth of a viable democratic process. As we shall see, the campaign speech by M. A. Ajasin, the incumbent UPN governor, communicated this vision quite clearly. On 16
August 1983, that myth, in Ondo State, was irreparably ruptured, and
the conventional distinctions between nation, state, and town collapsed. Seen not from Lagos, London, or Washington, but from within
Ayede, the events surrounding the 1983 elections can be analyzed to
reveal how popular protest in Ondo made sense not only as symbolic
drama, but also as effective political action. For, at least during the following four months—until Major-General Muhammadu Buhari's New
Year's Eve coup d'état dissolved all political parties by military
decree—the judiciary reversed Ondo State's vote and reinstated
Governor Ajasin.

●●

The events described and interpreted in this chapter occurred five
months after I arrived in Ayede. I had just started fieldwork and was
finding my feet when Ayede erupted into flames, baptizing me by fire
into political turmoil. Although normally received as a guest (and later
as a "son of the soil"), I was, during these turbulent events, a prisoner
of the town, which was physically sealed (like so many in Ondo State)
by roadblocks of felled trees monitored by armed hunters. When a
crowd of protesters first formed in the town, I followed with uneasy
fascination. As energies mounted and petrol was distributed to burn
NPN properties, I was summarily banished to my house (which was
fortunately owned by a UPN landlady), where I witnessed events from
my porch and received excited reports from my friends and research
assistants. As I pieced together the background to the federal and
gubernatorial elections, based on press releases, campaign speeches,
and popular wisdom, I saw how traditional models of political and ritual power shaped local political participation and the forms of opposition to rigged election results.

NATIONAL POLITICS

From the distant "bird's-eye" view of Nigerian politics, democracy has had a broken career. The First Republic, based on a Westminster model of parliamentary representation, organized Nigeria into three semi-autonomous regions, each associated with a dominant ethnic group and political party: the Yoruba Action Group (AG) opposition party in the West; the Ibo National Council of Nigeria and the Cameroons (NCNC) in the East (revised to the National Convention of Nigerian Citizens); and the Hausa-Fulani Northern People's Congress (NPC) in the North. To suggest that a one-to-one relationship existed between region, ethnicity, and political party is misleading, as classic studies of this period (and the formation of a Mid-Western Region of minorities) reveal (Post 1963; Sklar 1963); but a northern-dominated triangle of ethnopolitical blocs prevailed from 1960 to 1966 and reemerged after thirteen years of military rule in the 1979 elections of the Second Republic. The fragility of these federated regions, illustrated so tragically by the Biafran war, led to the creation of states. By 1979, the regional governments had been dissolved into first twelve and then nineteen states, within a constitutional framework that had shifted away from Westminster towards Washington, with a national presidency of up to two four-year terms, a Senate and House of Representatives at both federal and state levels, and state governors.

When General Olusegun Obasanjo returned Nigeria to civilian rule in 1979, the country was oil-rich and top-heavy. It boasted a $9 billion surplus in foreign exchange, based on federally controlled oil reserves which financed a growing civil service and professional class. Although the three former regions had been broken into states, ethnopolitical patterns persisted: the NPN succeeded the NPC as the party of the Hausa-Fulani in the North; the UPN succeeded the AG in the Yoruba West; and the Nigerian People's Party (NPP) succeeded the NCNC in the East. The historical connection of the UPN and NPP with the earlier "Yoruba" and "Ibo" parties was enhanced by the continuity of their leadership. Chief Obafemi Awolowo, who had founded the AG in 1951, led the UPN as its presidential candidate in 1979, while Dr. Nnamdi Azikiwe, founder of the NCNC (which was actually anti-regionalist at its inception), headed the NPP. The NPN compromise candidate, Shehu Shagari, was the new man on the scene, formerly minister of finance and backed by northern political bosses who brought him to power. The UPN under Awolowo still dominated the western states and elected Ajasin as governor in Ondo.

Shagari's first administration was a now-familiar story of government patronage, kickbacks, and corruption, along with an economic
collapse which was exacerbated by an international oil glut. Visible
signs included fleets of new cars for ministers and "contractors" amidst
construction projects which were abandoned when the funds ran out.
Overnight shortages of basic goods and medical supplies, longer
power failures, irrational price fluctuations, high inflation, and unpaid
government salaries were symptomatic of the more profound structural problems of an oil economy in which much was squandered and
very little produced. The net effect was an increased dependence on
the government's shrinking assets and an intensified scramble to get
what was left. The 1983 elections were seen as a zero-sum game in
which the winners would take all. Yoruba political strategies in 1983
reduced to two basic options: go with the UPN and receive the fruits
of an Awolowo victory, or sell out to Shagari and the NPN to gain
powerful friends likely to remain in high places. Uncertainty over
which strategy to follow was reflected by prominent figures in each
party decamping to the other side.

On 6 August 1983, presidential elections "reaffirmed" NPN control
of the country. Shagari won over twelve million votes; Awolowo came
in second with eight million votes, which were concentrated in the
West. More controversial, although less noticed abroad, were the state
gubernatorial elections held one week later. The NPN claimed victories
in twelve of the nineteen states, including staunchly UPN Oyo and
Ondo in the West and Azikiwe's NPP stronghold of Anambra in the
East. For voters in these states, Nigerian democracy was a mere ritual
of futile hopes and motions amidst forged voting slips, illegal polling
stations, and blatantly falsified counts. Petitions against the NPN "victories" in Anambra and Oyo were rejected in the Supreme Court by
junior judges selected for the task. Only Ondo State reversed its vote.
As seen from "above" by one London-based journalist, "The judicial
system succeeded in overturning the most ridiculous result: the victory
of the NPN gubernatorial candidate in Ondo State, where serious rioting claimed dozens of lives" (Q. Peel 1984). Against this thumbnail
sketch, we can examine the elections as perceived, experienced, and
opposed by the people of Ayede.

THE LOCAL FRAME

As we saw in chapter 2, Ayede was founded in the nineteenth century
by warriors who fought Nupe incursions from the north and joined the
Ekitiparapo against Ibadan's imperial invasions from the west.

Attracting groups of refugees seeking military protection, Ayede developed into a "traditional" Yoruba kingdom, organized into six *àdúgbò*, or quarters. Each quarter was stratified by age-sets and divided into lineages and compounds, and each had a dominant *òrìṣà* cult and a civil chief who regulated affairs within his quarter and sat with the other chiefs on the king's council. Whereas the king represented the unity of the kingdom, the chiefs expressed the sum of its parts; the council would unite in defense against external aggression and would divide as chiefs competed against each other in pursuit of parochial interests and favors from the king.

Like all Yoruba kings, the *Átá* of Ayede is sacred, tracing his dynastic pedigree back to ancient Ife. His sacred powers derive from special *jùjú* medicines, from installation ceremonies, from his privileged position "second to the gods," and from ritual sacrifices and annual festivals which ensure stability on the throne and good fortune in the town. These sociopolitical patterns and religious beliefs have persisted to the present day, responding to the incorporation of kingdoms into the wider structures of indirect rule; to the impact of Islam, Christianity, and formal education; to the new opportunities provided by cash cropping and occupational mobility; and to the dramatic vicissitudes of postcolonial party politics and military rule. As we have seen in Ayede, Yoruba kings still meet regularly with their chiefs, and the *òrìṣà* cults still regulate ritual power in their towns.

It was mainly Ayede's literate Christians, trained in Nigeria by the British and in some cases abroad, who first entered the national political scene. As we saw in chapter 7, this elite formed the Ayede Progressive Union, which consolidated AG support and sought government service and development grants. Mr. Longe, the president of the APU, became permanent secretary under Awolowo, who was then premier of the Western Region. With such a highly placed "son of the soil," Ayede secured a government hospital and grammar school. These concrete monuments of Ayede's progress strengthened Awolowo's local reputation and support and reinforced a popular conception of political success: just as a good town chief receives favors from the king, so a local party leader should have enough influence to bring progress to his town. National politics in the *local* frame has had less to do with nationalism and nation-building than with piped water and paved roads. There is nothing very mystical in this parochial notion of political clout. What is mystical are parochial notions of how people acquire such clout.

In competitive and individualistic Yoruba society, where social status is largely achieved and fortunes can change dramatically overnight, success and failure are attributed to a variety of mystical agencies (Barber 1981; Horton 1983). As explained by one Ayede Big Man who had served twice as an Action Group representative in the Western State House of Assembly, those who rise too high in politics are brought down with *jùjú* medicine. This same man described how he could not hug his children when he returned home from AG meetings because his protective *jùjú* medicines were "too hot."[4] Fortunes also change with the help of an *òrìṣà*, who exchanges powerful assistance for sacrificial offerings. Such views are not restricted to "illiterate pagans" (as the Christian elite sometimes refers to cult practitioners), but are shared by Yoruba Christians, Muslims, and physics professors as well. In Ayede, these ritual idioms and historical associations clothed the national drama of the 1983 elections in local dress.

A reelection campaign speech delivered by Governor Ajasin in Ayede illustrates concisely how Nigerian democracy was locally perceived. Since these speeches are designed to articulate such a local vision, they provide privileged data for the problem at hand. Ajasin was an old AG stalwart, having served as one of the party's four vice-presidents; his running with Awolowo on the UPN ticket emphasized a tradition of opposition to the ruling party. As state governor, poised between federal and local government frameworks, promising local access to the "national cake," his words literally and figuratively brought national politics to the people.

Ajasin spoke from a wooden podium erected next to Eshubiyi's town shrine in Ayede's central market, the locus of public assembly and town unity. The market is a ritual as well as secular meeting place, located opposite the palace, with sacrificial shrines to the major cult deities. The king was in fact present, together with all of his chiefs except Akerele, who had decamped to the NPN in January 1983 with Omoboriowo after the latter's defeat in the UPN primaries. Akerele had been the UPN organizer in Ayede and Ekiti-North generally; Omoboriowo had been Ajasin's UPN vice-deputy, but was now the NPN gubernatorial candidate. Their switch to the NPN was neither ideologically motivated nor based on NPN popularity in Ondo; rather, they were betting on a rigged victory which would reward them with access to national resources.[5]

Ajasin was joined on the podium by Ayede's Chief Ọ̀dọ̀fin, who had recently (and wisely, as events soon proved) decamped from the NPN to the UPN. The chief told the crowd that his former party was corrupt, urging all NPN members in the town to "retrace their steps" and "leave darkness for light." Ajasin then spoke, greeting the king and his chiefs, men and women, old and young, indigenes and strangers. His brief speech consisted of six basic points: the townspeople were (1) reminded that the national elections would be held on 6 August; (2) urged to take kerosene lamps to the polling booths to avoid rigging in case of a "timely" blackout; (3) exhorted to be nonviolent and peace-loving; and (4) told not to be corrupt and not to be bought off by the NPN. In addition, Ajasin (5) asked all present to make sure that the UPN ruled the nation, since the Shagari government had failed to implement its promises to build houses and roads, while its agricultural program—the so-called green revolution—was a symbol of theory with no practical results; and (6) emphasized the fundamental right and function of any electorate to reject a bad government by voting for another party.

Ajasin then introduced UPN leaders from Ayede and the local constituency, including representatives of marketwomen and traders. The chairwoman of all UPN women in Ekiti-North presented Ajasin with a broom so that "the UPN will sweep out corruption," with clay lamps to "show the light," and with three rooster pots containing alligator pepper, kola, and bitter kola "so that Ajasin will live long," adding that "when the rooster crows, everyone hears it . . . [so also] the UPN will be heard throughout the nation." Then she offered three calabashes of palm oil, salt, and honey. "Oil," she said, "is something soft, which everybody loves. Just as you can't cook without it, so everybody needs the UPN." Salt and honey, she said, would "sweeten" the UPN. After the presentation of these symbols, the hunters' masquerade entertained Ajasin, dancing to Ogun's drum rhythms and soon joined by the crowd.

Three aspects of this campaign event deserve special attention: the setting, the speech, and the symbolic "offerings." As a staged performance, Ajasin's visit to Ayede—like any major town ritual—organized the whole community both as spectators and as participants. Ayede's king and chiefs "received" Ajasin just as, in òrìṣà worship, they receive the ritual powers of deities which are brought into the town by cult specialists. In both cases, power is brought from outside the community into its very center, where it is regulated and controlled for the public good. Chief Akerele's *absence* from this event marked him off as a public enemy, an antisocial element who placed his own interests and ambitions before and against the UPN's revitalizing powers. At the same time, his own considerable power was politically divisive within the town, drawing its NPN minority away from Ayede's collective interest in UPN victory and thereby jeopardizing the town's regulation and control of party power.

Ajasin's speech was itself quite brief, establishing a set of ideologi-

cal oppositions associated with the UPN vs. the NPN which framed
Ayede's political identity in a series of widening political horizons.
Whereas the NPN is "dark," the UPN is "light," an attribute embodied
in the party's campaign symbol—a flame illuminating an outline map
of Nigeria—and concretized in the admonition to bring kerosene
lamps to the polling booths in case of a deliberate NPN blackout.
Whereas the UPN is morally pure, the NPN is morally corrupt. The
UPN is peace-loving, promoting prosperity and development; the
NPN is violent, promoting poverty and decline. These contrasts were
restated and personified in widening oppositions: between the UPN
chiefs and Chief Akerele in Ayede, between Ajasin and Omoboriowo
in Ondo State, and between Awolowo and Shagari in Nigeria at large.
The efficacy of Ajasin's rhetoric and the political vision which it sustained rested on the final point of his speech—that it is the right and
function of a democratic electorate to throw out a bad government by
voting in a new party. This fundamental principle of electoral freedom
authorized Ayede's role in self-improvement and promotion through
political participation.

The symbolic "offerings" to Ajasin after his speech communicated
a message of local support. The chairwoman of UPN women in the district employed overt political allegory as she explained each symbol for
the assembled audience—sweeping out corruption, long life for
Ajasin, a loud voice and "sweet" success for the UPN. Closer attention
to the symbols themselves, however, reveals a deeper level of unstated
meanings. Ritual power in òrìṣà worship is transported in calabashes
and decorated vessels, of which pots carved as roosters are a common
type. Carvings of women offering rooster pots to deities, found in
northern Ekiti cult shrines and palaces, are called olúmẹ̀yẹ, or "one who
knows honor," and they depict a "messenger of the spirits" offering a
sacrificial rooster to an òrìṣà. These carved objects contain kola nuts,
which "the king gives to his guests as an expression of hospitality"
(Pemberton and Fagg 1982:134, plate 41). In addition, alligator pepper
is valued for making one's speech "hot" and efficacious; cult priests
and priestesses—as well as politicians—eat it to add power to their incantations, prayers, and pronouncements. Honey, salt, and palm oil
are standard offerings to the òrìṣà, as ritual sweeteners and softeners
(ẹ̀rọ̀) which satisfy and "cool" the deities to enlist their support.

Thus the chairwoman of the UPN women fused an implicit ritual
role with her explicit political position. As a "messenger of the spirits,"
she offered a traditional sacrifice to the òrìṣà on Ajasin's behalf, providing him with kola nuts for long life and alligator pepper to make his
words—and hence the impact of his speech—more effective. Since the

offerings of the *olúmèyè* represent the implicit hospitality of the king, they indicated in this public forum his support of Ajasin. Implied, too, were the reciprocal obligations of ritual sacrifice—you give to the gods in exchange for their assistance, you make offerings for Ajasin's political success in exchange for his help as a powerful patron. The closing rhythms of the hunters' masquerade complemented the symbolic "offerings" of the UPN "priestess" with the male power of the hunter/ warrior cult—the armed guardians of the town—representing a collective strength and destructiveness which was soon to be unleashed.

VOTING BEHAVIOR

Shortly after Ajasin's speech, a general meeting was called at the palace to discuss growing concern about political violence. The elders discussed the town's violent proclivities in terms of its founding warlord and military past. They resolved that all weapons would be confiscated and that culprits harboring them should be punished. At the same time, allegations arose that certain NPN members in the town were responsible for recent deaths in UPN families by using witchcraft and *jùjú* medicines. Chief Akerele's absence became a sign of culpability; referred to as a witch and a wizard with powerful medicines, he personified the "evils" of the NPN. At a UPN meeting in Ayede just days before the presidential election, discussion centered on Akerele's *jùjú*, which would make him invisible and able to switch ballot boxes. The meeting resolved that everyone should carry mirrors which would catch his reflection in the polling booths.

On the day of the presidential elections, the UPN clearly dominated the town with local police support. Although polling booths were decentralized to prevent the formation of volatile crowds, isolated outbreaks of violence occurred. One of Chief Akerele's thugs was allegedly caught switching a ballot box; he was summarily beaten and jailed. Insults, curses, and abuse were hurled between partisan camps. The electoral process itself was a sham, with some people voting more than fifty times for Awolowo to counterbalance the NPN rigging which they correctly assumed. Nobody was surprised when Shagari was "reelected"; townspeople learned with satisfaction that in Ondo State, even with NPN rigging, he had received only 23 percent of the votes.[6]

With such a display of his party's strength, Governor Ajasin's reelection was virtually assured. While UPN minibuses broadcast campaign rhetoric, NPN vehicles were simply not on the scene. NPN members kept low profiles and walked cautiously during this period of mounting tension. On 13 August, the gubernatorial elections took place in much the same manner as the presidential elections held the previous week. On the morning of 16 August, when the results were announced, Ajasin was already being congratulated by the Ondo State Broadcasting Corporation when an announcer interrupted with a shaking voice to declare the official count in favor of Omoboriowo. The listeners were stunned. For the people of Ayede—and of Ondo State at large—the vision of democracy which Ajasin had promoted, democracy resting on the people's right to vote for the opposition, was fundamentally shattered by his electoral "defeat." Even NPN townspeople were surprised and bewildered, but they hardly had time to digest the news before they were fleeing for safety.

A crowd of mostly old and middle-aged women mobilized first, carrying sticks, cudgels, and yam-pounding pestles; they were quickly joined by young girls and boys. Their first act of protest was to overturn and set fire to a Peugeot station wagon owned by an NPN nurse. The nurse fled into the CMS Church, whereupon the pastor started ringing the bells—more a call to action than for help. Men and women joined the growing crowd after a man arrived in a taxi, reporting that other towns were "rioting for Awolowo." He said he came "from Ife," the locus of Yoruba creation and kingship, which gave moral sanction and cosmic closure to his message.[7] The crowd moved on to the marketplace, singing "Awò! Iná!" ("Awolowo! Fire!"), while hunters barricaded Ayede's main road, blocking the escape of NPN members but also the way in for the mobile police (colloquially referred to as "kill and go").

The crowd turned against NPN houses, while unlucky individuals who had not fled into the bush were routed from hiding places. Young boys beat a senior NPN member, slapping his face and chest with a stone while others jumped on him—an obvious inversion of customary respect for elders. Young girls screamed to burn houses and people as petrol was distributed for the demolition of NPN properties. "God is on our side," three young men proclaimed as they searched for an "arrogant" NPN girl to stab, beat, and rape.[8] As the crowd became a mob, it broke into sections, burning and gutting NPN beer parlors, compounds, motorcycles, and cars, drinking plundered beer, and smashing bottles. The atmosphere was sinister, festive, and frightening. But there was a method to the madness. Destruction followed a path of increasing social status and stature. First the "little people" were victimized: tenant farmers who had no influence in the town, and widows whose children had left for the cities, people who were marginals in the community and had responded to the "generosity" of NPN "gifts." Thereafter, pillage climbed the social hierarchy until by early afternoon, crowds convened at Akerele's three-story house—at once a monument of Big Manship, high estate *(ọlá)* and, for the majority of townspeople, NPN power and corruption.

Local testimony related that Chief Akerele's house would not catch fire until women urinated on his medicines, neutralizing their powers. Both his family shrine and his *jùjú* shrine to Osanyin—the *òrìṣà* of medicinal efficacy—were allegedly neutralized and burned, while other medicines (including a brass Ogboni chain) were brought to the palace to display to the king (who in the meantime prayed that the town would not destroy itself during his reign). Townspeople maintained that it was this *jùjú* medicine which prevented the king from owning a car—that someone wanting to give him one would forget because of Chief Akerele's *jùjú*. Human heads were allegedly unearthed in Akerele's compound—used for money making and protective medicines—although I never found anyone who admitted to seeing them. After burning and gutting the house, hunters performed a specialized sacrifice to further neutralize Akerele's powers, killing a goat by slicing its stomach and placing dry fish, pepper, salt, and ashes inside. Meanwhile, the women sang in Ayede dialect:

> *Òbó bo ọmọlẹ̀.*
> The Vagina which covered you in your life will bury you.

> *Akérélé kàa tí pè,*
> *Ógbó yẹríyẹrí kanlẹ̀ po.*
> Akerele who we called before,
> The masked spirit has destroyed to the ground completely.

> *Èrò ayé ewá werò ọrun,*
> *Akérélé lọ ò ìwé ìbò á gbe fò.*
> He is alive but we say he is dead,
> The voting card will take Akerele to heaven.

These songs were curses *(èpè)*, uttered by women with *àṣẹ* and alligator pepper in their mouths; these women proceeded, like priestesses, to the market shrines, where their words would "go straight." Chief Akerele's miraculous escape from this persecution was attributed to powerful medicines. Some say that he turned into a stick, others that he simply vanished. In the evening, less agile NPN members were fined, rounded up, and walked through the town carrying large stones on their heads, crying "Awò!" and "Come and buy beancake!" *(wá r'àkàrà*, signifying that the NPN sold them stones and cinder blocks for food—i.e., a load of rubbish and false promises) while they were beaten with sticks. Brought to the central shrine in the market, they were forced to swear allegiance to Awolowo and to forswear their association with Akerele and the NPN. Despite the plunder and persecution, nobody was killed during the riots in Ayede, although deaths were reported elsewhere. The town turned inward, not against itself, but against the state.

●●

One must neither romanticize local violence as exalted struggle nor abuse the ethnographer's questionable role as privileged voyeur. There was much that was cruel, opportunistic, and simply ugly during the 1983 election riots. But to return to my initial concern with the symbolic construction of microcosmic idioms and the instrumental logic of destructive acts, events *were* meaningful and targeted toward specific ends. The "deconstruction" of Akerele's three-story house attacked a symbol as well as a man: a symbol of "bigness," prestige, and power associated with NPN corruption, electoral rigging, and the ruin of the nation. By neutralizing his *jùjú* medicines, women and hunters not only brought Akerele down, but purged and purified the community. As with traditional ritual idioms, collective purification demands political unity. Whereas in a public *òrìṣà* festival the king and chiefs are united at the market and palace, the election riots culminated in public oaths at market shrines. These oaths were not mere punishments. They guaranteed with ritual sanctions the unity of the town, the demise of the NPN, increased support for Ajasin and Awolowo, and a revitalized Nigeria "purified" by the UPN. Just as *òrìṣà* worship transforms the town into a microcosm of the Yoruba world, in which the king receives primordial powers, the secular ritual of local violence transformed the town into a microcosm of the national state. Although incited by Ajasin's electoral "defeat," the townspeople rioted "for Awolowo" and their country's future.

There are less visionary explanations of similar events. David Laitin (1986:132) has argued recently that the Yoruba town as an "ancestral city" remains "the dominant metaphor for political interpretation within Yorubaland," observing that NPN support among the Yoruba in 1983 was "entirely based on the exploitation of ancestral city fissures." This certainly was true in Ife, where violence erupted between UPN Ife indigenes and NPN Oyo immigrants of Modakeke quarter; and also in Ibadan, "where violence between Oyos and Ijebus broke out in the wake of voting" (ibid.). But in Ayede, the dominant fissure was created by the political parties themselves. Of the town's six quarters, four were indigenous and two were considered strangers; neither side had a particular commitment to the NPN. Chief Akerele's faction recruited indigenes and strangers, Muslims and Christians, literates and illiterates, rich and poor; their only common interest was in the NPN itself. It was precisely the cleavage of partisan politics which transcended all others, turning friends, neighbors, and kinsmen against each other.

The big question is why. J. D. Y. Peel (1983:253) has characterized party politics in Ilesha as "a hierarchy of communities . . . none of whose levels was fixed, and each of which opened up to a yet higher level of power and resources." The *key* to Yoruba political complexity, he argues, is the concept of a community simultaneously divided into competitive subunits but united with respect to the "outside" sociopolitical environment (ibid., 222). This paradigm, we have seen in chapters 6 and 7, is grounded in Yoruba cosmology and underlies Yoruba perceptions of the nation as well, appearing in Ajasin's campaign speech as a series of widening political horizons. When Shagari was "reelected," the UPN Yoruba of Ondo State were disappointed but not surprised. When Ajasin was "defeated," they rebelled. In terms of Peel's paradigm, the UPN in Ondo State lost its access to the national-government structures and resources which a real election would have sustained.

Fighting the NPN at state and federal levels, UPN towns could not tolerate internal schisms between parties. As the case of protest in Ayede reveals, town communities asserted themselves as centers of power because the vision of democracy and its horizons collapsed; ritual techniques and violent persecution "neutralized" the NPN because the electoral process had clearly failed. The strategy was unpleasant, but unlike democracy, it worked.

9

Yoruba Culture and Black Texts

The argument that Yoruba religion is a critical practice—one that structures history, politics, ritual, and knowledge, as well as popular resistance against hegemony—has general implications for black critical theory which we are now in a position to develop. That the Yoruba hermeneutics of power is also a textual hermeneutics in the most literal and traditional senses of the term emerges in what I call "rewriting paganism"—the representation, in missionary prose, of "pagan" and "heathen" Yoruba practices by indigenous Christian converts. Such writing was no mere brainwashing exercise, but harnessed the critical powers of "paganism"—ultimately grounded in òrìṣà worship itself—to the colonizing language of the church, thereby establishing an African voice within official Africanist discourse. To consider the result a hybrid is wrong, since the very opposition between Christian and "pagan" is itself a product of the missionary mind.[1] The critical difference lies even deeper, between the restricted knowledge of black African religions and the "pagan" masks which were assumed for the whites.[2]

To Gates's (1984:3) challenging questions—"How do the canonical texts in the black traditions relate to canonical texts in the Western literatures?" and "How are we to read black texts?"—the works and lives of two nineteenth-century Yoruba missionaries, Bishop Samuel Ajayi Crowther and the Reverend Samuel Johnson, suggest culturally and historically specific answers which continue to illuminate black textual strategies and the formation of an "oppositional," or "marked," literary

193

canon. Both Crowther and Johnson were among the mission-educated Yoruba to write major ethnographies in English of their own and neighboring traditions and societies, adopting the official Christian view of "pagans" and "heathens" while subverting that view in "deeper" discourses.

Bishop Crowther's early experiences—captured and enslaved by Muslims, resold to Portuguese slave traders, "liberated" at sea by the British, and relocated in Sierra Leone—represent, in his first narrative, the problematic relations between freedom and bondage, relations transcended on one level but reproduced on another by British intervention in West Africa. Clearly Bishop Crowther, who met Queen Victoria in 1851, was no ecumenical radical. Awarded the degree of D.D. from Oxford University in 1864 and a Gold Medal of the Royal Geographical Society in 1876, the first African bishop affirmed central values of European missionary and commercial ideology—that Africans did possess souls and could be "saved" to serve the "higher" interests of "civilization."[3] But Crowther's outward affirmation of this ideology concealed the more critical consequences of his Christian conversion. These consequences were permitted freer reign in Crowther's other major project—the development of a Yoruba grammar and orthography to promote literacy in Yoruba and the spread of the Christian Gospel in his Yoruba translations of the Bible from English, Hebrew, Latin, and Greek (Crowther 1843, 1851, 1852). For Crowther, the Christian conversion of Yoruba "pagans" led to the African's appropriation of Christianity as a strategy of self-recognition and self-determination. Despite his conservative reputation throughout a long lifetime of service to the Church Missionary Society, he was stripped of his powers in his final years and became "a symbol of race on trial" (Ajayi 1970c:12) for African Christians.

Rev. Samuel Johnson's textual genesis involved an almost equally hegemonic drama with overtones of colonial sabotage and anticolonial "revisionary" critique. Dedicated to Rev. David Hinderer, the original manuscript of his *History of the Yorubas* was lost in 1899 by the Church Missionary Society—three years after the *Pax Britannica*. The author died in 1901, but his text was rewritten by his brother "from the copious notes and rough drafts left behind by the author" (Johnson 1921:ix). It was finally published, after a second transatlantic seizure, in 1921. For Yoruba scholars, this text is a "bible" of traditional knowledge and cultural documentation. But its rhetorical relationship to the sacred texts of Islam and Christianity prefigured an Afrocentric discursive critique polarized, for instance, by the liberating theologies of Malcolm X and Dr. Martin Luther King, Jr. and reformulated in the "voodoo" of Zora

Neale Hurston; in the "sorcery" and "Neo Hoodoo" of Cecil Brown, Jones/Baraka, Toni Morrison, and Ishmael Reed; and in the extremely critical hermeneutics of Wole Soyinka, A. K. Armah, and other giants of the black literary canon. If "rewriting paganism" refers to specific texts of the first African clergymen, it identifies not only the critical moment of their literary production, but also a critical method of black writing and voicing which has developed under related conditions of oppressed alterity. Even the concept of "black canon" itself refigures this difference between "pagan" (black) and Christian (canonical).

MASTERS AND SLAVES

Samuel Crowther's first literary success was his "Letter of Mr. Samuel Crowther to the Rev. William Jowett, in 1837, Then Secretary of the Church Missionary Society, Detailing the Circumstances Connected with his Being Sold as a Slave." the letter was published as an appendix in 1842 to the *Journals of Schön and Crowther*, which describes their famous expedition up the Niger the year before. The letter had clearly impressed the CMS not only for its violent imagery and poignant prose, but also because it told the missionaries what they wanted to hear. Samuel Crowther's explicit message was that his liberation from slavery was only the first step toward true freedom in Christ. He even recalls his capture c. 1821 (at age fifteen) as "unhappy" but "blessed":

> I call it *unhappy* day, because it was the day in which I was
> violently turned out of my father's house, and separated from
> my relations; and in which I was made to experience what is
> called to be in slavery:—with regard to its being *blessed*, it being
> the day which Providence had marked out for me to set out on
> my journey from the land of heathenism, superstition, and vice,
> to a place where His Gospel is preached ([1842] 1970b:372).

If Crowther opens his account with redemptive gratitude, he closes it with equally obedient dogma: "May I ever have a fresh desire to be engaged in the service of Christ, for it is *perfect freedom!*" (ibid., 384). And he concludes, "That the time may come when the Heathen shall be fully given to Christ for His inheritance, and the uttermost part of the earth for His possession, is the earnest prayer of [and he signs] Your humble, thankful, and obedient Servant, Samuel Crowther" (ibid., 385).

Thus ideologically framed, "Christ," "His inheritance," and "the uttermost part of the earth for His possession" have this-worldly analogues in British religious and commercial interests and possessions. Crowther furnished both living and written proof that British intervention, urged and partially funded by the African Civilization Society and its colonial venture called the Model Farm, was morally necessary and economically promising (Ajayi 1970a:vii–xi). But between the opening and closing statements of his letter, Crowther narrates the "unhappy" events. Captured by Oyo Yoruba under the sway of Fulani *jihad*, Crowther—here we do not learn his Yoruba name—was sold and re-sold, bartered once for a horse and again for "tobacco, rum, and other articles," and finally sold to the Portuguese (ibid., 378).[4] After initial attempts to strangle himself ("May the Lord forgive me this sin!") and marching for months through "four different dialects," Crowther's first "contact" with the "White Man" involved new extremes of incarceration:

> It was not without a great fear and trembling that I received, for the first time, the touch of a White Man, who examined me whether I was sound or not. Men and boys were at first chained together, with a chain about six fathoms in length, thrust through an iron fetter on the neck of every individual, and fastened at both ends with padlocks. In this situation the boys suffered the most: the men sometimes, getting angry, would draw the chain so violently, as seldom went without bruises on their poor little necks; especially the time to sleep, when they drew the chain so close to ease themselves of its weight, in order to be able to lie more conveniently, that we were almost suffocated, or bruised to death, in a room with one door, which was fastened as soon as we entered in, with no other passage of communicating the air, than the openings under the eaves-drop . . . Thus we were for nearly four months (ibid., 380-81).

Here the white man is marked as undifferentiated other, as invading captor, torturer, and oppressor. At this time in Crowther's discourse, all whites are the same. There is no meaningful difference between Portuguese and British. When two British men-of-war intercepted the slaver after its first day on the open sea, the enslaved cargo were prepared for the worst: "On the next day we found ourselves in the hands of new conquerors, whom we at first very much dreaded, they being armed with long swords" (ibid., 381).

There follows a remarkable literary moment, a reversal of Eurocentric interpretations and fears of the African other. As the slaves were "transshipped" to British vessels, Crowther held back with several "friends in affliction," who together were conveyed to the *Myrmidon*. There they found "not any trace" of those shipped out before them:

We soon came to a conclusion of what had become of them,
when we saw parts of a hog hanging, the skin of which was
white—a thing we never saw before; for a hog was always
roasted on a fire, to clear it of the hair, in my country;—and a
number of cannon-shots were arranged along the deck. The
former we supposed to be the flesh and the latter the heads of
the individuals who had been killed for meat. But we were soon
undeceived, by a close examination of the flesh with cloven foot,
which resembled that of a hog; and, by a cautious approach to
the shot, that they were iron (ibid., 382).

Here it is not Africans but Europeans who eat human flesh. The black
man perceives the white man as cannibal. This conclusion is dismissed
as a frightened mistake, but in a deeper sense it remains valid. White
man's slavery "consumes" black flesh. This knowledge inspired
Crowther to commit his only recorded act of violence and revenge
against the "master race." It is a moment when not only images but situations are reversed:

Our Portuguese owner and his son were brought over into the
same vessel, bound in fetters; and, thinking that I should no
more get into his hand, I had the boldness to strike him on the
head, while he was shaving by his son—an act, however, very
wicked and unkind in its nature (ibid., 383).

The sublation of this master-slave dialectic establishes a critical textual
precedent.[5] As "white" discourse, it sets the British up as saviors and
blames slavery on the Portuguese. It also initiates Crowther's "progress" toward the "truth"—that the British are not cannibals; that
"liberated" Christians do not strike their tormentors; and, most importantly, that "unenlightened" Africans are "wicked and unkind." But on
a deeper level it signifies something else. The significant difference is
between black and white. The black man is free, the white man is fet-
tered. The black man is master, the white man is slave. For at least one
moment in his life, Crowther physically struck out against the figure of
oppression which presumed to shape Africa's destiny. In his text, he
established a "pagan" literary voice which subverts and decenters occi-
dental hegemony while outwardly following its rhetorical forms.

Crowther's career in the CMS recapitulated the logic of his earliest
essay throughout the rest of his life. As a "good Christian," he rose to
the rank of Bishop of Western Africa, approved by the Archbishop of
Canterbury. But Crowther was denied jurisdiction over Lagos,

Abeokuta, and Ibadan. The white missionaries there, in the last instance, could not accept the religious authority of an African. His "perfect freedom" in Christ was restricted by racism and was recognized only "in places not yet occupied by European missionaries," mainly the Niger (indeed "Black") Mission to the east of Yorubaland (Ajayi 1965:207). It was during efforts of missionary expansion up the Niger River—on three separate expeditions in 1841, 1854, and 1857–59, when Crowther was employed by the British as linguist, translator, and ethnographer of riverine peoples—that he wrote his journals.

Crowther's accounts of "other peoples" are literary masterpieces of official Africanist discourse; the "other" has "strange superstitions" and "curious habits," including ludicrous ways of wearing European clothes. Crowther is definitely a member of the missionary team, and he regards the "natives" with the proper pity, distance, and disdain. Consistent with "pagan" ruptures in his texts, however, the substantive conclusions which he draws from his observations promote the autonomy, responsibilities, and freedom of African missionaries (1841) and recommend (1854) the controversial policy of training "uneducated" elders instead of "young, inexperienced, college-trained men" to spread the Gospel among local chiefs.[6] By 1852 Crowther had published his *Grammar and Vocabulary of the Yoruba Language* and his Yoruba translations of St. Luke, Acts, St. Peter, and St. James. Crowther's subsequent literary strategy was less with the African elite largely brainwashed by privilege and more with the "vernacular." His "Christian" and "pagan" discourse, in a sense, developed into a diglossic situation, with English above Yoruba in the white world and Yoruba on top in the "black interior"—Crowther's recognized regional jurisdiction but also his topos of inner experience.

CROWTHER RECONSIDERED

If this "radical" reading appears pushed or contrived, I do not mean to suggest that Crowther was a closet pagan in clerical drag. Crowther's sincerity as a Christian is beyond dispute, but to reduce our interpretation to what he really "intended" or "believed" invokes a psychological essentialism—a veritable symptom of officializing discourse in the West—which misses the subtleties of Yoruba selfhood and identity and distorts the basic logic of Yoruba religious discourse. Furthermore, evidence from Crowther's childhood, translation methodology, and philosophy of conversion indicates his profound understanding of "traditional" wisdom. And finally, Crowther's resistance to the growing imperialist policy of the CMS church and his radicalizing impact on the "native" Christian community reveal how his critical vision was received at the time and why it became so important.

The question of the author's intention requires a brief digression into indigenous ideas about intentionality. Yoruba notions of personal identity index multiple levels of the self in relation to different hermeneutical levels. The Yoruba concept of *orí* (lit. "head") refers to the metaphysical self as a personal (and prenatal) destiny, objectified into an *òrìṣà* as the spiritual locus of the empirical ego; it subdivides into *orí-ọdẹ*, or "outer head," and *orí-inú*, or "inner head." This distinction is itself metaphysical and deep, but can be roughly glossed as the outer, public self—how others see you—and the inner, private self, or how you "really" see others (cf. Abiodun 1987; Lawal 1985). Crudely put, the outer head corresponds to public, authoritative discourse (e.g., praises voiced but not offered with sincerity) which masks the secret intentions of the inner head, embodied in subversive readings of ritual symbols which restructure authority, in curses against enemies, in harbored jealousies, or in the hidden languages of ritual specialists. Beneath *orí*, however, lies an even deeper and more fundamental spiritual identity, called *ìpọ̀nrí*. It is this innermost self which an *òrìṣà* seizes when a person falls into a state of possession, becoming a vessel for the *òrìṣà*—speaking in its voice, foretelling the future, issuing its commands, and dancing or swooning under its power. *Ìpọ̀nrí* also refers to the painted spot on an initiate's shaven head which marks the *òrìṣà*'s precise point of entry into the devotee (see Drewal 1977; Verger 1982, plate 194).

If we apply this model to Crowther's texts, we can account for his multiple "intentions" according to Yoruba concepts of personal identity. Whereas Crowther's official Christian voice represents his outer head, his less orthodox departures reveal his inner head, which doubles in Protestant theology as the Christian inner self and its immanent understanding *sola fide*, by faith alone. We can say these departures were intentional in the Yoruba senses of the term. But his most dramatic reversals—and here I include the most radical readings, which Crowther himself might have explicitly disavowed—represent, in Yoruba, his *ìpọ̀nrí*, that innermost essence as it was seized by an *òrìṣà* and used as a vessel for the deity's voice. I am not implying that this actually happened, invoking personal claims of mystical participation, or what Mudimbe (1988:136, passim) calls *Einfühlung*. But in deep Yoruba terms, it could have happened. My point is simply that a Yoruba hermeneutical perspective can account for a powerful discourse voiced by Crowther which he did not consciously intend, but one which he could not control, since he was not in possession of his innermost self. Thus my radical readings of Crowther remain valid in Yoruba cosmological terms.

Keeping with this Yoruba reading, we can ask which òrìṣà possessed him. It could be any òrìṣà, but chances are it was Obatala, the deity of political displacement (see chapter 1). Some Yoruba scholars liken Obatala to Jesus, as both suffered humiliation from captors in order to ritually empower their people—an accurate portrayal of Crowther's own life. "Circumstantial" evidence is provided by Page (1908:7), who tells us that the young Crowther's mother was a priestess of Obatala and that when the family house caught fire, "Adjai promptly rushed through the flaming doorway and brought all the idols back to safety, amid the cheers of the neighbours, who cried out, 'This child will be a great worshipper of the gods; he will one day restore the gods to our nation.'" Thus it appears that "little Ajayi" accumulated some credit with the òrìṣà, particularly Obatala, and may have even received Obatala's powers after converting to Christianity. Shifting back to a Western psychological orientation, we could say that the biographical evidence of Crowther's intimate involvement with the deities assures us of one thing—that at an early, highly impressionable and formative age, Crowther was indeed exposed to the fundaments of Yoruba òrìṣà worship; that the seeds of his Yoruba religious understanding were planted in his youth. Was it not prophesied by his neighbors that "he will one day restore the gods to our nation"?

This fact is significant in light of Crowther's later translations of the Bible into Yoruba. We know from J. F. Ade Ajayi's archival research that Crowther took great pains to find "deep" Yoruba equivalents of Christian vocabulary; that he sought out "traditional priests" among the Yoruba of Freetown (in Sierra Leone, where Crowther was then living) to "study their practices and liturgies" (Ajayi 1970c:8); that he "'watched the mouth' of the elders and, while discussing theology and other serious matters with them, noted down 'suitable and significant words'" (Ajayi 1965:128). In a journal extract from 1844, he wrote, "In tracing out words and their various uses, I am now and then led to search at length into some traditions or customs of the Yorubas" (quoted in ibid.), and he refers to his specific research on Egúngún and Ifá (ibid.). Crowther's linguistic sensitivity to deep Yoruba concepts revived his interest in Yoruba religion, including the "oral literature, proverbs and idioms of the people" (Ajayi 1970c:12) and influenced his later ideas about Christian conversion.

In a lecture delivered at Lakoja in 1869, Crowther advocated an "assimilationist" evangelical strategy unpopular among most white missionaries:

It should be borne in mind that Christianity does not undertake to destroy national assimilation; where there are any degrading and superstitious defects, it corrects them; where they are connected with politics, such corrections should be introduced with due caution and with all meekness of wisdom, that there may be good and perfect understanding between us and the powers that be that while we render unto all their dues, we may regard it our bounded duty to stand firm in rendering to God the things that are God's (quoted in Ajayi 1965:224).

At a time when some white missionaries were burning "*jùjú* houses," destroying "fetishes," and razing *òrìṣà* cults in campaigns against "the devil," Crowther's call for a more enlightened approach to traditional culture was radical indeed. His text is carefully framed in a rhetoric of conversion which preserves religious difference with scriptural authority. Where traditional religion has "degrading and superstitious defects," it should be "corrected," not destroyed. Where it is "connected with politics," such corrections should be introduced with caution, respect, and "with the meekness of wisdom" demanded by Christianity. Such a method will establish a "good and perfect understanding between us and the powers that be," and here Crowther's text conveys an important double meaning. In official discourse, these "powers" refer to traditional chiefs and elders, whose authority must be recognized and cooperation sought. But in a deeper Yoruba discourse, do these "powers" extend to the "pagan" deities which constitute the religious bases of chiefly authority—and which, by extension, must also be respected?

The immediate audience of this particular address was Crowther's own African clergy, and perhaps they sensed this deeper message. The whites who read his text could be assured that Crowther was following a precedent set by Jesus—of rendering to Caesar the things that are Caesar's and to God the things that are God's (Matthew 22:21). But this scriptural allusion indexes the deepest subversion of all. Like Jesus defending the faith against hostile Pharisees, Crowther was defending the true Christianity—one that recognized the things that are Africans'—against the racist zealots (called the "young purifiers") in the CMS church who were soon to take over his Niger Mission. Crowther continued to preach respect for indigenous wisdom, including "fables, story-telling, proverbs and songs which may be regarded as stores of their [i.e., Africans'] national education in which they exercise the power of their thinking"; he added that "their religious terms and ceremonies should be carefully observed; the wrong use made of

Figure 9.1. The Bishop and His Native Clergy (1908).

such terms does not depreciate their real value, but renders them more valid when we adopt them in expressing Scriptural terms in their right senses and places" (quoted in Ajayi 1965:224). As Crowther rewrote "paganism" into Christianity, he reaffirmed the critical power of "pagan" knowledge by deploying its vernacular lexicon—literally re-writing Christianity into the language of Yoruba elders and ritual spe-cialists to promote the role of Africans in running their own religious and political affairs.

It is in this latter struggle for African autonomy that Crowther's "subversion" of official church policy would have made immediate sense to his African allies. From 1877 to 1891, the consolidation of the Royal Niger Company and the organization of Nigeria into three Brit-ish protectorates transformed the labors of white missionaries in Nigeria, who were urged "not only to trade with Africans but also to rule over them" (ibid., 233). During this time, CMS racism intensified, as did the conviction that Africans could not be entrusted with the re-sponsibilities of Christian leadership. Crowther's success with his Niger Mission, winning souls in the interior while promoting riverine trade, became a threat to growing imperial claims—in ideological as well as economic and political terms. These transformations precipi-tated the Niger Mission crisis, when Crowther's authority was effec-tively reduced to a sinecure and his black clergy displaced by white "purifiers." In 1890 Crowther was put on trial and told that his Mission was "the work of the devil" (Ayandele 1970:237). The backlash was im-mediate, unleashing a united African Christian front against the CMS and leading to the founding of an independent Delta Pastorate Church and, in 1891, the United Native African Church. In his final days, "the most submissive Bishop in the C.M.S. experience, who had before obeyed 'orders', associated himself with the greatest rebellion against the C.M.S." (ibid., 243).

In the year of his death, the black bishop became a rallying symbol of antiwhite protest and Christian schism. Here, J. F. Ade Ajayi (1961) and E. A. Ayandele (1970) have argued, lie the foundations of Nigerian nationalism. Whether or not Crowther *intended* his rewriting of "pa-ganism" to precipitate such political momentum is not really the point. The fact that he fueled growing opposition to an increasingly imperi-alistic British and CMS policy suggests how the critical power of his deeper discourse inspired effective resistance during a fundamental turning point in Nigerian history. We might even say that Crowther's revisionary critique established the turning point itself—a rhetorical turning, to be sure—whereby "the alien colonialist project of appropriation was matched by an indigenous nationalist project of counter-appropriation" (Guha 1989:212).

SAMUEL JOHNSON IN AFRICA

In a line of almost direct descent from Crowther, Samuel Johnson's monumental *History of the Yorubas* continued to rewrite "paganism" in Africanist discourse. Johnson's decentering strategy becomes even clearer to the "initiated" eye, while the text's literary history recapitulates his rhetoric of revision.

The subtitle of Johnson's *History* reads *From the Earliest Times to the Beginning of the British Protectorate*, already establishing two "beginnings": one "earliest" and black, the other "British" and white. Johnson's discursive repossession decenters British hegemony by re-centering history in Yoruba traditions and myths of origin. The author's preface of 1897 opens with an indignant reproach against the educated African's lack of self-awareness:

> Educated natives of Yoruba are well acquainted with the history
> of England and with that of Rome and Greece, but of the history
> of their own country they know nothing whatever! This
> reproach it is one of the author's objects to remove (Johnson
> 1921:vii).

But Johnson's goal was repeatedly sabotaged and delayed by a series of strange interventions. In the editor's preface to the first edition, we learn of the "singular misfortune" which "befel the original manuscript of this history, in consequence of which the author never lived to see in print his more than 20 years of labour" (ibid., ix). We are introduced to a serious confrontation which indicts the British church and Crown in a muted accusation of murder and of trying to silence the African voice. "The manuscripts were forwarded to a well-known English publisher through one of the great Missionary Societies in 1899 and—*mirabile dictu*—nothing more was heard of them!" (ibid.). Then follows an attempted payoff:

> The editor who was all along in collaboration with the author
> had occasion to visit England in 1900, and called on the
> publisher, but could get nothing more from him than that the
> manuscripts had been misplaced, that they could not be found,
> and that he was prepared to pay for them! This seemed to the
> editor and all his friends who heard of it so strange that one

could not help thinking that there was more in it than appeared
on the surface, especially because of other circumstances
connected with the so-called loss of the manuscripts (ibid.).

Johnson's brother and editor, Obadiah Johnson, suspected foul play,
but he turned to the task of reconstructing the text: "Some chapters had
to be rewritten, some curtailed, others amplified, and new ones added
when necessary" (ibid., ix–x), so that we never really know which
Johnson wrote what. But even the reconstructed text was appropriated:

> When at last the task of re-writing it was completed, it was
> forwarded to England by the *Appam*, which left Lagos on the
> 2nd of January, 1916. The *Appam* was at first supposed to be lost,
> but was afterwards found in America, having been captured by
> the raider *Moewe*. Nothing was heard of the manuscripts for
> nearly two years, when they were at last delivered to the
> printers! (ibid., x).

Whether factually accurate or structured purely by rhetoric, the history
of Johnson's *History* echoes Crowther's ultimate "payoff" by the
British—who effectively sold him "up the river"—and his "recapture," "transshipment," and final "delivery" at sea. But this time
America defines a point in what Fox (1987:2) calls "the triangle of European desire"; it is the economic basis of "black dispossession" but also a
model of black "double-consciousness" achieved by discursive repossession. In the editor's preface, "paganism" is rewritten twice,
stolen twice, and finally returns to Africa, where it fulfills "the earnest
desire of the original author."

The editor signs the preface with two names: as the enlightened O.
Johnson and as Ajagbe Ogun, a compound of his *oríkì* (praise name)
and *orílè* (family stock, origins), which have important Yoruba meanings. *Àjàgbé* means "he who fights to take" (Abraham 1962:487); we
could say "retake," or "repossess" in this context. Ogun is of course the
Pan-Yoruba *òrìṣà* of war and hunting, a violent, "hot," vengeful hero
who vanquishes towns, kills commoners and kings, and subverts hierarchies of chiefs.[7] By reconstructing his brother's text, Ajagbe Ogun is
drawing on his "pagan" power—in his fight against white "protection"—to repossess his origins. That this struggle is consistent with
Samuel Johnson's original desire is signified by his Yoruba name on *his*
preface. Samuel Johnson, a lexicographer like his famous English
namesake, is also Anla Ogun, a "pagan" Yoruba warrior who died
while fighting by the pen. In white discourse, he is a CMS reverend
and pastor of Oyo. Writing in black, he represents the Ogun cult of

warriors and records the (in fact Oyo-centric) history of Yoruba origins and empires.

Johnson's *History* divides into four major periods, glossed mythological, expansionist, revolutionary, and protectionist. These correspond to traditions of origin, the rise of the Oyo empire, the collapse of Oyo and the rise of Ibadan, and the advent of British overrule. The explicit thrust of this structure is that the Yoruba people developed a great empire which was subverted by Islam from without and political treachery from within, disintegrating thereafter into internecine conflict and civil war which was "providentially" checked by British intervention. Like Crowther's *Letter*, Johnson's *History* concludes its 642 pages of text with the proper genuflection to authority:

> When we have allowed for all the difficulties of a transition state
> the disadvantages that must of necessity arise by the
> applications of rules and ideas of a highly civilized people to one
> of another race, degree of civilization, and of different ideas, we
> should hope the net result will be a distinct gain to the
> country . . . and above all that Christianity should be the
> principal religion in the land—paganism and Mohammedanism
> having had their full trial—should be the wish and prayer of
> every true son of Yoruba (Johnson 1921:642).

Johnson's introduction is similarly structured by protectionist rhetoric; in fact it opens, after a brief description of geographic topography locating the Yoruba in longitudes and latitudes, with a "valuable letter" written by Rev. Samuel Crowther to Her Britannic Majesty's consul. In this quoted letter, Crowther is again the "faithful servant," documenting the Yoruba "sub-tribes" and "limited monarchies" which were soon to be incorporated into indirect rule. Johnson continues to describe the Africanist landscape—its physical features, flora, and fauna—but when he gets to the people, racial difference is both preserved and erased:

> As far as it is possible for one race to be characteristically like
> another, from which it differs in every physical aspect, the
> Yorubas—it has been noted—are not unlike the English in many
> of their traits and characteristics. It would appear that what the
> one is among the whites the other is among the blacks. Love of
> independence, a feeling of superiority over all others, a keen
> commercial spirit, and of indefatigable enterprise, that quality of
> never being able to admit or consent to defeat . . . are some of
> the qualities peculiar to them, and no matter under what

circumstances they are placed, Yorubas will display them (ibid., xxii).

The official Christian, or "white" reading is still clear. Yorubas are to other Africans what the English are among Europeans—at the top of the hierarchy of nations—by virtue of shared traits and characteristics. The inferiority of black to white, however, is implicitly assumed. Or is it? On this point, a deeper reading asserts something else. Yorubas, like the English, love their independence. Like the English, they feel superior to all others, are stubborn and enterprising, and above all will never consent to defeat "no matter under what circumstances they are placed." When these circumstances include British overrule, *mutatis mutandis*, the Yoruba will protect their independence, feel superior, and never accept defeat. The black text confronts white hegemony from a stance of original purity:

> The whole people are imbued with a deep religious spirit,
> reverential in manners, showing deference to superiors and
> respect to age, where they have not been corrupted by foreign
> intercourse (ibid.).

The religious spirit is a "pagan" code corrupted by contact with "foreign intercourse," suggesting sexual and racial as well as discursive crossings which contaminate the original. The subversive project of Johnson's *History,* like Crowther's interior language, is the overthrow of British hegemony, the revaluing of official racial tropes to turn the discourse upside down.

The project begins with traditions of origin. As we saw in chapter 1, most Yoruba creation myths state that in the beginning, Olodumare, the Yoruba High God, had a son, Oduduwa, who climbed down a chain from heaven to an uninhabited world. Since the world was covered with water, Oduduwa placed a handful of earth on it and a rooster on top of the earth. As the rooster began to scratch and kick the earth about, land spread out across the water. According to this myth, Ile-Ife is the sacred locus of Oduduwa's original descent, where he founded Yoruba kingship and fathered future generations through sixteen sons.[8]

Johnson's *History* avoids this account, partly to downplay Ife's political importance and promote Oyo's dynastic claims, but more importantly to canonize a migration myth which rewrites "paganism" in both content and form. Johnson's "revisionist" strategy is in fact revolutionary; by introducing a "false" tradition which he then "corrects," he reformulates popular conceptions of Yoruba origins as a pagan response to Islam and Christianity. In his account, Yoruba origins spring from religions of the book; the question of which religion and which book shifts in a series of textual quotations and substitutions which subvert canonical Christian readings.

Johnson "documents" a "commonly received" tradition that the Yoruba "sprung from Lamurudu, one of the kings of Mecca," whose offspring included Oduduwa. Thus the Yoruba High God (Olodumare) is initially displaced by a Meccan king as Oduduwa's father, locating Yoruba origins outside of the Ife-centric cosmological scheme. Lamurudu ruled "after Mohomet" as an Islamic king. His son, the Crown Prince Oduduwa, "relapsed into idolatry" and attracted many followers. "His purpose," Johnson (1921:3) writes, "was to transform the state religion into paganism, and hence he converted the great mosque of the city into an idol temple." A civil war eventually broke out between Muslims and pagans; Lamurudu was killed but the Muslims prevailed, while "Oduduwa and his children escaped with two idols to Ile-Ife" (ibid., 4). During their escape, they defeated a detachment which had set out to destroy them, and they seized among the booty "a copy of the Koran." The Koran was thereafter "written" into "paganism," textually relocated in Ile-Ife's central shrines, where it "was not only venerated by succeeding generations as a sacred relic, but is even worshipped to this day under the name of Ìdì, signifying Something tied up" (ibid.). Thus Yoruba origins are historically grounded in a pagan revolution (and implicit parricide/regicide) against an Islamic king and kingdom. In the process, Islam's sacred text is appropriated, re-fetishized, and incorporated into a central pagan shrine, where it remains hidden and "tied up."

In this "commonly received account among this intelligent although unlettered people," Johnson identifies "traces of error," which he "corrects" in a series of nested quotations. That the Yorubas came from the East he believes, but he doubts that they descended from an "Arabian family" in Mecca. Mecca is dismissed as a symbol of the East, not the name of a specific city. Johnson consults "the only written record we have on this subject," a text written by the Fulani Sultan Belo of Sokoto, a prominent crusader of Islamic *jihad*, and quoted by the English captain (and Christian crusader) Hugh Clapperton in his *Travels and Discoveries in Northern and Central Africa, 1822–1824*. Here we have Samuel Johnson, who is a Christian Yoruba, quoting an English Christian quoting a Fulani Muslim to reconstruct pagan Yoruba origins. Christian discourse suffers a double subversion in this chain of transmission: first, because it is parasitic to Islamic sources—as such it is secondary to an original text—but more significantly, because by Clapperton's shifting "hand" it is implicated in the slave trade. Quoting the sultan, Clapperton writes, "By the side of this [Yarba] province there is an anchorage or harbour for the ships of the Christians, who used to go there and purchase slaves" (ibid., 5). Like the "pagan" voice of the young Samuel Crowther, this passage identifies the Christians as slavers, rupturing the myth of Christian liberation and salvation in a quotation of one of its British proponents.

Johnson's metaquotation of Clapperton continues with a Canaanite theory of Yoruba origins which traces back to Nimrod. In this figure, Islam and Christianity begin to converge. Johnson cites references to Nimrod in both religions, conceding the possibility that both the Koranic and Biblical descriptions "belong to one and the same person" (ibid., 6). In his "correction" of the tradition, Johnson concludes:

1. that the Yoruba sprang from Upper Egypt or Nubia,

2. that they were subjects of the Egyptian conqueror Nimrod, who was of Phoenician origin, and that they followed him in his wars of conquest as far as Arabia, where they settled for a time,

3. that from Arabia they were driven, on account of their practicing their own form of worship, which was either paganism or more likely a corrupt form of Eastern Christianity (which allowed of image worship, so distasteful to Moslems) (ibid., 6–7).

Lastly, Johnson questions the claim that the "sacred relic called Idi" was "a copy of the Koran" (ibid., 7). Instead, he "cannot resist" concluding "that the book was not the Koran at all, but a copy of the Holy Scriptures in *rolls*, the form in which ancient manuscripts were preserved" (ibid., 7). After being erased, religious difference between Islam (Orientalism) and Christianity (Occidentalism) is textually resurrected—gradually, in a "corrupt" form of Coptic Christianity, then more clearly, in rolled manuscripts of the Holy Scriptures enshrined in Ile-Ife. Christianity, not Islam, is now appropriated by "paganism" and written into its very center, where it remains a "closed" book. What looks like a Christian reading of Yoruba origins doubles as a "pagan" appropriation of Christianity, a "conversion" of Christianity into "paganism" before the missionaries' eyes. Johnson continues to document the traditions of various Yoruba kingdoms and the essentials of Yoruba religion and government. But the "closed book" remains at the center of his *History*, rolled and tied shut because—as a deep discourse—it subverts the Christian canon which it outwardly enshrines.[9]

●●

As "formal revision" (Gates 1984:285), rewriting "paganism" is a particular mode of "signifyin(g)" (ibid., 286, passim) in Africanist discourse. Like toasting, Santería, and "mumbo jumbo" in the New World, it represents black discourse in relation to something else, as marked, oppositional, subversive, and powerful in its ability to restructure official, "white" discourse.[10] This, I believe, was the "vernacular" contribution of Bishop Crowther and Rev. Samuel Johnson to the Africanist discourse of the British church and state. It was also an African contribution, specifically a Yoruba contribution. The "double voicing" (ibid., 294), "repetition of formal structures" (ibid., 285), and the representation of black experience ("paganism") (ibid., 295) so artfully woven into Crowther's journals and Johnson's *History* deploy critical strategies of Yoruba ritual. Besides the polyvocality of the òrìṣà themselves and of the secret languages of their priests and priestesses, Yoruba ritual represents on multiple levels: one official and transparent *(funfun)*, the others hidden and opaque *(dúdú)*.[11] To have "deep" ritual knowledge—access to the "essences" of cult secrets and symbols—is to possess a dangerous power which is lost if revealed. Such power is dangerous because it subverts official discourse and hierarchy: as Ogun's sword, it decapitates chiefs; as Shango's lightning, it deposes kings; as Eshu the trickish mediator, it propagates chaos and anarchy.

Both Soyinka (1976) and Gates (1984) use Yoruba òrìṣà worship as a paradigm of the "African world" and the "black cultural matrix." Soyinka's *Myth, Literature and the African World*, its explicit project of "self-apprehension," is in fact another rewriting of Yoruba "paganism" which appropriates Greek gods and oracles to subvert the classical canon. But whether we perceive metaphysical confrontation, critical parody at play, or some vibrant combination of both at different moments of the ritual process, the point cannot be overemphasized that the power of Yoruba religion is grounded in its own, indigenous, critical hermeneutics which structures interpretation in the public domain. The oppositional, revisionary, and subversive dimensions of Crowther and Johnson are not just responses to foreign intervention; they ultimately derive from the hermeneutical structure of Yoruba religion itself. As we saw in chapters 4, 5, and 6, ritual knowledge is that privileged access to what the official discourse of homespun oppression really signifies; paradoxical, dangerous, revolutionary, and empty, such knowledge cannot be publicly disclosed.

Powerful in Yoruba society because it can restructure political hierarchy, this hermeneutical principle entered Africanist discourse to disseminate an Afrocentric critical voice which today has grown much louder and has broken many chains. I do not wish merely to "historicize" the Yoruba connection to black critical theory and canonical texts, although the historical connection is clearly important. Certainly other "tribes" have other "scribes" on both sides of the Atlantic. Rather, the history of Yoruba "self-apprehension"—from "pagan" ritual through Christian "enlightenment" to Nobel Prize–winning poetry, drama, and prose—is itself paradigmatic of the black literary canon, its fictions, its facts, its theory and practice.

CONCLUSION

But though all our knowledge begins with experience, it does not follow that it all arises out of experience.

Immanuel Kant, *Critique of Pure Reason*

One cannot say that the petty bourgeois has never read anything. On the contrary, he has read everything. Only, his brain functions after the fashion of certain elementary types of digestive systems. It filters. And the filter lets through only what can nourish the thick skin of the bourgeois' clear conscience.

Aimé Césaire *Discourse on Colonialism*

Bí òwe, bí òwe ní à ń lu ìlù Ògìdìgbó. Ológbón ni í jo ó. Omòràn ni í si í mò ó.
The rhythm of Ogidigbo drumming is proverbial. Only the wise can dance to it. Only the discerning are able to understand and interpret it.

Yoruba proverb (Roland Abiodun)

Awó j'awo lọ, awo lè gb'áwo mì torí-torí.
Secret surpasses secret, secret can swallow secret completely.

Yoruba *arò*

If, as Giddens (1984:374) says, all social science is a "double hermeneutic" consisting of "the meaningful social world as constituted by lay actors and the metalanguages invented by social scientists," I have sought to penetrate the first, in this case Yoruba, hermeneutic, rather than dwell extensively on the metalevel of theory per se. However, as Giddens points out, there is a "constant slippage" from one to the other—an inevitable consequence, perhaps even virtue, of the hermeneutical circle—and I conclude by making this slippage explicit, examining what the Yoruba hermeneutics of power implies for anthropological theory.

RITUAL, POWER, AND HISTORY

The major thesis which this study has developed is that Yoruba ritual is a *critical practice* that is based on a hermeneutics of power. I have focused on ritual in the "grand" tradition of sacred kingship and elaborate symbolic drama not to highlight the "sensational" productions of an "exotic" society (like some of our Africanist forebears), but because the Yoruba possess such a grand tradition and proudly acclaim both its history and power. I have offered at best a partial vision, neglecting the more intimate bonds between devotees, deities, and their individual clients in favor of a more ostensibly political focus on the public performances of òrìṣà cults because it is here that the critical relations between knowledge and power are paradoxically most visible and invisible. Public ritual remains a privileged site in Yoruba society precisely because it engages communities in collective, and indeed contested, empowerment. My goal has been to understand this empowerment as real—not in mystical and symbolic terms which make cultural sense to "them," or in material and instrumental terms which make theoretical sense to "us," but in critical terms which establish a shared understanding for both "sides" of the double hermeneutic.

In so doing, I hope to have challenged a prevailing Western vision of cultural death and dissolution, so clearly expressed by Parrinder's (1953:1) claim that "the ancient pagan religion of the country is declining . . . so that one cannot now speak of the land as 'heathen' or 'untouched.'" Let us hope that we can no longer think of Yoruba religion as "heathen" or "untouched," either today or before, in some myth of a pristine past. As the historical and ethnographic record reveals, Yoruba ritual and religious change implies dynamic transformation—particularly in response to Christianity and colonialism—and not a dwindling away of "tradition" in the face of modernity. Even if particular rituals and òrìṣà cults die out, new ones emerge, in the traditional "dress" of closed corporations or, more subtly, in idioms of Christian enlightenment and political protest. In Nigeria today, even the most "modern" Yoruba towns engage in "traditional" ritual. The ruling Elékọ̀lé of Ikole—a self-professed Christian—has been criticized for refusing to eat the heart of his predecessor. But his kingmakers know better. Public claims need not concur with private, hidden, esoteric practices, particularly those of a Christian ọba.

It is the hidden and deep which this study has explored, not as a sacred transcript of gnostic wisdom, but as a critical space for reconfiguring power. If this space is intellectual, safeguarding a place for critical thinking, it is not merely so, but has concrete political implications when put into ritual practice. We know from Van Gennep (1909) and Victor Turner (1967) that the "work" of ritual is one of passage—from one social status to another, as in rites de passage narrowly conceived; or from one "state" or condition to another, as in rites of collective regeneration and renewal. When a major *òrìṣà* festival is performed, the kingdom and its contesting parts are selectively reborn. Ties between metropolitan centers and subordinate towns may be established, reaffirmed, or severed. Relationships between civil chiefs may be reproduced or revised. While refusal to participate signals political fission, new players on the scene indicate alliance and fusion. This remains as true today as it was in the past: when Old Oyo expanded its empire and its subject territories resisted; when the *Àtá* Eshubiyi first allied and then broke with Ibadan, and when he displaced the Iye chiefs; or when Ayede's cult of Orisha Iyagba boycotted the palace to depose the *Àtá* Gabriel Osho in 1934. Such options are guaranteed by a hermeneutical vision which maintains the power of deep knowledge-claims as dangerous, paradoxical, transgressive, and above all efficacious.

It is with such efficacy in mind that we can fruitfully return to Victor Turner's work on liminality, for it contains insights which can be further developed. Turner's (1967) focus on liminality broke new ground because it identified specific relationships between symbolic processes and social dynamics.[1] Liminal symbols are chaotic and unhinged because they signify a state of antistructure, a condition of pure disorder and negativity which exists outside of society, in violation of social and semantic taxonomies. Hence the confounding of *prima materia*—filth, feces, menses, and decay, signifying social death from a previous status—with regenerative substances such as semen and breast milk, which indicate movement toward social rebirth. Liminal figures, moreover, are polluting and powerful because they embody both sets of denotata at once. They are simultaneously dead and alive, male and female, human and animal, singular and plural, and ultimately destructive and regenerative. Their condition, says Turner, "is one of ambiguity and paradox, a confusion of all the customary categories" (ibid., 97). It is, moreover, a powerful condition, because, like anarchy, it allows pure freedom from constraint.

The beauty of this insight is that it makes sense in both cultural and sociological terms. In ritual experience, liminality constitutes "close connection with deity or with superhuman power, with what is, in fact, often regarded as the unbounded, the infinite, the limitless" (ibid., 98). Recall the king's empowerment in chapter 4, when contact with Yemoja's calabash established a moment of pure synthesis—of death and rebirth, witchcraft and fertility, maleness and femaleness, pollution and purification, mortality and divinity, multiplicity and singularity, all in a transitory fusion with the *òrìṣà* herself. It is a moment, moreover, when all difference is erased, when all social groups and categories become one body politic. Liminality is simultaneously a semantic and social condition of erasure. It sanctions a sociopolitical as well as symbolic freedom which can run amok if let loose.

The point I wish to emphasize—and it is one which has been curiously overlooked—is that Turner's theory of liminality identifies ritual power with critical reflection. Consider the following quotations. "Liminality may perhaps be regarded as the Nay to all positive structural assertions, but as in some sense the source of them all, and more than that, *as a realm of pure possibility whence novel configurations of ideas and relations may arise*" (ibid., 97, my emphasis). Like deep Yoruba knowledge, liminality establishes conditions of "pure possibility" which negate the official (i.e., ideological) and natural (i.e., hegemonic) orders and which generate "novel configurations." And again, during the passage between social states, "undoing, dissolution, decomposition are accompanied by processes of growth, transformation, and *the reformulation of old elements in new patterns*" (ibid., 99, my emphasis), or what amounts to a deconstructive and revisionary practice.[2] Furthermore, such thinking is socially restricted; it is "arcane knowledge or *'gnosis'*" (ibid., 102), represented by iconographic *sacra* which serve as "objects of reflection" (ibid., 103). It is here that Turner's critical theory begins to emerge; "Liminality may be partly described as a stage of reflection" in which "neophytes are alternately forced and encouraged to think about their society, their cosmos, *and the powers that generate and sustain them*" (ibid., 105, my emphasis).

Turner thus characterizes liminality and *gnosis* as a form of pure possibility and negation, one which reconfigures signs, inspires new insights, and reflects on the powers which generate and sustain society. In the dangerous context of antistructure, such thought itself is powerful, since it allows for social as well as symbolic revision. And it is here that I take Turner one step further, by equating liminality with power itself. Throughout my study I have defined power negatively, as subversion and transgression, as that which revises and transforms authority.[3] This negative relation to authority is dialectical, as we saw in local politics (chapter 3) and in ritual (chapters 4, 5, and 6). In politics, power comes from below, from the segmentary nature of competing blocs and individuals seeking to *make a difference*. Similarly, in ritual it comes from below, from the earth *(ilè)*, from the dead, from ponds and streams, and from the *deep* knowledge which subverts official orthodoxies. This distinction between politics and ritual is, of course, relative, since there is always ritual in politics and politics in ritual. How could it be otherwise, since both are predicated on a negative dialectic that is shaped and sustained by a hermeneutical vision?

What, then, about power from above—such as state power, dictatorship, or the power of a ruling class? Here I would argue that the definition still holds. State power remains oppositional in its capacity to put down the people; such power is meaningless without opposition or resistance from below, and it in effect appropriates it. Power from above is often masked by rules of authority, but, *qua* power, it can always rewrite the rules. Is not authoritarianism about regimes which "author" their own authority, like Hobbes's sovereign (a "Mortall God" and supreme "author" [1986:227]), monopolizing official truth? Under such extreme conditions, the critics and intellectuals go to jail precisely because their voices are powerful, contesting the regime's authoritative illusions. Wole Soyinka's *The Man Died* remains an eloquent testament to the fate of the critic under Gowon. Recently the Babangida regime in Nigeria *decreed* that no military officer could be tried for embezzling state funds. It is also throwing prominent scholars in prison. Yet Nigerians are not fooled. It is obvious to everyone what is going on, but the prospects of elections scheduled for 1992 appear to outweigh the desirability of a countercoup. Nor are such abuses alien to Western democracies; they are built into the logic of effective government itself. Occasionally they surface into spectacular scandals. During Watergate, Nixon's break-in and wiretaps destroyed his presidency. As with Shango, who in one myth was playing with medicines and immolated himself and the palace with a bolt of lightning (Johnson 1921:150–51), Nixon's power undermined his authority. Reagan was luckier. His "Irangate" scandal formed, as one analyst put it, a "government within a government" to bypass Congress and illegally aid the Nicaraguan *contras*. Only John Poindexter served any jail time. In this case Reagan's ignorance proved to be his greatest asset, but few were deceived. In the last instance, Reagan wielded the power to violate the law with personal impunity and still finish his second term.

These examples illustrate a basic point: just as power is meaningful when structured by authority—an institutional as well as semantic structuring, to be sure—so meanings and discourses are powerful when they oppose, revise, or violate such authority. This dialectical relationship informs the guiding question of my study, which was to determine the conditions which render deep knowledge powerful. As we have seen, these conditions are both social, since powerful knowledge is restricted to specific groups and statuses, and epistemological, since restricted knowledge rests on privileged access to paradoxical truths. For the Yoruba, the deepest knowledge of all is formless, inchoate, and empty—pure negativity, in Turner's (and Hegel's) terms. It is not, as I have emphasized, a strict secret doctrine (although these may be posited at more "mediate" hermeneutical levels, in variable guises), but an interpretive space for the construction of difference. If deep knowledge is true by definition—original, safeguarded, ritually sanctioned, and cosmologically essential—it is conceived of as powerful because it *is* powerful, by virtue of its critical, revisionary, and even revolutionary possibilities, and more importantly by virtue of its concrete actualizations in political struggle and change.

These latter actualizations of hermeneutical *praxis*—including those examples which I identified between the rise of the Oyo empire and the 1983 elections—illustrate Yoruba history as one of sociopolitical transformation, as actual change in the "real" world, as critical difference (*différance?*) in motion. Clearly there are other Yoruba histories of this time—of private life, prejudices, sexuality, agricultural production, etiquette, or even historiography, to name a few. Historical topics are, of course, infinitely selectable and segmentable. But if we consider history in its most elementary sense, as "significant" social change over time (barring for the moment the question "significant for whom?"), the abstract definition of power as negation acquires an important diachronic value. Placed in whatever spatiotemporal frame—the local, the regional, or *la longue durée*—power as negation (revision, transgression, transformation, revolution) is what makes history itself, *qua* difference over time. Such unfoldings, of course, do not occur through the abstract agency of a totalizing *Geist*, but through the manifold activities of real people in the world. Whatever the specific historical interpretation, mediated as it must be through culture and politics, I am for now talking about history in its most abstract sense, as nothing other than some kind of social (including cultural, economic, political, etc.) transformation— that is, a history without content.

My intent is to extend the equation of liminality (antistructure) and power to include history as well, and to illustrate how and where they converge. If power as negation transforms society over time, and if abstract history is sociocultural change, we can say that power makes history; or, to rephrase Marx (and paraphrase Foucault), that all history is the history of power. Such history is of course blind, lacking specificity and meaning, and refers at this abstract level to a diachronic *property* of sociocultural systems. But if we posit this property as that which is conditioned—culturally segmented into spatiotemporal categories which include causes, effects, events, and contingencies—we see not only how history is made meaningful, but more importantly how history is made. Such a perspective makes no assumptions about historical objectivity, other than that transformation (however major or minor) is an objective property of sociocultural systems. The content of history is always culturally mediated; hence specific accounts of what "actually" happened—in fact, the "events" themselves, as Sahlins (1981, 1985) so cogently illustrates—can never be separated from cultural logics and schemes. The content of history is not "objective" but intersubjective; it is a form of interpretation which recalls and "documents" the past and which shapes the power of the past to bear upon the present.

History in this sense is always political because in recalling the past, it invokes political claims and can even precipitate change. The hermeneutics of power is necessarily a historiography as well, and on this the Yoruba historians have much to say. Deep history *(itàn)*, we have seen, is dangerous and subversive because it contradicts historical charters of kingship, chiefly rank, and lesser authoritative hierarchies with rival accounts of origins and deeds. The Yoruba historian, moreover, does not merely "tell" *(ní)* history, but "utters" *(pà)* it (as in *pà + itàn)*, just as one utters a command *(pà + àṣẹ)* or an incantation *(pà + ọfọ̀)* or invokes the power of an *òrìṣà*. In fact, the deepest histories of all, I was told, are expressed strictly in incantations—esoteric formulae which can actualize and kill. The verb *pà* also means "to kill" or "to strike," and in this sense we can say that deep history *strikes* with the hidden power to make a critical difference—to kill rivals, subvert authority, and in effect to make history. The secrets of *òrìṣà* cults are hidden histories narrated in fragments during ritual performances: in the songs, praises, invocations, and incantations of excited spectators and possessed devotees, and in the iconography of ritual *sacra*. These histories are literally powerful because they make the unthinkable audible, visible, possible, and when conditions are right, actual.

Deep history is thus history from "below" in the ritual and political sense of the term. If it carries the claims of an "original" truth tracing back to Ile-Ife, it also supports the interests of rivals—of the dominated, the dispossessed, or the dangerously ambitious. Unlike official history (such as Whig history), which "writes" present authority structures into the past (much like any mythic or historical character) to legitimize the status quo, deep history "rewrites" the past to contest, destabilize, and transform the present. Deep history is revisionary and powerful because it sees official history for what it is—the "noble" lies of sacred kings and their loyal subjects and followers. It negates the official past with deeper historical insight to produce a different future.

The empty center of Yoruba cosmology—the deepest level of its hermeneutical vision—is where meaning, power, and history converge and where the kingdom is ritually remade. In Turner's terms, we could say that ritual liminality, what we have equated with power itself, is the circumscribed site of history in the making. Its liberation from social and semantic constraints negates the king with the power of the past, which *is* the power to remake society and thus make history again. There follows a precarious "reconstructive" moment, when, if all goes well, the king is ritually reborn and recrowned. Is this not how the king is praised, in parts and wholes, with multiple histories and identities, embodying the power of his enemies and ancestors, the living terminus of an "original" genealogy which extends *ad futurum*?

I do not mean to suggest that ritual is the only site of historical practice, only that it is a privileged passage in time because it self-consciously remakes the social order, capturing the power of the past to refashion the present. Nor are such rituals restricted to town quarters and kingdoms, for the logic of empowerment extends to the limits of the meaningful world. During the 1983 elections, Ayede's priestesses sacrificed for a UPN victory to make a better Nigeria.[4] And after Buhari's military coup, they again invoked the òrìṣà to help control his soldiers. This is not to say that local rituals actually remake national policy. But on occasion they can, when they mobilize the power to wage effective protest against the state.

HEGEMONY AND RESISTANCE

Like the logic of ritual empowerment itself, the theory of ritual outlined above embraces larger discursive fields, and here I turn to consider its general import for the study of hegemony and resistance. I have used the term *hegemony* rather loosely throughout this study, to mean the domination and overrule of subject territories and populations, be it Yoruba, Christian, colonial, or statist. But as the growing literature attests, hegemony is a complex and slippery concept, whether we genuflect to Gramsci or return to the Greeks.[5] In current anthropological parlance, hegemony has come to mean a form of habituated and embodied knowledge which defines the given or "natural" world in ways which normalize everyday practices and thereby govern thought and action. The power of hegemony is exerted from above, by the totalizing visions of ruling elites and classes which silently inform the minds and bodies of their subjects. Hegemony is not a self-conscious strategy of domination, but, like Bourdieu's (1977) "habitus," it is internalized unwittingly by all. As defined by the Comaroffs (1991:23), hegemony refers to

> that order of signs and practices, relations and distinctions,
> images and epistemologies—drawn from an historically situated

field—that comes to be taken-for-granted as the natural and
received shape of the world and everything that inhabits it. It
consists, to paraphrase Bourdieu (1977:167) of things that go
without saying because being axiomatic, they come without
saying; things that, being presumptively shared, are not
normally the subject of explication or argument (1977:94). This is
why its power has so often been seen to lie in what it silences,
what it prevents people from thinking and saying, what it puts
beyond the limits of the rational and credible.

Hegemony is thus paradigmatically uncritical and mute. Once its hidden and axiomatic terms are exposed to discursive articulation and
negotiation, it "becomes something other than itself"–namely, the object of symbolic and ideological struggle (Comaroff and Comaroff
1991:24). Herein lie the roots of resistance, as contestation of the given
world and as the revision and revaluation of its most essential forms.

It is not resistance, however, but ideology which establishes the
most basic opposition to hegemony for the Comaroffs; not a binary
opposition, they emphasize, but "as the ends of a continuum" (ibid.,
28). Citing Raymond Williams (1977:109), they define ideology as "an
articulated system of meanings, values and beliefs of a kind that can be
abstracted as [the] 'worldview' of any social grouping," as that which
"provides an organizing scheme (a master narrative?) for collective symbolic production" and "is likely to be protected, even enforced, to the full
extent of the power of those who claim it for their own" (Comaroff and
Comaroff 1991:24). Whereas hegemony is "unconscious" in the sense
that it is "unseen," "submerged," and "unrecognized," ideology is
"conscious" in that it is "seen," "apprehended," and explicitly "cognized" (ibid., 29). The continuum leading from hegemony to ideology
thus defines a *"chain of consciousness"* (ibid.), in which different modalities of power (nonagentive and agentive) achieve increased clarity and
expression. Shared hegemonic structures are so deeply buried in cultural practices that their "meanings" reduce to the *formal* distinctions of
implicit taxonomies and basic cultural categories. Ideology establishes
the *content* of these forms, the beliefs and values of the meaningful world
as articulated in explicit and sometimes programmatic claims (ibid., 30).

One of the virtues of this analytical formulation is that it de-
ontologizes class as the exclusive site of hegemony and ideology,
although class division remains extremely salient when and where it
develops and must be historically situated (J. L. Comaroff 1982;
J. Comaroff 1985; Comaroff and Comaroff 1991). For the Comaroffs,
hegemony and ideology are constitutive modalities of *all* sociocultural

systems—as these systems exist in analytic "isolation," develop over time, and articulate with each other in more inclusive political and economic relations. Hegemony and ideology furthermore exist "in reciprocal interdependence" (Comaroff and Comaroff 1991:25)—if hegemony represents ideology naturalized, ideology represents hegemony conceptualized, in the prevailing visions of a dominant group or in the heterodox discourses of the excluded or oppressed. Since ideologies (whether dominant or dissenting) unmake hegemony, hegemony must constantly be remade (ibid.), in "the assertion of control over various modes of symbolic production; over such things as educational and ritual processes, patterns of socialization, political and legal procedures, canons of style and self-representation, public communication, health and bodily discipline, and so on" (ibid.). It is, moreover, in the "liminal space" between hegemony and ideology, the unconscious and conscious—a space of "partial recognition, of inchoate awareness, of ambiguous perception, and, sometimes, of creative tension" (ibid., 29)—that "new relations are forged between form and content" (ibid., 30) and thereby reconfigure power.

It is these reconfigurations, whether partially cognized or programmatically launched, which constitute variable modes of resistance per se, from counter-hegemonic bodily practices to overt ideological struggles. The question becomes not what is or is not resistance, but what forms it takes and with what political consequences. As recent research in Africa illustrates, the forms are predominantly (but not exclusively) religious because it is through idioms of ritual healing and empowerment that sociopolitical contradictions are re-cognized and controlled—with variable degrees of success and failure, to be sure, but practically apprehended nonetheless.[6] For it is precisely by constructing liminal moments that power can be seized to make a difference, in hegemony, ideology, history, and historical consciousness. In this sense resistance lies at the empty center of ritual, where it unites with power and history. In Yoruba ritual, the commanding heights are appropriated by òrìṣà cults, recentered in their shrines and reinvested with new meanings which reconfigure the dominant order. As we have seen, subject kingdoms resisted the Oyo empire, civil chiefs resisted their kings, òrìṣà cults throughout Yorubaland resisted Christianity and colonialism and, more recently, the Nigerian state. I am not suggesting that òrìṣà cults hold a monopoly on resistance. The proliferation of African churches—Aladura, Cherubim and Seraphim, and the Celestial Church of Christ, among the most prominent—has produced new sites and idioms of collective symbolic struggle. But here the same hermeneutical principles are at work, restructuring

Yoruba and Christian cosmologies and recombining their codes to invoke new spirits of resistance.[7]

Located within the hegemony-ideology continuum, the critical power of deep Yoruba knowledge at first appears paradoxical. Like hegemony, it is hidden, submerged, and embodied—quite literally inscribed on the bodies of initiates and devotees. And like hegemony, it "opposes" official ideology since, analytically speaking, deep knowledge retreats as public discourse approaches. But it also opposes ideology critically, by revaluing its signs with subversive interpretations. If the deepest knowledge, like hegemony, is semantically empty, it is, unlike hegemony, self-conscious of its emptiness and of the conditions which make such emptiness powerful. When Barber (1981) explains "how man makes God in West Africa," she identifies the place of self-conscious agency in Yoruba religion: the ability of the devotee to impress upon her deity, to abandon her spiritual patron for another, and thus to restructure the balance of religious debts and obligations. For in the last instance, as every Yoruba knows, the òrìṣà depend on people—on their capacity to feed them, glorify them, and keep their secrets secret. This insight extends to the public domain. Just as the individual can change his or her relationship to a particular òrìṣà, so can the polity, collectively and through its segments, revise the pantheon of òrìṣà on which it is based. In so doing, it mobilizes hidden powers, subversive interpretations, and rival factions to reproduce and transform political hierarchies. If the contradictions of effective government are "mystified" by official religious claims, they are self-consciously mystified by those cult elders who understand the powerful implications of their public roles and of the deeper wisdom, or *gnosis*, which remakes the world.

Deep knowledge is thus paradoxical because, though empty and hegemonic, it is also critically reflexive—more "conscious," in fact, than the explicit discourse of a dominant ideology. But this paradox actually demonstrates the dialectic of hegemony and ideology at work, revealing the conceptual space where each remakes the other, as well as the power deployed in the process. Hegemonically hidden within the unseen forces of the Yoruba world, deep knowledge is ideologically acknowledged as too profound and dangerous to openly articulate. When deployed in rituals of regeneration and renewal—"fertility rites," as the early ethnographers perceived them (and ideologically speaking they were correct)—deep knowledge literally transforms the body politic, bringing hegemonic form and the power of its sanctioned possibilities to shape new political realities. The logic of such transfiguration was not erased by Christians and colonizers, for their own categories and narratives fed right into it. As we saw in the texts of Bishop Crowther and Samuel Johnson, mastering the canons of Christian learning and culture did not entail blind allegiance to its dictates (or proselytizers), but rather a deeper conversion toward an independent church and eventually an independent Nigeria. Yoruba "readings" of Christian dogma turned its messages around, creating new possibilities of collective empowerment as colonialism intensified.

In the New World this process has developed with an even greater energy, where the spiritual agents of Catholic saints have been identified with specific òrìṣà and "African powers." Beneath the icons of Saint Anthony, Saint Lazarus, Saint Barbara, and Saint Regla we find Ogun, Obatala, Shango, and Yemoja. Such associations are not static or fixed, but like the indeterminate identities of the Yoruba òrìṣà, they vary locally, regionally, nationally, and over time (Herskovits 1966). This appropriation of Catholicism (a "hegemonic" religion if there ever was one) by African gods has played a well-documented role in black revolution and resistance—first against slavery and later against discrimination and class oppression, although today it is growing throughout all sectors of these societies. The old issues of New World "syncretism" and "acculturation" are ripe for rethinking, along the more hermeneutical lines developed in this study. The question of whose hermeneutics, and its history and development, are "hot" topics today because they touch on the production of new counterhegemonies and ideological struggles.

THE CHALLENGE OF POSTMODERNISM

This latter question of "whose hermeneutics?" brings the argument of this study back full circle and releases the demons of postmodern criticism. I will not review this literature and its debates, save only to highlight its most basic implications for Africanist anthropology. Foremost is the interrogation of ethnographic discourse—of ethnography's construction of an "exotic" alterity by hidden rhetorical forms. Narrative conventions such as the ethnographic present, invocations of ethnographic authority, divisions of cultures into "kinship," "politics," "religion," "economy," etc., as well as staging the scenes of everyday life, coloring ethnographic landscapes, locating peoples in longitudes and latitudes, and, perhaps most importantly, imposing theoretical closure on the lives of a people—all are among the many strategies which silently shape the other and appropriate its voices in the name of speaking "for them."[8] Critiques of these conventions are powerful because they bring the discursive forms of Western hegemony into open ideological confrontation. Solutions to this challenge have, to date, been largely negative. Ethnography is either impossible, consigned evermore to history and literature; or it is experimental, reproducing the fragmentary chaos of fieldwork in postmodern pastiches and novels.

The most radical and stimulating critique of Africanist discourse comes from Mudimbe (1988), to whom, I will argue, the Yoruba still have something to say. Mudimbe identifies African philosophy as *gnosis*, including methods of inquiry and knowing which emphasize a "higher and esoteric knowledge . . . under specific procedures for its use as well as transmission" (ibid., ix). This *gnosis* is what the Yoruba would call deep knowledge. But here lies the catch. *Gnosis* for Mudimbe is a duplicitous category, anchoring the form and content of vernacular African philosophies within those Western discourses which purport to represent them. *Gnosis* is as much the product of Africanist discourses as the object of their inquiry, and it is the images, inventions, and "translations" of African alterity by the West which command Mudimbe's critical attention. Of the African worlds portrayed by Western scholarship, Mudimbe asks, "Is not this reality distorted in the expression of African modalities in non-African languages? Is it not inverted, modified by anthropological and philosophical categories used by specialists in dominant discourses?" (ibid., 186). This critique is not limited to Western scholars, but extends to African intellectuals who remain unwitting heirs to a colonial mentality (ibid., 69).

There is much more to Mudimbe's brilliant exposition, but this argument is central and poses a fundamental challenge to any study of an African culture's hermeneutics, whatever its ethnic or regional attribution. Briefly stated, how do we know that "their" hermeneutics of power is really theirs and not "ours"? The invocation of Giddens's "double hermeneutic" may provide a methodological solution, but is it theoretically defensible? Are not the very forms of "our" understanding shaped by the legacy of colonial conquest and infused with the conceits of a liberal imagination which exposes its paternalism in cultivated sympathy and "mystical participation" (ibid., 145)? These are disturbing questions which cannot be sidestepped and which have no satisfactory answers—at least not for Africanists who still believe in anthropology. I hold no illusions about the error built into the ethnographic gaze; but I can respond with two political counterarguments, since it is issues about power and its representation which are at stake.

Both counterarguments are extremely simple. The first replaces Mudimbe's "all or nothing" method (one proposed by Plato in the *Phaedo* [100a]) with Aristotle's "method of more and less" (Wells 1977:12). We know from logic (Quine 1960:26–79) and critical theory (e.g., Derrida 1976) that perfect linguistic (and by extension cultural) translation is impossible. But this should not blind us to the empirical fact that some translations are "better"—more culturally accurate, less ideologically loaded—than others. By this account, if perfect ethnography is clearly impossible, bad ethnography is not. From this less than auspicious beginning, we can continue to write better ethnography—if not politically innocent, at least more conscious of its implications and sensitive to its distortions.

Mudimbe, however, is arguing from foundations, not facts, and he might not accept this argument. For him, the validity of Africanist anthropology is undermined by its historical genesis and development, in that its "facts" are forged by the very hegemonies which invented the African other. To this most fundamental challenge, I can only reply that the alternative is even worse. There is a danger that the denial of "Africa" silences Africans' voices in their conversations with the West and allows for an even greater play of grotesque Western fantasies. This is not what Mudimbe's own work entails, since the debates which he and like-minded critics have inspired are *about* (among other things) African philosophy and do produce meaningful dialogues about decolonizing the mind.[9] His radical critique is powerful precisely because it forces Africanist discourse to examine its limits. If as a philosophy it leads us down Hegel's "highway of despair" (Hegel [1807] 1967:135), as a methodological tool its positive function is to produce more sensitive research and discussion. This might be Mudimbe's response to my political counterarguments.

It is in this spirit that I have ventured into a hermeneutics of power, not knowingly or willingly at first, but out of necessity. The "data" on Yoruba òrìṣà worship which I set out to "collect" were not forthcoming, for reasons which only gradually became clear. The power of deep knowledge was real enough, since it dominated and thwarted my efforts. But how real, and in what ways, emerged much later. The multiple discourses of Yoruba ritual—with its revisionary logic, fragmented histories, ironic voices, and infinite depth—challenge postmodernism with an empty center which still holds. And the conditions of its holding are critical. As one *babaláwo* gleefully explained, addressing me by my Yoruba name: "Ogundele, it is only because we love you that you are not dead."

NOTES

Introduction

1. See Hountondji 1983 for a sustained critique of the ethnophilosophical project as developed by Tempels [1945] 1959 and Griaule [1948] 1965. See also Mudimbe 1988:135–86.

2. The literature on black diaspora cultures is vast. Basic studies include Abrahams and Szwed 1983; Barnes 1989; Bascom 1950, 1972, 1980; Bastide 1971, 1978; Cabrera 1975; Harris 1982; Herskovits 1966; Hurston 1938; Kilson and Rotberg 1975; Murphy 1988; Simpson 1978; R. F. Thompson 1983; V. B. Thompson 1987; and Verger 1957, 1982.

3. These and other seminal studies include Abimbola 1976; Abiodun 1987; Afolayan 1982; Ajayi 1965; Akinjogbin 1967; Akintoye 1971; Asiwaju 1976; Atanda 1973; Awe 1964, 1965; Ayandele 1966, 1970; Babalola 1966; Biobaku 1957, 1973; Fadipe 1970; Gbadamosi 1978; Ogunba 1967; and Olatunji 1984.

4. See Brown 1989 for one of the most sensitive and ambitious studies of Santería sacred idioms and ritual kinship.

5. Landmarks of the Griaule school which focus on vernacular texts and traditions include Griaule 1938, [1948] 1965; Griaule and Dieterlen 1951, 1965; Dieterlen 1951; Leiris 1948; Rouch 1960; and Calame-Griaule 1965.

6. By *hermeneutics* I mean a set of interpretive strategies which disclose multiple levels of the "truth" within a text, discourse, or other symbolic expression. These truths cannot be truth-functionally defined, since the "deeper" levels are not consistently disclosed but allow agents to assert their restricted access to hidden knowledge and powers instead. In this sense, the levels are more adequately described by assertibility conditions (see Appiah 1985:157) and felicity conditions. The hermeneutical system can thus be described as an increasingly restricted series of pragmatic metalevels (or orders) which form a hierarchy of logical types. This perspective "solves" what otherwise appear as paradoxical interpretations of the same ritual activity by associating the "deeper" meanings with "higher" metalevels (the way Bertrand Russell solves the Cretan's paradox). Ritual itself—acknowledged publicly and transparently as instrumental activity—is the first metalevel (second order) in relation to the ordinary discourse of secular life. The knowledge of the initiate ascends the hierarchy of levels—each of which reflects on the level "below" it—according to different assertibility and felicity conditions, which are social and political as well as semantic. This may at least partially account for why the most important ritual symbols and expressions are metaphorical and metapragmatic as well as socially and politically efficacious. I believe that this was the direction that Bateson began to explore in his 1958 epilogue to *Naven;* his attention, however,

focused more on the metalevels of his own explanatory framework than on those of the Iatmul interpretations themselves. In his posthumous *Angels Fear* (1987), Bateson develops a more positive logical theory of the sacred along these lines.

More generally, the history of hermeneutics from biblical scholasticism to modern Continental philosophy and social science lies beyond the scope of this study, although it remains relevant to the Yoruba material, including the Yoruba missionary texts discussed in chapter 9. Useful studies include Bauman 1978; Gadamer 1976; Hekman 1986; Proudfoot 1985:48–60; J. B. Thompson 1981; and Ricoeur 1981.

7. My use of "heterodox" discourse derives from Bourdieu's (1977:168–69) formulation—as conscious opposition to official dogma—but differs in that contests for power (implied by all forms of political segmentation and sectional competition) rather than class division per se constitute its "objective conditions." Whereas Bourdieu would argue that heterodox discourses could not arise in precapitalist Yorubaland, I argue that they remained enshrined in "deep" knowledge, as a latent political resource for mobilizing collective action and structural change. When such oppositional discourses are officialized (into a new orthodoxy) by successful mobilization, such as a ruling dynastic shift or reranking of chieftaincy titles, they immediately confront the heterodox challenges of rivals.

8. By "Yoruba society" I mean an abstract field of social relations and representations which underlie empirical variations in specific kingdoms and communities and which inform Yoruba conceptions of their common ethnic identity and social life. It is neither a colonial construction like "tribe" nor an essentialist reification like "race." It is an analytical construction which unifies the bewildering variety of subcultural variations for theoretical discussion. What, indeed, is the alternative? "Among the Yoruba people" (substituted for "Yoruba society") is one possibility, but it suggests a false empiricism which accomplishes the same task in a clumsier way. To be sure, Yoruba society is transformed by colonialism, Christianity, and global markets, but this only illustrates the utility of the concept. Without it, the transformations cannot be traced.

9. Indigenous ritual and cosmological responses to Islamic *jihad* and its religious institutionalization in Yorubaland (from 1804 to the present) are glaringly absent in this study; they represent a rich topic for further research. Since Ekitiland (unlike, for example, Oyo North) is predominantly Christian, I was not well placed to pursue such a topic. See Gbadamosi 1978 and Laitin 1986:38–42, 51–75.

Chapter One

1. By *historiography* I mean the method of writing history. The structural study of myth, in this context, applies more to the comparison of variant myths

than to their historical interpretation. For a cogent critique of structuralist methodology in African history, see Vansina 1983.

2. This "puzzle" is most recently discussed in Horton 1979:119–28.

3. Lloyd 1955:21; Law 1973. Cf. Agiri (1975:7), who glosses creation myths as "cosmological" and migration myths as "political"—a misleading distinction, since both types have political implications.

4. Cf. Obayemi 1979 for the strongest critique of the early Ile-Ife hegemony thesis. Obayemi argues that Ife became important as the manufacturing center of a glass *sègi* beads used to make the beaded crowns of sacred Yoruba kings.

5. Folk etymologies of kingship and chiefship titles are really statements about political status and are usually without sound linguistic foundation. See J. D. Y. Peel 1980:225–35, passim for general features of Yoruba political titles and particular features of the Ilesha title system.

6. I collected an interesting variant of this tradition in Akure, merging the Ife and Oyo versions, in which the first *Ọ̀ni* was the son of a female slave who was impregnated by Oduduwa.

7. For Ede, compare MacRow 1955:239 and Johnson 1921:125; for Egba, compare Biobaku 1957:4 and Johnson 1921:8, for Ijebu, compare Lloyd 1961:7 and Johnson 1921:20.

8. I have discussed the semiotics of tonal transfer in Yoruba *dùndún* and *bàtá* drum languages and the performative functions of their utterances in two working papers: "Tone-bearing Units in Yoruba Speech Surrogates" (1982) and "Yoruba Talking Drums and Ritual Communication" (1981). The best ethnological study of Yoruba drums is Thieme 1969.

9. J. D. Y. Peel's observation (1979:132) that in Ilesha "the sequence of the festivals of royal ancestors might seem likely to preserve the order of succession, perhaps even be oral tradition's mnemonic for it" illustrates how a ritual sequence can recapitulate and preserve sequence in oral tradition.

10. Lloyd (1955:25) writes that "when an oba is installed he often re-enacts the final part of the journey of his ancestor to the town . . . Along the route are often shrines at which annual sacrifices must be made, each such action recalling the myth which describes the original purpose of the shrine. It is for these reasons that the route is only remembered within the kingdom." Agiri (1975:3) relates that among the *Aláàfin*'s praise-singers *(arọkin)*, "it is the duty of the *Ológbò* to recite at one of the crucial installation ceremonies of the new *Aláàfin* the legend concerning the migration of the ancestors of the Oyo kings," and that "in the precolonial times, any unsatisfactory rendering of the traditions on this occasion carried very dire consequences."

11. William Bascom (1944) classified *òrìṣà* cults into two types, "single-sib" and "multi-sib." Whereas single-sib cults represent agnatic descent groups, multi-sib cults transcend unilineal principles of recruitment, and there Bascom let the matter stand. Had he realized that corporate descent groups ("sibs," in his terminology) constitute the political segments of quarters *(àdúgbò)* and that

these constitute political segments of towns, he would have identified political segmentation as the unifying principle of "single-sib" and "multi-sib" òrìṣà cults.

12. Cf. Ajayi 1974; Lloyd 1954; Ogunba 1967; J. D. Y. Peel 1983; Barber 1981.

13. According to Lloyd (1955:25), "The subordinate towns usually retain their original myths, but any attempt to assert them, and thus threaten the integrity of the kingdom, was, in the past, met by raiding and possible destruction of the town."

14. Based on Wescott and Morton-Williams 1958. Cf. Beier 1958 for an account of a similar subordinate-town ritual—that of Iragbaji in relation to Ilesha.

15. Not all subordinate towns were conquered; some originated as farm settlements, while others sought the protection of more powerful allies.

16. The formal relations I identify in this chapter between capital and subordinate towns and their dominant òrìṣà cults also obtain between lineages and their cults within quarters and between quarters and their cults within towns (see Apter 1987). Each political unit has its own historical traditions (ìtàn), reproduced by ritual, which rival the ọba's official history of the kingdom.

17. Important studies of Old Oyo include Ajayi 1974; Akinjogbin 1966; Law 1977; Lloyd 1971; Morton-Williams 1967.

18. According to Mabogunje and Omer-Cooper (1971:17), "The Alafin's position as representative of Sango was exploited to the full as a means of supporting his authority. The Sango cult was spread to every town under Oyo influence and organised in a hierarchy centered in the palace at Oyo. The Alafin's Ajele were often themselves Sango priests. This added to their authority at the courts of vassal rulers who were nevertheless divine kings in their own right. By passing into a state of spiritual possession, the Ajele whose personal status was the lowly one of a palace slave, would participate in divinity and be in a position to exercise authority equal to that of a vassal king."

19. Fear of Shango did not always deter political revolt. The successful revolt of the Egba against Oyo, led by Lisabi sometime between 1775 and 1780, began with the massacre of the ìlàrí throughout Egbaland. See Biobaku 1957:8–9.

20. According to Abimbola (1975:2–4), iyèrè chanting preserves the "true" Ifa text against "spurious" revisions:

> The chanting of iyèrè is a well-developed art among Ifa priests and it is usually done in choral form, led by someone who is a good chanter. To every complete sentence chanted correctly by the leader of the chant, the other Ifa priests chant han-in, meaning "Yes, that is right". However, if a leader has chanted a sentence wrongly, the other priests inform him of this and tell him to correct his mistake. If he makes another mistake, he might be shouted down and he who is sure of himself immediately takes over from him. Where a priest makes serious mistakes while chanting and refused to stop chanting in defiance of the wishes of the congrega-

tion, he might even be thrown out of the meeting in shame. By this rigid insistence on the correct recital of Ifa texts, Ifa priests have made it almost impossible for spurious passages to appear in the Ifa literary corpus.

Such a statement reflects more the ideological importance of the text's "authenticity" than its philological achievement, a point developed in the chapter's conclusion.

21. See Beier 1959; Johnson 1921:156; Law 1977:36, 86, passim.

22. The second priest, the *Olúnwi*, is also referred to as *Jagun* (warrior) in Beier 1956a.

23. Verger (1957:459) mentions that Osalufon is the name given to Obatala in Ifon, but Beier may have been unaware of this particular derivation.

24. From Beier 1959:14; Verger 1957:443; and Adedeji 1966.

25. The struggle between Oduduwa and Obatala may well refer to a dispute over the kingship in Ife between two rival factions. See Adedeji 1966:90; and Verger 1982:252–54, in which "Obatala" may have solicited Igbo support.

26. Iconographic associations between Eshu and Shango on the *làbà* panel are documented and discussed by Wescott and Morton-Williams (1962). Also note how Eshu's spilling of palm oil on Osalufon's (i.e., Obatala's) white cloth would change the cloth to red and white, which are Shango's colors.

27. Notice how Shango remains blameless, since the mistake is made by his "servants." The Oyo empire is thus not held politically responsible for Obatala's (Osalufon's) incarceration.

28. See Beier 1959:14; Verger 1957:440, 473–75; Verger 1982:255–65. Law (1977:88) documents that Ejigbo was once an Ife town that was later incorporated into Oyo.

29. See Verger 1982:252. Johnson (1921:27) suggests that Orishanla is the "generic" deity designated by Orisha Oluofin at Iwofin; Orishako at Oko; Orishakire at Ikire; Orishagiyan at Ejigbo; Orishaeguin at Eguin; Orisharowu at Owu; Orishajaye at Ijaye; and Obatala at Oba. If the dominant *òrìṣà* of local kingdoms are thereby appropriated and subsumed by the Oyo empire, they never completely lose their distinct identities. The theory that Obatala represents a cult of ritual surrender to the *Aláàfin* is further supported by Belasco's (1980:123) claim that "Obatala's revolutionary fragmentation is to be understood in the context of Oyo's emerging imperial thrusts to the coast," but he uncritically accepts Beier's thesis that Obatala represents "an ancestral autochthonous culture" (ibid., 109), an assumption which is not required by the ritual-field theory.

30. Not all ritualized mock battles are by implication records of conquest. J. D. Y. Peel (1980:236–38) argues that ritualized conflict in Ilesha's Iwude Ogun ceremony represents an actual conflict between the *Qwálùṣẹ* (a former Ilesha king) and his townspeople which became the paradigm for the "stereotypical reproduction" of similar conflicts and of the contested relationship between king and people in general.

31. See Law 1977:59. Obayemi (1979:171), who accepts Beier's aboriginal theory, estimates that the Oduduwa "revolution" occurred in the eleventh or twelfth century.

32. Note how "post-fifteenth century" Ife really concerns Ife from the mid-seventeenth century to the fall of Old Oyo c. 1830.

33. Horton argues that this interpretation also accounts for two otherwise-inexplicable features of Yoruba religion: (1) the homogeneity of the *odù* of Ifa throughout Yorubaland; and (2) the coexistence in Yoruba kingdoms of both pan-Yoruba and purely local *òrìṣà* rites and traditions. Though I cannot engage in a protracted argument here, I would maintain that the ritual-field theory accounts for the first feature as an ideological claim (which is all that it is) and for the second feature as built into the very logic of the Ife-centric ritual field.

Chapter Two

1. Johnson (1921:23) ranks the *Àtá* of Ayede as tenth among the sixteen "original" kings; cf. Oguntuyi (1979:49).

2. Like the *Ọwá* of Ilesha, no *ọba* tracing descent from Oduduwa through a maternal link can wear a beaded crown with a bird on it *(adé Olókun)*.

3. In the neighboring town of Ishan, the fusion of three *àrẹ* grades into one is called *àrẹ mẹ̀tà* (three *àrẹ*).

4. This tradition *(itàn)* was narrated to explain how the *Olú*'s title, initially vested in Imela lineage of Owaiye quarter, came to rotate between quarters. After the *Olú*'s deposition (whereby he became an *òrìṣà*), his wives returned to their fathers' compounds with their children, thereby activating claims to the title through complementary filiation.

5. When the present *Àtá* of Ayede, Samson Omotosho II, was questioned by the Ondo State Chieftaincy Review Commission about Eshubiyi's paternity in order to determine the genealogical depth and span of the ruling house, he replied under oath that he did not know (Ondo State Chieftaincy Review Commission on Daily Proceedings, no. 153, 16 August, 1978:43–44).

6. May's mission was to open up a direct route between Lagos or the sea and the trading post at the confluence of "the Kwora and Binue" (i.e., Kwara and Benue) rivers (May 1860:213–14).

7. Ote-muru is the place-name of the Orisha Ojuna cult's sacred water in Ikole and later in Ayede.

8. The title actually comes from the *Àtá* of Igala (Idah), a warrior-king whom Eshubiyi allegedly befriended and later betrayed. The title might have appealed to Eshubiyi because it represents, in Igala kingship, a dynastic break from the *Ọba* of Benin (Boston 1968:13; Akintoye 1971:65). One of Eshubiyi's praises is *jagun bí Àtá ní Gara*, or "warrior like the *Àtá* of Gara" (where Gara [Gbara] is the capital of Igala).

9. Omole-Akodi means roughly "those under the protection of a powerful person." The "powerful person" refers to the war chief *Balógun Èkìtì*, who came from Opin, not the *Balógun À\\àfin* from Alu.

10. The same belief applies to lineage cults within quarters. The relative poverty of Inisa lineage in Ishan's Irefin quarter and the deaths of some of its younger members in the last decade are attributed to the decline of its Oshun cult.

11. Many of these herbalists come from Ilaaro quarter, whose chief, the *Obáàrò*, occupies an important post as the king's herbalist.

12. These consist of dog (except for devotees of Ogun), day-old pounded yam *(iyán àná)*, and food "talked over" while prepared, because of saliva which could enter into it.

13. The figure of a crossroads in this tradition represents the liminality, danger, threshold, and crossing which make crossroads within any town the privileged place of sacrifice. In political terms, crossroads represent the intersection of chiefly jurisdictions; in ritual terms, they constitute sites of communication with Eshu, witches, and other *òrìṣà*.

14. This is the same Elegunmi who became a military chief in Ayede and holds a post in the Orisha Ojuna cult.

15. A complex association is here developed between sacred water—which, contained by an animal horn (called *àṣẹ*), possesses *àṣẹ* (the capacity of speech to influence the future)—and the founding of the kingdom.

16. *Ìdìyá* is the locus of Ayede's origin, where Eshubiyi allegedly threw his spear into a tree (or, alternatively, the ground) and declared that he would establish the town.

Chapter Three

1. Where Smith uses the terms *bushmen* and *bushman band*, I use *San kindreds* instead. For an excellent critique of the "bushman" trope of the primitive, see Wilmsen 1989.

2. Cf. Abraham 1962:222. Jacob Ade Ajayi has informed me that this interpretation of *àfóbàjé* is incorrect; the word is in fact a contraction of *a fí ọba jẹ* (we take the king to eat). This meaning is even more dangerous and subversive, as we shall see in chapters 4 and 5.

3. The confrontation in Okuku between Elemona and the *ọba* may well have been ritually staged every year. Pemberton (1979:90) describes a similar confrontation in Ila between a civil chief called *Ẹlẹ̀mọ̀nà* (representing the senior town chiefs) and the *ọba* which takes place during the town's Ogun festival.

4. The importance of slaves for traditional Big Manship is illustrated by a story about the *Ọ̀tún* Osinkolu, the wealthy military chief who survived Eshubiyi and ruled as a regent (see fig. 3.1). In 1901, after the British decreed that all slaves be set free, he allegedly "died one hour after hearing the news."

Chapter Four

1. It is not by chance that the resident NEPA (National Electrical Power Authority) official in Ayede worships Shango, although the official is also a mem-

ber of the local Aladura Church. Since he works with power lines and surging electrical currents, he seeks Shango's protection against fatal shocks.

2. Yam which flies out of the mortar *(odó)* while pounded "belongs" to Eshu, probably because it refuses to be contained.

3. Reading the kola is an esoteric skill based on a variety of systems and techniques. The priestesses in Ayede split kola into four pieces, two "male" and two "female," each of which can fall "up" or "down." The sixteen combinatorial possibilities invoke the sixteen *odù* of Ifa, although how precisely I was unable to determine. A good toss is two pieces up and two down; but the best tosses are either three up and one down (Father) or one up and three down (Mother). The worst tosses are either all four up or all four down; they are associated with false spirits such as *ikú* (death), *àrùn* (disease), *òfò* (loss), *èse* (accident), *èwòn* (bondage), *àjé* (witches), and other pernicious manifestations.

4. The proverb cited by R. F. Thompson (1976, frontispiece) as a cardinal principle of Yoruba aesthetics expresses this bond between gods and kings: *Tí a kò bá da omi s'íwájú, a kò lè te ilè tútù*, which translates roughly as "When we don't pour water down in front, we can't walk on cool [i.e., safe, level] ground." Sabotaging a ritual calabash is a common theme in discussions of inter-kingdom conflict. One of my friends in Ayede proudly related how his father, a powerful hunter, shot a ritual calabash during the royal Agunlele festival in the neighboring kingdom of Itaji in order to help settle a land dispute in Ayede's favor. My friend explained that Itaji lost the case in court because his father had sabotaged their festival, but added that his father soon died from the calabash's protective medicines and powers.

5. The ritual salute, or homage *(ìjúbà)*, extends the right foot forward to touch the ground three times, with arms raised forward and hands closed. Lead priestesses walking with a staff *(opa olósorò)* will strike the ground with its base to produce a rattling sound while the front foot touches down.

6. For the general importance of seniority in Yoruba society, see Bascom 1942.

7. I owe this fragment of an incantation to Roland Abiodun, who suggested its association with the *abèbè* icon. The incantation illustrates the morphosyntax of *àse*—the power of actualization—by abstracting the reduplicated *bè* in *abèbè* to form the verb of the utterance ("to beg [cool]") and thereby activate its power.

8. I suspect that the subversive number three of the Ogboni "earth" cult is also signified during two critical moments of ritual already described—when the ram's severed head is lifted and lowered three times during the king's sacrifice, and when the Yemoja priestess with the calabash on her head turns toward and away from the king three times. These are both liminal moments of the king's revitalization, veritable thresholds of his political survival, during which the Ogboni cult may be ultimately in charge. I know that the two top priestesses of the Yemoja cult hold senior titles in the Ogboni cult as well, as do the *àwòrò*; but I was unable to determine the precise articulation between the Ogboni cult and the *òrìṣà* cults as ritual corporations. Such information is high-

ly classified. For an attempted sketch of these relations in Old Oyo, see Morton-Williams 1964.

9. Other accounts (e.g., Johnson 1921) state that parrot eggs (not feathers) are sent in a calabash to command the king's suicide. Whether the feathers stand for eggs by association or represent the command in and of themselves is impossible for me to determine. I can only record what I was told by a cult member.

10. Some of the deepest ritual secrets concern the preparation of powerful medicines from the deceased king's body parts. I would like to discuss these procedures (how and where the corpse is cut and dismembered, buried, exhumed, and cooked) to deepen my analysis and strengthen my argument, but on this very touchy subject I feel obliged to keep quiet.

11. The same parallelism may well extend to the accompanying priestesses with "water" on their heads, in that their "putting down" of water at the town shrine corresponds to the breaking of water in the labor of childbirth. This interpretation is obliquely supported by a story from one of the priestesses. When I asked her if she knew of a time when a priestess dropped her "water" during the festival, she said no, but that once when the ọlọ́ọ̀tun of Orisha Ojuna were carrying their water, a witch suddenly seized an ọ̀tun bottle from a priestess's head and left it suspended in the air for one hour. The festival was held up until the bottle was "released' with incantations (at which point a bird fell dead from a tree) and returned without mishap to its carrier. This story reveals an interesting association between the normal role of witches in sabotaging childbirth and the role of this particular witch in sabotaging the priestess's "delivery" of water.

12. Note how witchcraft subverts fertility in this explanation by inverting with near-perfect symmetry the "normal" logic of insemination and sexual reproduction. I mention this because it supports the idea that witchcraft and fertility are inversely related as irreducible values of female power. For a more symbolic but less politically grounded analysis of the "structurally female," see Matory 1986:61–68. See also Oyesakin 1982 for a thematic discussion of witchcraft and fertility (and related values) in Ifa divination texts.

13. Cf. Pemberton 1988:62 for an Ijebu Yoruba permutation of this theme in the Agemo festival. I should add that the witchcraft and fertility of female power also relate to women's economic roles in markets, where women block the flow of capital through accumulation (eating the "blood" of market circulation) as they exchange their husbands' produce and other products in sales. Furthermore, as they accumulate wealth, they can "snatch" their children from paternal control through lineage optation and can precipitate domestic strife through competition for inherited wealth between groups of full siblings (ọmọ̀ìyá) in a polygynous household. I have discussed these dynamics in "Atinga Revisited: Yoruba Witchcraft and the Cocoa Economy, 1950–1951" (forthcoming). See also Belasco 1980 for an elaboration of some of these themes.

14. In Iye dialect; "Ṣ'óo rí baba t'ó jókòó ìí, iye ọjọ́ó kù lámọ̀ọ́dún baba ti mọ̀ ọ́n, àmọ́é tì ní sọ ọ́ fún a."

15. Thus, installation rituals require that a new king ingest the "heart" of his predecessor (actually, it is more than just the heart), ensuring that he too will be "eaten" when his time comes. Continuity of bodily substance is thereby sustained throughout the "line" of kings and traces back to original kingship at Ile-Ife.

Chapter Five

1. My Yoruba is by no means proficient enough to translate these texts, which pose interpretive challenges to many Yoruba as well. For their transcription into Yoruba and translation into English, I am indebted to Michael 'Dejo Afolayan's diligent assistance during the summer of 1988 in New Haven, Conn. The observation that àṣẹ is associated with utterances in which nouns reduplicate monosyllabic verbs, thereby nominalizing activity and agency through repetition (and vice versa, with verbs "activating" nominal powers), is his. Cf. Drewal and Drewal 1987:226 and Olatunji 1984:152–64.

2. E.g., Ẹkún ìyàwó (bridal chants); see Barber 1986.

3. The oríkì technically refers to the goddess Yemoja; in this ritual context it also refers to the Àtá of Ayede, thereby merging both identities.

4. Jí can mean "wake up" or "shock," as in òjìjí (electric eel); e.g., "Òjìjí jí mi lọ́wọ́" ("I got an electric shock from the electric eel") (in Abraham 1962:347).

5. I cannot disclose which body parts without revealing extremely closely guarded secrets. Suffice it to say that these parts are subsequently unburied, cooked, and pulverized into black powder to make the most powerful àṣẹ medicine of all.

Chapter Six

1. Horton's translation of àgbànlá as "ancestor" is extremely idiosyncratic— no Yoruba I have asked accepts it (nor does it appear in any major Yoruba dictionary). In Ilesha, Àgbànlá denotes the senior grade of civil chiefs (what are termed ìwàrèfà in standard models of Yoruba government) and appears to have a link with the Ogboni society (see J. D. Y. Peel 1980:228–31).

2. The cluster concept is closely related to Wittgenstein's concept of "family resemblances" (Wittgenstein 1958:32). Cf. the discussion of cluster theory in Searle 1969:162–74.

3. The idiom of the rebellious slave in this tradition may refer to the rise of Old Oyo from a subordinate town of Owu (Law 1977:37) to a great empire. More generally, it provides a mythic charter for the subversion or usurpation of metropolitan centers by subordinate towns. The image of a slave living in a hut characterizes the status of a subordinate town vis-à-vis a metropolitan center, a parallel which is morphologically supported by the derivation of abúlé (subordinate town, village) from abà (farm shack, hut) in Abraham 1962:10.

4. For a spirited critique of Yoruba pantheon models, see Matory 1986:18–24.

5. An Orisha Iyagba priestess said of Ẹ̀kùn, "He doesn't know what he is saying or doing. The *ìmọlẹ̀* [in this context, the "spirit" of the *òrìṣà*] is directing him. Ẹ̀kùn can make predictions; for example, he will tell a person to sacrifice a white cock to Ogun and Osanyin to prevent an accident while traveling, and the person must kill it in front of the house—then the person will go free without accident. Ẹ̀kùn can also predict for the king; he will tell the king to buy a keg of palm wine to share among his chiefs, so that he will not lose cases in court, cross an enemy, or fall when he walks."

6. The Esi-Onigogo shrine resembles Eshu shrines in markets throughout Yorubaland; it is alleged to contain the corpse of an albino cut into four pieces by Eshubiyi and placed within the mound. The "spirit" is primarily protective of the town and will wander at night to seize troublemakers. The nearby Ogun shrine is specifically associated with the Àtá of Ayede's ancestors. Unlike most Ogun shrines, which are associated with civil chiefs and receive sacrifices of decapitated dogs, the Àtá's Ogun shrine, associated with a ruling lineage, requires the decapitation of a dog which is already dead. The shrine also serves as the focus of the king's New Yam ceremony. Ayede's hunters sacrifice at a separate Ogun shrine.

7. The "food" of these spears is kola nut rubbed with shea butter (*òrí*) and palm oil and then stuck on the tip of the blade.

8. During the deposition proceedings against the Àtá Gabriel Osho, for example, the Orisha Iyagba cult avoided him. Representatives of Ayede's Yagba towns amassed in Ayede in a powerful public display which glorified the *Balógun Ààfin* but refused to *júbà* at the market and palace. The Yagba towns and strangers in Ayede were prepared to secede from Ayede District; the cult's festival "separated" Omole-Akodi quarter from the town but boycotted the subsequent routine of reintegration. The ritual performance was thus technically incomplete. After Gabriel Osho's deposition, the Yagba towns agreed to remain in the district, and the Orisha Iyagba cult restored its full ritual program in Ayede. Similarly, in neighboring Itaji kingdom, I witnessed the deterioration of ritual relations as Imojo, a subordinate town, asserted its independence. When Imojo belonged to Itaji, I was told, they cooked their festival food together, while their *egúngún* masquerades came out on the same day. In June of 1984, however, Imojo performed its *egúngún* festival separately, and it sent only two of its masqueraders to dance before the *Onítaji* instead of the customary six—much to the *Onítaji's* chagrin.

Chapter Seven

1. This song is sung in the Babatigbo cult's Ora dialect.

2. The late Baba Ayeni of Ejigbo quarter recalled these ritual texts during long discussions about Ayede and Iye. As a former District Court judge, he remembered some of these texts quoted as legal testimony.

3. Relevant novels in Yoruba and English are too numerous to cite. Some of

the classics are Tutuola 1953, 1954, 1958, 1982; Fagunwa 1982; and Soyinka 1963. The plate comes from Ogundele 1961:13.

4. The two carved effigies of white colonial officers in the Àtá's official chamber may well represent objects of ritual control—of tapping into and manipulating the white man's considerable power. Such effigies are in fact quite common throughout West Africa, as Africanist art historians are now documenting.

Chapter Eight

1. Important exceptions include Dent 1966; J. D. Y. Peel 1983:219–54; and Anifowose 1982.

2. For example, Coleman and Rosberg 1964; Lewis 1965. In both works, however, violence is peripheral to their considerable interest in one-party states. Cf. also Young 1982 and Diamond 1982.

3. Even where the "symbolic factor" in African politics is discussed, the focus remains on political elites—e.g., Cohen 1981; Hayward and Dumbuya 1983; Owusu 1986; and Sylvester 1986.

4. Throughout Obafemi Awolowo's campaign for the presidency, I heard rumors that he possessed a "fantastic jùjú" which protected him from rivals and intimidated his closest associates.

5. The irony of this situation is that Omoboriowo may well have defeated Ajasin in the UPN primaries, which some UPN politicians maintained were rigged for Ajasin. In other words, his reasons for decamping to the NPN may have involved sincere frustration with the UPN as well as political opportunism.

6. Since the electoral laws required Shagari to win 25 percent of the votes in two-thirds of the states, his 23 percent in Ondo represented a politically significant defeat.

7. Subsequent discussion with the man who arrived "from Ife" revealed that he had actually traveled from Ijero, the last leg of the road from Ife. The ideological importance of his Ife-centric statement is heightened by its factual inaccuracy.

8. These were their stated intentions. Fortunately, the girl had already escaped from the town.

Chapter Nine

1. Actually, it *is* a hybrid in Bhabha's (1985:153) "theory of 'hybridization' of discourse and power," which analyzes "hybridity" as "a *problematic* of colonial representation and individuation that reverses the effects of the colonialist disavowal, so that other 'denied' knowledges enter upon the dominant discourse and estrange the basis of its authority" (ibid., 156). Since this use of *hybrid* is counterintuitive, I avoid its signifier and explicate its signified as a form of revision or "rewriting" instead.

2. In the "research" section of her autobiography, Hurston ([1942] 1984b:205) thus explains that in Haiti, "the Sect Rouge, also known as the Cochon Gris (gray pig) and Ving Bra-Ding (from the sound of the small drum), a cannibalistic society there, has taken cover under the name of voodoo, but the two things are in no wise the same."

3. Soyinka (1976:xii) disdains "the colonial mentality of an Ajayi Crowther, West Africa's first black bishop, who grovelled before his white missionary superiors in a plea for patience, and understanding for his 'backward, heathen, brutish' brothers," especially because of the persistent neocolonial mentality in Nigeria today (cf. Soyinka 1984, particularly pp. 31–32 and his trenchant metacritique of Nigerian leftocracy); but I shall argue that at least seeds of subversion were disseminated by the man J. F. Ade Ajayi (1970a:xiii) describes as a "rather shadowy figure." Was this why Soyinka (1981:5), in his childhood, was haunted by Crowther's "strange transformations" and asked, "Was Bishop Crowther an *oro* [i.e., a "pagan" spirit]?" (ibid., 8).

4. The slave narrative of Cudjo Lewis's 1859 capture and sale to American slavers recorded by Hurston ([1942] 1984b:198–205) may be fruitfully compared with Crowther's narrative and read in a similar fashion (cf. also Stepto 1984 for a discussion of Frederick Douglass's "heroic slave" as an Afro-American narrative convention). Cudjo Lewis's claim that "his Nigerian religion was the same as Christianity" (Hurston [1942] 1984b:198) also resembles Johnson's "pagan" appropriation of Christianity (which follows) and Hurston's appropriation of Exodus in *Moses: Man of the Mountain* ([1939] 1984a).

5. See Hegel's ([1807] 1967:229–30) discussion of "sublation" and its *double entente* in the master-slave dialectic for a remarkable paradigm of doubling discourse which, ironically, transcends his racism.

6. See particularly Crowther's letter of 2 November 1841 to the CMS secretaries ([1842] 1970b:347–50); and his letter of 2 December 1854 to Rev. H. Venn ([1855] 1970c:xiii–xviii). See also Ajayi 1965:221–23 for historical clarification.

7. See, for example, Beier 1980:36–41; Soyinka 1976:26–32; Pemberton 1979.

8. In addition to the myths in Johnson's *History*, for interpretation of Ile-Ife in Yoruba creation and founding myths cf. Agiri 1975; Beier 1955; Horton 1979:119–28; Lloyd 1955; Obayemi 1979.

9. Like Ishmael Reed's *Mumbo Jumbo*, Johnson's *History* quite clearly "is both a book about texts and a book of texts, a composite narrative composed of sub-texts, pre-texts, post-texts and narratives-within-narratives" (Gates 1984:299).

10. Despite his sophistication as a reader, I think that Eco misses the "black" discourse of Candomble in "Whose Side Are the Orixa On?" (1986:103–22). Eco's misgiving that the cult serves "white" ideology is valid only when limited to "white" readings.

11. These voices also correspond to the concepts of "outer head" *(orí-ọdẹ)* and "inner head" *(orí-inú)* in Yoruba metaphysics and ideas of personal identity

discussed by Abiodun (1987). The public outer head masks the more sincere or subversive intentions of the private inner head.

Conclusion

1. The concept of liminality evolved considerably in Turner's later work (e.g., 1969, 1974, 1982). I focus on his classic article "Betwixt and Between: The Liminal Period in *Rites de Passage*" (first published in 1964) because of its paradigmatic clarity.

2. Note the similarity of this recombinatory logic to Lévi-Strauss's concept of bricolage, which J. Comaroff (1985:198) reworks into a more practical concept of "subversive bricolage" *qua* innovative symbolic practices which "deconstruct existing syntagmatic chains[,] . . . disrupt paradigmatic associations and, therefore . . . undermine the very coherence of the system they contest." Such practices, she adds, always perpetuate aspects of the symbolic order which they reconfigure, producing syncretistic forms in the Kingdom of Zion.

3. I derive this definition from M. G. Smith (1975:85), as the "capacity for effective action" which extends "beyond the requirements of rules or in the face of opposition," although I push the logic of this concept to equate power *sui generis* with subversion itself—a step which Smith rejects (personal communication).

4. The text, recorded in Yemoja's bush shrine *(igbó Yemoja)*, was produced when a local UPN representative came to thank the Yemoja priestesses for their campaign contributions and ritual protection against NPN intimidation. The representative said, "All members of the Party of Light [UPN] in Ayede-Ekiti have sent me to come and express my gratitude to you. We are aware of your activities day and night since all these problems started! You are our Mothers!" ("Gbogbo ẹgbẹ́ imọlẹ̀ l'Ayédé-Èkìtì ló ní kí ń wá dúpé lọ́wọ́ yín láti 'jọ́ làálàá àtí wàhálà yìí ti bẹ̀rẹ̀, a mà rí 'un tí ẹ ń ṣe lọsàn-án ló-ruù! Èyìn ló bí wa!") To this the priestesses responded with a powerful incantation of female power:

O dọwọ́ọmú méjì,

Òbò á bò ó!

Let the shield of power emanate from the two breasts,

The vagina will envelop him [the enemy]!

Note how the verb *bò* (to envelop) activates the power of the vagina *(òbò)* through morphemic repetition, one of the most salient features of powerful speech *(àṣẹ)*. The full text cannot be quoted without compromising the confidentiality to which I was—and remain—held, although the political crisis is officially settled in Ayede.

5. Important perspectives include Gramsci 1971; Nelson and Grossberg 1988; Scott 1985; Laitin 1986; Laclau and Mouffe [1985] 1989; and Williams 1977.

6. See, for example, Abu-Lughod 1990; Boddy 1989; J. Comaroff 1985; Lan 1985; Fernandez 1982; and MacGaffey 1983, 1986.

7. For example, I have seen church choir girls wearing the mortarboard caps of the university graduate, young "officers" of a church in militaristic soldier-of-God uniforms boasting the red and white colors of òrìṣà priests and priestesses, and a dreadlocked prophet reading his sermon from the type of office file folder that is found in all government bureaucracies.

8. Thus for Hountondji (1983:34), "The black man continues to be the very opposite of an interlocuter; he remains a topic, a voiceless face under private investigation, an object to be defined and not the subject of a possible discourse." Although this statement directly attacks Tempels's *Bantu Philosophy*, it applies, in Hountondji's larger argument, as a general critique of anthropology.

9. I have in mind an extremely stimulating panel, "The Invention of Africa," at the 1989 African Studies Association meeting in Atlanta, Georgia, which included Kwame Anthony Appiah, Abiola Irele, Jonathon Ngate, Paulin Hountondji, and Valentin Mudimbe himself. See also Appiah 1988 and Miller 1990.

GLOSSARY OF YORUBA TERMS

adé	Crown. Cf. *adé ìlú* (king's beaded crown) and *adé imọlẹ̀* (ritual crown belonging to an *òrìṣa* cult).
àdúgbò	Quarter or ward of a town, composed of several local descent groups.
àfọ́bàjẹ́	Kingmakers, town chiefs, and ritual specialists who install the *ọba*.
àgàdà	Brass cutlasses brandished by warrior Yagba priestesses *(ọlọ́ọ̀mẹhin)*.
àjẹ́	Witch.
ajẹ́lẹ́	Administrative officer of precolonial kingdoms sent by the king to oversee subordinate territories, particularly important in the Oyo and Ibadan empires.
aládé	"Owners of the crown"; can refer to *àfọ́bàjẹ́* or cult members.
ààfin	King's palace (*aafin* in North Ekiti dialect).
ará ayé	Mortals; beings on earth or of this world.
ará ọ̀run	Beings of heaven or sky; spirits, including ancestors and *òrìṣà*.
àrẹ	Age-sets; military regiments.
àṣẹ	Ritual power, command, authority, efficacious speech; also, the name of a medicine to empower speech and incantations.
Àtá	The title of Ayede's king.
awo	Secret; sacred mystery; spiritual power.
àwòrò	High priest of an *òrìṣà* cult.
baálé	Authoritative head of a lineage or compound, lit. "father of the house."
baálẹ̀	Authoritative head of a subordinate town, lit. "father of the earth."
baba	Grandfather; senior elder.
babaláwo	Ifa diviner, lit. "father of secrets."
Balógun	War officer, often a civil chieftaincy title.

Balógun Ààfin	Powerful military chief under Eshubiyi who became civil head of Omole-Akodi quarter in Ayede. Also the owner of the Orisha Iyagba cult in Ayede.
egúngún	Masquerade representatives of the dead, usually organized by lineage.
ẹhin	Behind, in back of (cf. *iwájú*).
Ẹkùn	Leopard (ritual office in Orisha Iyagba cult).
Empé	Senior association of titled elders in Iye, at the apex of the *àrẹ* system. A military and judicial tribunal.
Èyémọlẹ̀ (Yèyémọlẹ̀)	Priestess of civic composure in Orisha Ojuna and Orisha Iyagba cults, lit. "grandmother of the possession priestesses."
idílé	Lineage, descent group.
igbá	Calabash, important ritual vessel.
igbó	Uncultivated bush.
igbó imọlẹ̀	Cult shrine or clearing in the bush.
igharẹ	Senior grade of civil chiefs; the North Ekiti equivalent of *iwàrẹ̀fà* chiefs, but usually rotating among lineages.
ijúbà	To salute with ritual respect; to swear fealty.
ikó odídẹ	Red parrot feathers, used in medicines and ritual.
ilú	Town; kingdom.
imọ jinlẹ̀	"Deep" knowledge.
imọlẹ̀	Possession priest or priestess; spirit of an *òrìṣà*.
ipara	Town shrine of an *òrìṣà* cult.
ipọnmi	Act of carrying water.
itàn	History, mytho-historical narrative.
iwájú	Ahead, in front of (cf. *ẹhin*).
iwàrẹ̀fà	Senior grade of civil chiefs under a king.
ìyá	Mother.
Ìyáolókun	Olokun priestess in Ayede's Yemoja cult; lit. "Mother of Olokun."
Ìyá Ṣàngó	Shango priestess in Ayede's Yemoja cult; lit. "Mother of Shango."
Iyálòde	Female chief of the market; also, a title in Ayede's Yemoja cult.
ìyàwó	Wife.
Ìyàwó Ọ̀sun	Oshun priestess, lit. "Wife of Oshun."

jùjú	Medicine, verbal and herbal.
ọba	King.
ọdẹ	Hunter; also a grade of female "hunters" in *òrìṣà* cults.
odù	One of sixteen division of the Ifa divinatory corpus.
ọdún	Year; annual festival.
ofọ̀	Incantation.
Ògbóni	Secret society of "owners of the earth."
ọjọ́ ipọnmi	Day of carrying water during an *òrìṣà* festival; *ijọ́ ipọnmi* in Ekiti dialect.
Olókun	*Òrìṣà* of the deep, the ocean, associated with Yemoja's ritual calabash and with one of the king's beaded crowns (in Ayede).
ọlọọ̀mẹyin (*ọlọọ̀mẹhin*)	"Warrior" priestesses in Ayede's Orisha Ojuna and Orisha Iyagba cults.
ọlọọ̀tun	Carriers of ritual water (cf. *ọtun*).
olórí àrẹ	Leader of an age-set.
olórí awo	Head of diviners.
Olú	Generic kingship title among North Ekiti, Akoko, and Iyagba Yoruba.
omi	Water.
omi imọlẹ̀	Sacred pool of an *òrìṣà*, which devotees tend.
ọmọ	Child.
ọmọdé	Children of junior status.
ọmọìyá	Child of one mother.
òpìtàn	Historian.
orí	Head; personal destiny; spiritual double.
oríkì	Praise name; attributive poetry.
òrìṣà	Deity; god, goddess, or both; deified person.
Oròyeye	"Grandmothers' cult" which sings songs of abuse against offensive individuals in Ayede.
òrun	Sky; heaven.
ọtun	Renewal; revitalizing ritual water (cf. *ọlọọ̀tun*).
yèyé	Grandmother; old woman.
Yèyéolókun	High priestess of the Yemoja cult in Ayede.

BIBLIOGRAPHY

Abimbola, Wande
1976 *Ifa: An Exposition of the Literary Corpus*. Nigeria: Oxford University Press.
1975 *Sixteen Great Poems of Ifa*. Zaria: UNESCO.

Abiodun, Roland
1987 "Verbal and Visual Metaphors: Mythical Allusions in Yoruba Ritualistic Art of Orí." *Word and Image* 3(3):252–70.

Abraham, R. C.
1962 [1946] *Dictionary of Modern Yoruba*. London: Hodder and Stoughton.

Abrahams, R. D., and Szwed, J. F.
1983 *After Africa*. New Haven: Yale University Press.

Abu-Lughod, Lila
1990 "The Romance of Resistance: Tracing Transformations of Power through Bedouin Women." *American Ethnologist* 17(1):41–55.

Adedeji, J. A.
1966 "The Place of Drama in Yoruba Religious Observance." *Odu* 3:88–94.

Adeniji, D. A. A.
1980 *Ọfọ̀ Rere (Àgbà Oògùn)*. Ibadan: Ibadan University Press.

Afolayan, Adebisi
1982 Ed. *Yoruba Language and Literature*. Ife: University of Ife Press; Ibadan: University Press Ltd.

Agiri, B. A.
1975 "Early Oyo History." *History in Africa* 2:1–16.

Ajayi, J. F. Ade
1974 "The Aftermath of the Fall of Old Oyo." In *History of West Africa*, ed. J. Ajayi and M. Crowder, 2:129–66. New York: Longmans Group.
1970a Introduction to *Journals of the Rev. James Frederick Schön and Mr. Samuel Crowther*. 2d ed. Missionary Researches and Travels Series no. 18. London: Frank Cass.
1970b Introduction to *Journal of an Expedition up the Niger and Tshadda Rivers . . . in 1854*, by Samuel Crowther. 2d ed. Missionary Researches and Travels Series no. 15. London: Frank Cass.
1970c "Bishop Crowther: An Assessment." *Odu* 4:3–17.
1965 *Christian Missions in Nigeria, 1841–1891*. London: Longmans Group.
1964 "The Ijaye War, 1860–65." In *Yoruba Warfare in the Nineteenth Century*, ed. J. F. A. Ajayi and R. S. Smith, 59–149. Cambridge: Cambridge University Press.

1961 "Nineteenth Century Origins of Nigerian Nationalism." *Journal of the Historical Society of Nigeria* 2(2):196–210.

1960 "How Yoruba Was Reduced to Writing." *Odu* 8:49–58.

Ajayi, J. F. Ade, and Smith, Robert S.

1964 *Yoruba Warfare in the Nineteenth Century.* Cambridge: Cambridge University Press.

Akinjogbin, I. A.

1971 "The Expansion of Oyo and the Rise of Dahomey, 1600–1800." In *History of West Africa*, ed. J. Ajayi and M. Crowder, 1:374–412. New York: Longmans Group.

1967 *Dahomey and Its Neighbours, 1708–1818.* Cambridge: Cambridge University Press.

1966 "The Oyo Empire in the Eighteenth Century–A Reassessment." *Journal of the Historical Society of Nigeria* 3(3):449–60.

Akintoye, S.

1971 *Revolution and Power Politics in Yorubaland, 1840–1893.* London: Longmans Group.

1970 "Obas of the Ekiti Confederacy since the Advent of the British." In *West African Chiefs: Their Changing Status under Colonial Rule and Independence*, ed. M. Crowder and O. Ikime. Ife: University of Ife Press.

Anifowose, Remi

1982 *Violence and Politics in Nigeria: The Tiv and Yoruba Experience.* New York; Nok Publishers Int.

Appiah, Anthony

1988 "Out of Africa: Topologies of Nativism." *Yale Journal of Criticism* 2(1):153–78.

1985 *Assertion and Conditionals.* Cambridge: Cambridge University Press.

Apter, Andrew

1987 "Rituals of Power: The Politics of *Orisa* Worship in Yoruba Society." Ph.D. diss., Yale University.

1985 Review of *Oedipus and Job in West African Religion*, by Meyer Fortes with an essay by Robin Horton. *Anthropology* 8(2):131–33.

1983 "In Dispraise of the King: Rituals 'Against' Rebellion in South-East Africa." *Man*, n.s. 18(3):521–34.

Asante, M.

1987 *The Afrocentric Idea.* Philadelphia: Temple University Press.

Asiwaju, Anthony I.

1976 *Western Yorubaland under European Rule, 1889–1945.* London: Longmans.

Atanda, J. A.

1973 "The Yoruba Ogboni Cult: Did It Exist in Old Oyo?" *Journal of the Historical Society of Nigeria* 5(4):477–90.

Augé, Marc

1982 *Génie du paganisme.* Paris: Editions Gallimard.

1979 "Towards a Rejection of the Meaning-Function Alternative." *Critique of Anthropology* 13/14:61–75.

1975 *Théorie des pouvoirs et idéologie: Etude de cas en Côte d'Ivoire.* Paris: Hermann.

Awe, Bolanle

1965 "The End of an Experiment: The Collapse of the Ibadan Empire, 1877–1893." *Journal of the Historical Society of Nigeria* 3(2):221–30.

1964 "The Ajele System: A Study of Ibadan Imperialism in the Nineteenth Century." *Journal of the Historical Society of Nigeria* 3(1):47–71.

Awolalu, J.

1979 *Yoruba Beliefs and Sacrificial Rites.* London: Longmans Group.

Ayandele, E. A.

1970 *Holy Johnson: Pioneer of African Nationalism, 1836–1917.* New York: Humanities Press.

1966 *The Missionary Impact on Modern Nigeria.* London: Longmans.

Babalola, S. A.

1966 *The Content and Form of Yoruba Ijala.* Oxford: Clarendon Press.

Bailey, F. G.

1969 *Stratagems and Spoils: A Social Anthropology of Politics.* New York; Schocken Books.

Baker, H., Jr.

1984 *Blues, Ideology, and Afro-American Literature: A Vernacular Theory.* Chicago: University of Chicago Press.

Baker, H., Jr., and Redmond, P., eds.

1989 *Afro-American Literary Study in the 1990's.* Chicago: University of Chicago Press.

Barber, Karin

1986 "Ẹkún Ìyàwó: Bridal Chants." In *Readings in Yoruba Chants,* ed. O. O. Olatunji. Ibadan: Heinemann Educational Books.

1984 "Yoruba *Oríkì* and Deconstructive Criticism." *Research in African Literatures* 13(4):497–518.

1981 "How Man Makes God in West Africa: Yoruba Attitudes Toward the Òrìṣà." *Africa* 51(3):724–45.

Barnes, Sandra T. ed.

1989 *Africa's Ogun: Old World and New.* Bloomington: Indiana University Press.

Bascom, William

1980 *Sixteen Cowries: Yoruba Divination from Africa to the New World.* Bloomington: Indiana University Press.

1972 *Shango in the New World.* Austin: The African and Afro-American Research Institute.

1969 *Ifa Divination: Communication Between Gods and Men.* Bloomington: Indiana University Press.

1950 "The Focus of the Cuban Santeria." *Southwestern Journal of Anthropology* 6(1):64–68.

1944 "The Sociological Role of the Yoruba Cult Group." *American Anthropologist*, n.s. 46 (no. 1, pt. 2, Memoires 63): 1–75.

1942 "The Principle of Seniority in the Social Structure of the Yoruba." *American Anthropologist*, n.s. 44:37–46.

Bastide, Roger

1978 *The African Religions of Brazil: Towards a Sociology of the Interpenetration of Civilizations*. Trans. H. Sebba. Baltimore: Johns Hopkins University Press.

1971 *African Civilizations in the New World*. Trans. Peter Green. New York: Harper Torchbooks.

Bateson, G.

1958 [1936] *Naven: A Survey of the Problems Suggested by a Composite Picture of a New Guinea Tribe from Three Points of View*. Reprint. Stanford: Stanford University Press.

Bateson, G., and Bateson, M.

1987 *Angels Fear: Towards an Epistemology of the Sacred*. New York: Macmillan.

Bauman, Zygmunt

1978 *Hermeneutics and Social Science*. New York: Columbia University Press.

Beidelman, Tom

1986 *Moral Imagination in Kaguru Modes of Thought*. Bloomington: Indiana University Press.

1966 "Swazi Royal Ritual." *Africa* 36:373–405.

Beier, Ulli

1982 *Yoruba Beaded Crowns: Sacred Regalia of the Olokuku of Okuku*. London: Ethnographica.

1980 *Yoruba Myths*. Cambridge: Cambridge University Press.

1959 *A Year of Sacred Festivals in One Yoruba Town*. Lagos: Nigeria Magazine Special Publication.

1958 "Ori-Oke Festival, Iragbaji." *Nigeria Magazine* 56:65–83.

1956a "The Oba's Festival, Ondo." *Nigeria Magazine* 50:238–59.

1956b "Obatala Festival." *Nigeria Magazine* 52:10–28.

1955 "The Historical and Psychological Significance of Yoruba Myths." *Odu* 1:17–25.

1953 "Festival of Images." *Nigeria Magazine* 45:14–20.

n.d. "Before Oduduwa." *Odu* 3:25–31.

Belasco, B. I.

1980 *The Entrepreneur as Culture Hero*. New York: Praeger Publishers.

Bender, D. R.

1970 "Agnatic or Cognatic? A Re-evaluation of Ondo Descent." *Man*, n.s. 5(1):71–87.

Bhabha, Homi K.

1985 "Signs Taken for Wonders: Questions of Ambivalence and Authority under a Tree Outside Delhi, May 1817." In *"Race," Writing and Difference,* ed. Henry Louis Gates, Jr. *Critical Inquiry* 12(1):144–65.

Biobaku, S. O.
1973 Ed. *The Sources of Yoruba History.* Oxford: Clarendon Press.
1957 *The Egba and Their Neighbours, 1842–1872.* Oxford: Clarendon Press.

Boddy, Janice
1989 *Wombs and Alien Spirits: Women, Men, and the Zar Cult in Northern Sudan.* Madison: University of Wisconsin Press.

Boston, J. S.
1968 *The Igala Kingdom.* Ibadan [New York]: Oxford Univ. Press for the Nigerian Institute for Social and Economic Research.

Bourdieu, Pierre
1979 "Symbolic Power." *Critique of Anthropology* 13/14:77–86.
1977 *Outline of a Theory of Practice.* Trans. Richard Nice. Cambridge: Cambridge University Press.

Bovell-Jones, T. B.
1935 Letter to the District Officer, Ekiti Division, Ado-Ekiti, June 21. Nigerian National Archives, University of Ibadan, Iabadan, Nigeria.

Brown, David H.
1989 "Garden in the Machine: Afro-Cuban Sacred Art and Performance in Urban New Jersey and New York." Ph.D. diss., Yale University.

Buckley, Anthony D.
1985 *Yoruba Medicine.* Oxford: Clarendon Press.

Cabrera, Lydia
1975 *El Monte: Notas sobre las religiones, la magia, las supersticiones y el folklore de los negros criollos y del pueblo de Cuba.* Miami: New House Publishers.

Calame-Griaule, G.
1965 *Ethnologie et language: La parole chez les Dogon.* Paris: Editions Gallimard.

Césaire, Aimé
1972 [1955] *Discourse on Colonialism.* Trans. J. Pinkham. New York: Monthly Review Press.

Clifford, J.
1988 *The Predicament of Culture: Twentieth Century Ethnography, Literature, and Art.* Cambridge, Mass.: Harvard University Press.
1983 "Power and Dialogue in Ethnography: Marcel Griaule's Initiation." In *Observers Observed: Essays on Ethnographic Fieldwork,* ed. George Stocking, 121–56. Madison: University of Wisconsin Press.

Cohen, A.
1981 *The Politics of Elite Culture: Explorations in the Dramaturgy of Power in a Modern African Culture.* Berkeley: University of California Press.

Coleman, J., and Rosberg, C., eds.
1964 *Political Parties and National Integration in Africa.* Berkeley: University of California Press.

Comaroff, J.
1985 *Body of Power, Spirit of Resistance: The Culture and History of a South African People.* Chicago: University of Chicago Press.
Comaroff, J., and Comaroff, J. L.
1991 *Of Revelation and Revolution.* Chicago: University of Chicago Press.
Comaroff, J. L.
1982 "Dialectical Systems, History and Anthropology: Units of Study and Questions of Theory." *Journal of Southern African Studies* 8(2):143–72.

Crowther, Samuel Ajayi
1970a [1842] "Journal of Mr. Samuel Crowther." In *Journals of the Rev. James Frederick Schön and Mr. Samuel Crowther,* 255–344. Missionary Researches and Travels Series no. 18. London: Frank Cass.
1970b [1842] "Letter of Mr. Samuel Crowther to the Rev. William Jowett, in 1837, Then Secretary of the Church Missionary Society, Detailing the Circumstances Connected with his Being Sold as a Slave." In *Journals of the Rev. James Frederick Schön and Mr. Samuel Crowther,* Missionary Researches and Travels Series no. 18. London: Frank Cass.
1970c [1855] *Journal of an Expedition up the Niger and Tshadda Rivers . . . in 1854.* Missionary Researches and Travels Series no. 15. London: Frank Cass.
1968 [1859] "Journal of the Rev. S. Crowther." In *The Gospel on the Banks of the Niger,* by Samuel Crowther and Christopher Taylor, 1–240, 385–445. London: Dawsons.
1852 *Vocabulary of the Yoruba Language.* London: C.M.S.
1851 *St. Luke, Acts of the Apostles, St. James, and St. Peter in Yoruba.* London: C.M.S.
1843 *Grammar and Vocabulary of the Yoruba Language.* London: C.M.S.
Curtin, P. D.
1964 *The Image of Africa: British Ideas and Action, 1780–1850.* Vol. 1. Madison: University of Wisconsin Press.
Daramola, O., and Jeje, A.
1967 *Àwọn Àṣà àtí Òrìṣà Ilẹ̀ Yorùbá.* Ibadan: Onibon-Oje Press.
Davies, Carol, and Graves, Anne, eds.
1986 *Ngambika: Studies of Women in African Literature.* Trenton: Africa World Press.
Dennett, R.
1910 *Nigerian Studies.* London: Macmillan.
Dent, M. J.
1966 "A Minority Party—the UMBC." In *Nigerian Government and Politics,* ed. J. P. Macintosh, 461–507. Evanston: Northwestern University Press.

Derrida, Jacques
   1988 "Like the Sound of the Sea Deep within a Shell: Paul de Man's War."
      Critical Inquiry 14(3):590–652.
   1976 *Of Grammatology*. Trans. Gayatri Spivak. Baltimore: Johns Hopkins
      University Press.

Diamond, L.
   1982 "Cleavage, Conflict, and Anxiety in the Second Nigerian Republic."
      Journal of Modern African Studies 20(4):629–68.

Dieterlen, G.
   1951 *Essai sur la religion Bambara*. Paris: Presses universitaires de France.
   1941 *Les âmes de Dogon*. Paris: Institut d'ethnologie.

Dirks, Nicholas
   1987 *The Hollow Crown: Ethnohistory of an Indian Kingdom*. Cambridge: Cam-
      bridge University Press.

Dougals, M.
   1980 *Edward Evans-Pritchard*. New York: Viking Press.

Drewal, M.
   1977 "Projections from the Top in Yoruba Art." *African Arts* 11(1):43–49, 91–92.

Drewal, H., and Drewal, M.
   1987 "Composing Time and space in Yoruba Art." *Word and Image* 3(3):225–
      51.
   1983 *Gẹlẹdẹ: Art and Female Power among the Yoruba*. Bloomington: Indiana
      University Press.

Durkheim, Emile
   1965 [1915] *The Elementary Forms of the Religious Life*. Trans. J. W. Swain. New
      York: Free Press.

Eco, Umberto.
   1986 *Travels in Hyperreality*. Trans. William Weaver. New York: Harcourt
      Brace Jovanovich.

Ellis, A. B.
   1894 *The Yoruba-Speaking Peoples of the Slave Coast of West Africa*. London:
      Chapman and Hall.

Evans-Pritchard, E. E.
   1956 *Nuer Religion*. New York: Oxford University Press.
   1937 *Witchcraft, Oracles, and Magic among the Azande*. Oxford: Clarendon
      Press.

Fadipe, N. A.
   1970 *The Sociology of the Yoruba*. Ibadan: Ibadan University Press.

Fagunwa, D. O.
   1982 *Forest of a Thousand Daemons*. Trans. Wole Soyinka. New York: Random
      House.

Farrow, Stephen
   1926 *Faith, Fancies, and Fetich, or Yoruba Paganism*. New York: Macmillan.

Fernandez, J.
  1982 *Bwiti: An Ethnography of the Religious Imagination in Africa*. Princeton: Princeton University Press.
Fields, Karen
  1985 *Revival and Rebellion in Colonial Central Africa*. Princeton: Princeton University Press.
Finnegan, R.
  1969 "How to Do Things with Words: Performative Utterances among the Limba of Sierra Leone," *Man*, n.s. 4(4):537–52.
Forde, D.
  1951 *The Yoruba Speaking Peoples of Southwestern Nigeria*. London: International African Institute.
Fortes, Meyer
  1959 *Oedipus and Job in West African Religion*. Cambridge: Cambridge University Press.
  1945 *The Dynamics of Clanship among the Tallensi*. London: Oxford University Press.
Fortes, Meyer, and Dieterlen, Germaine, eds.
  1965 *African Systems of Thought*. London: Oxford University Press for the International African Institute.
Fortes, Meyer, and Evans-Pritchard, E. E., eds.
  1940 *African Political Systems*. London: Oxford University Press for the International African Institute.
Fox, Robert E.
  1987 *Conscientious Sorcerers: The Black Postmodernist Fiction of LeRoi Jones/ Amiri Baraka, Ishmael Reed, and Samuel R. Delany*. Contributions in Afro-American and African Studies, no. 106. New York: Greenwood Press.
Frobenius, L.
  1968 [1913] *The Voice of Africa*. Trans. Rudolf Blind. Reprint. New York and London: Benjamin Blom.
Gadamer, Hans
  1976 *Philosophical Hermeneutics*. Trans. D. Lige. Berkeley: University of California Press.
Gates, Henry Louis, Jr.
  1988 *The Signifying Monkey*. New York: Oxford University Press.
  1987 "Authority, (White) Power and the (Black) Critic: It's All Greek to Me." *Cultural Critique* 7:19–46.
  1985 Ed. *"Race," Writing and Difference*. *Critical Inquiry* 12(1).
  1984 Ed. *Black Literature and Literary Theory*. New York and London: Methuen.
Gbadamosi, T. G. O.
  1978 *The Growth of Islam among the Yoruba, 1841–1908*. Atlantic Highlands, N.J.: Humanities Press.

Geertz, Clifford
    1980 *Negara: The Theatre State in Nineteenth-Century Bali.* Princeton: Princeton University Press.
    1973 "Religion as a Cultural System." Pp. 87–125 in *The Interpretation of Cultures.* New York: Basic Books.

Giddens, Anthony
    1984 *The Constitution of Society.* Berkeley: University of California Press.
    1979 *Central Problems in Social Theory.* London and Berkeley: University of California Press.

Girard, René
    1977 [1972] *Violence and the Sacred.* Trans. P. Gregory. Baltimore: Johns Hopkins University Press.

Gleason, Judith
    1973 *A Recitation of Ifa, Oracle of the Yoruba.* New York: Grossman Publishers.

Gluckman, Max
    1954 *Rituals of Rebellion in South-East Africa.* Manchester: University of Manchester Press.

Goody, J.
    1966 Ed. *Succession to High Office.* Cambridge: Cambridge University Press.
    1962 *Death, Property, and the Ancestors: A Study of the Mortuary Customs of the Lodagaa of West Africa.* London: Tavistock.

Gramsci, A.
    1971 *Selections from the Prison Notebooks.* Trans. and ed. Q. Hoare and G. N. Smith. New York: International Publishers.

Griaule, M.
    1948 *Dieu d'eau: Entretiens avec Ogotemmeli.* Paris: Editions du chêne. Published as *Conversations with Ogotemmeli,* Oxford University Press for the International African Institute, 1965.
    1938 *Masques Dogons.* Paris: Institut d'ethnologie.

Griaule, M., and Dieterlen, G.
    1965 *Le Renard Pâle.* Paris: Institut d'ethnologie.
    1951 *Signes graphiques soudanais.* Paris: L'Homme.

Guha, Ranajit
    1989 "Dominance without Hegemony and Its Historiography." In *Subaltern Studies VI: Writings on South Asian History and Society,* 210–309. Delhi: Oxford University Press.

Harms, Robert
    1983 "The Wars of August: Diagonal Narrative in African History." *The American Historical Review* 88:809–34.

Harris, Joseph, ed.
    1982 *Global Dimensions of the African Diaspora.* Washington, D.C.: Howard University Press.

Hayward, M., and Dumbuya, A. R.
1983 "Political Legitimacy, Political Symbols, and National Leadership in West Africa." *Journal of Modern African Studies* 21(4):645–71.

Hegel, G. W. F.
1967 [1807] *The Phenomenology of Mind.* Trans. J. B. Baillie. New York: Harper and Row.

Hekman, Susan J.
1986 *Hermeneutics and the Sociology of Knowledge.* Cambridge: Polity.

Herskovits, Melville J.
1966 *The New World Negro: Selected Papers in Afro-American Studies.* Bloomington: Indiana University Press.

Heusch, L. de.
1985 *Sacrifice in Africa.* Bloomington: Indiana University Press.
1982 [1972] *The Drunken King.* Reprint. Bloomington: Indiana University Press.

Hobbes, Thomas
1986 [1651] *Leviathan.* Ed. C. B. Macpherson. Aylesbury: Penguin Books.

Horton, Robin
1983 "Social Psychologies: African and Western." In *Oedipus and Job in West African Religion,* by Meyer Fortes. Cambridge: Cambridge University Press.
1979 "Ancient Ife: A Reassessment." *Journal of the Historical Society of Nigeria* 9(4):69–149.

Hountondji, P.
1983 *African Philosophy: Myth and Reality.* Bloomington: Indiana University Press.

Hurston, Zora Neale.
1984a [1939] *Moses: Man of the Mountain.* Reprint. Urbana: University of Illinois Press.
1984b [1942] *Dust Tracks on a Road.* Reprint. Urbana: University of Illinois Press.
1978 [1935] *Mules and Men.* Reprint. Bloomington: Indiana University Press.
1938 *Tell My Horse.* Philadelphia: J. B. Lippincott.

Idowu, B.
1962 *Olodumare: God in Yoruba Belief.* London: Longmans, Green and Co.

Johnson, S.
1921 *The History of the Yorubas.* Lagos: C.M.S. Bookshops.

Kantorowicz, Ernst H.
1957 *The King's Two Bodies: A Study in Medieval Political Theology.* Princeton: Princeton University Press.

Karp, I., and Bird, C., eds.
1980 *Explorations in African Systems of Thought.* Bloomington: Indiana University Press.

Kilson, M., and Rotberg, R., eds.
   1975 *The African Diaspora: Interpretive Essays.* Cambridge, Mass.: Harvard
      University Press.
Laclau, Ernesto, and Mouffe, Chantal
   1989 [1985] *Hegemony and Socialist Strategy: Towards a Radical Democratic Poli-
      tics.* Reprint. London: Verso.
Laitin, D.
   1986 *Hegemony and Culture: Politics and Religious Change among the Yoruba.*
      Chicago: University of Chicago Press.
Lan, D.
   1985 *Guns and Rain: Guerrillas and Spirit Mediums in Zimbabwe.* Berkeley:
      University of California Press.
Langer, S.
   1953 *Feeling and Form.* New York: Charles Scribner's Sons.
Law, R. C. C.
   1977 *The Oyo Empire c. 1600–1836.* Oxford: Clarendon Press.
   1975 "A West African Cavalry State: The Kingdom of Oyo." *Journal of Afri-
      can History* 16(1):1–15.
   1973 "Traditional History." In *Sources of Yoruba History,* ed. S. O. Biobaku,
      25–40. Oxford: Clarendon Press.
   1971 "The Constitutional Troubles of Oyo in the Eighteenth Century." *Jour-
      nal of African History* 14(2):25–44.
Lawal, Babatunde
   1985 "Ori: The Significance of the Head in Yoruba Sculpture." *Journal of An-
      thropological Research* 41:91–103.
Leach, E.
   1968 Ed. *Dialectic in Practical Religion.* Cambridge: Cambridge University
      Press.
   1961 "Rethinking Anthropology." In *Rethinking Anthropology,* 1–27. Lon-
      don: Athlone Press.
   1954 *Political Systems of Highland Burma: A Study of Kachin Social Structure.*
      Cambridge, Mass.: Harvard University Press.
Leiris, M.
   1948 *La langue secrète des Dogons de Sanga.* Paris: Institut d'ethnologie.
Levy, M., Jr.
   1952 *The Structure of Society.* Princeton: Princeton University Press.
Lewis, W. Arthur
   1965 *Politics in West Africa.* Oxford: Oxford University Press.
Lienhardt, Godfrey
   1961 *Divinity and Experience: The Religion of the Dinka.* Oxford: Clarendon
      Press.
Lloyd, P. C.
   1971 *The Political Development of Yoruba Kingdoms in the Eighteenth and Nine-*

teenth Centuries. London: Royal Anthropological Institute Occasional Paper no. 31.

1968 "Conflict Theory and Yoruba Kingdoms." In *History and Social Anthropology,* ed. I. M. Lewis. London: Tavistock.

1966 "Agnatic and Cognatic Descent among the Yoruba." *Man,* n.s. 1(4):484–500.

1962 *Yoruba Land Law.* London: Oxford University Press.

1961 "Installing the Awujale." *Ibadan* 12:7–10.

1960 "Sacred Kingship and Government among the Yoruba." *Africa* 30(3):221–38.

1955 "Yoruba Myths—A Sociologist's Interpretation." *Odu* 2:20–28.

1954 "The Traditional Political System of the Yoruba." *Southwestern Journal of Anthropology* 10:366–84.

Lucas, J. O.
1948 *The Religion of the Yoruba.* Lagos: C.M.S. Bookshops.

Mabogunje, A. L., and Omer-Cooper, J. D.
1971 *Owu in Yoruba History.* Ibadan: Ibadan University Press.

McClelland, E. M.
1966 "The Significance of Number in Odu of Ifa." *Africa* 36:421–31.

MacGaffey, W.
1986 *Religion and Society in Central Africa: The Bakongo of Lower Zaire.* Chicago: University of Chicago Press.

1983 *Modern Kongo Prophets: Religion in a Plural Society.* Bloomington: Indiana University Press.

McKenzie, P. R.
1976 "Yoruba *Orisa* Cults: Some Marginal Notes concerning Their Cosmology and Concept of Deity." *Journal of Religion in Africa* 8(3):189–207.

MacRow, D. W.
1955 "Natural Ruler: A Yoruba Conception of Monarchy." *Nigeria Magazine* 47:233–45.

Marti, Palau
1960 *Essai sur la notion de roi chez les Yoruba et les Aja-Fon.* Paris: Editions Berger-Levrault.

Mason, Michael
1970 "The *Jihad* in the South: An Outline of the Nineteenth Century Nupe Hegemony in North-Eastern Yorubaland and Afenmai." *Journal of the Historical Society of Nigeria* 5(2):191–207.

Matory, J. L.
1986 "Vessels of Power: The Dialectical Symbolism of Power in Yoruba Religion and Polity." Master's thesis, University of Chicago.

May, D.
1860 "Journey in the Yoruba and Nupe Countries in 1858." *Journal of the Royal Geographic Society* 30:212–33.

Middleton, J.
  1968 "Conflict and Variation in Lugbaraland." In *Local Level Politics: Social and Cultural Perspectives,* ed. M. Swartz, 151–62. Chicago: Aldine.
  1960 *Lugbara Religion: Ritual and Authority among an East African People.* London: Oxford University Press for the International African Institute.

Miller, C. L.
  1990 *Theories of Africans: Francophone Literature and Anthropology in Africa.* Chicago: University of Chicago Press.
  1985 *Blank Darkness: Africanist Discourse in French.* Chicago: University of Chicago Press.

Miller, J. C., ed.
  1980 *The African Past Speaks: Essays on Oral Tradition and History.* Hamden: Archon Press.

Morton-Williams, P.
  1967 "The Yoruba Kingdom in Oyo." In *West African Kingdoms in the Nineteenth Century,* ed. D. Forde and P. Kaberry, 36–69. London: Oxford University Press for the International African Institute.
  1964 "An Outline of the Cult Organization and Cosmology of Old Oyo." *Africa* 34(3):243–61.
  1960 "The Yoruba Ogboni Cult in Oyo." *Africa* 30(4):362–74.

Mudimbe, V. Y.
  1988 *The Invention of Africa: Gnosis, Philosophy, and the Order of Knowledge.* Bloomington: Indiana University Press.
  1973 *L'autre face du royaume: Une introduction à la critique des languages en folie.* Lausanne: L'age d'homme.

Murphy, Joseph
  1988 *Santería: An African Religion in America.* Boston: Beacon Press.

Nadel, S. F.
  1970 [1954] *Nupe Religion: Traditional Beliefs and the Influence of Islam in a West African Chiefdom.* Reprint. New York: Schocken Books.
  1942 *A Black Byzantium: The Kingdom of the Nupe in Nigeria.* London: Oxford University Press for the International African Institute.

Nelson, Cary, and Grossberg, Lawrence
  1988 Eds. *Marxism and the Interpretation of Culture.* Urbana: University of Illinois Press.

Obayemi, A.
  1979 "Ancient Ife: Another Cultural-Historical Interpretation." *Journal of the Historical Society of Nigeria* 9(4):151–85.
  1971 "The Yoruba and Edo-speaking Peoples and Their Neighbours Before 1600." In *History of West Africa,* ed. J. Ajayi and M. Crowder, 1:196–263. New York: Longmans Group.

Ogunba, Oyin
  1973 "Ceremonies." In *Sources of Yoruba History,* ed. S. O. Biobaku, 87–110. Oxford: Clarendon Press.

1967 "Ritual Drama of the Ijebu People: A Study of Indigenous Festivals."
Ph.D. diss., University of Ibadan.

Ogundele, J. O.
1961 *Ibu-Olokun.* London: University of London Press.

Oguntuyi, A.
1979 *A Short History of Ado-Ekiti,* part 2. Ado-Ekiti: Bamgboye Press.
1970 *History of the Catholic Church in the Diocese of Ondo.* Ibadan: Claverianum Press.

Ojo, G. A.
1966a *Yoruba Palaces.* London: University of London Press.
1966b *Yoruba Culture.* London: University of London Press.

Ojo, J. R. O.
1977 "The Hierarchy of Yoruba Cults: An aspect of Yoruba Cosmology." Paper presented in the seminar series of the Department of African Languages and Literatures, University of Ife, Nigeria.

Olatunji, Olatunde
1984 *Features of Yoruba Oral Poetry.* Ibadan: University Press Ltd.
1982 "Classification of Yoruba Oral Poetry." In *Yoruba Language and Literature,* ed. A. Afolayan, 57–72. Ibadan: University of Ife Press.

Olupona, J.
1983 "A Phenomenological/Anthropological Analysis of the Religion of the Ondo-Yoruba of Nigeria." Ph.D. diss., Boston University.

Oni, J. O.
n.d. *A History of Ijeshaland.* Ife.

Ortner, Sherry
1984 "Theory in Anthropology since the Sixties." *Comparative Studies in Society and History* 26:126–61.

Owusu, Maxwell
1986 "Custom and Coups: A Juridical Interpretation of Civil Order and Disorder in Ghana." *Journal of Modern African Studies* 24(1):69–99.

Oyesakin, A.
1982 "The Image of Women in Ifa Literary Corpus." *Nigeria Magazine* 141:16–23.

Page, J.
1908 *The Black Bishop: Samuel Adjai Crowther.* London: Hodder and Stoughton.

Parrinder, G.
1953 *Religion in an African City.* London: Oxford University Press.

Peel, J. D. Y.
1984 "Making History: The Past in the Ijesha Present." *Man,* n.s. 19:111–32.
1983 *Ijeshas and Nigerians: The Incorporation of a Nigerian Kingdom, 1890's to 1970's.* Cambridge: Cambridge University Press.

1980 "Kings, Titles and Quarters: A Conjectural History of Ilesha." Part 2, "Institutional Growth." *History in Africa* 7:225–57.
1979 "Kings, Titles and Quarters: A Conjectural History of Ilesha." Part 1, "The Traditions Reviewed." *History in Africa* 6:109–52.
1968 *Aladura: A Religious Movement among the Yoruba.* London: Oxford University Press, for the International African Institute.

Peel, Quentin
1984 "Obituary for an Election." *The Financial Times,* 23 January, p. 4.

Pemberton, J.
1988 "The King and the Chameleon: Odun Agemo." *Ife: Annals of the Institute of Cultural Studies* 2:47–64.
1979 "Sacred Kingship and the Violent God." *Berkshire Review* 14:85–106.

Pemberton, J., and Fagg, W.
1982 *Yoruba Sculpture of West Africa.* London: William Collins Sons and Co.

Post, K.
1963 *The Nigerian Federal Election of 1959.* London: Oxford University Press for the Nigerian Institute for Social and Economic Research.

Prince, R.
1961 "The Yoruba Image of the Witch." *The Journal of Mental Science* 107:795–805.

Proudfoot, W.
1985 *Religious Experience.* Berkeley: University of California Press.

Pryse, Marjorie, and Spillers, Hortense, eds.
1985 *Conjuring: Black Women, Fiction, and Literary Tradition.* Bloomington: Indiana University Press.

Putnam, H.
1971 "The Analytic and the Synthetic." In *Readings in the Philosophy of Language,* ed. J. Rosenberg and C. Travis, 94–126. Englewood Cliffs, N.J.: Prentice-Hall.

Quine, W.
1960 *Word and Object.* Cambridge, Mass.: MIT Press.

Radcliffe-Brown, A. R.
1952 *Structure and Function in Primitive Society.* London: Cohen and West.
1950 Introduction to *African Systems of Kinship and Marriage,* ed. A. R. Radcliffe-Brown and Daryll Forde, 1–85. London: Oxford University Press for the International African Institute.

Ricoeur, P.
1981 *Hermeneutics and the Human Sciences: Essays on Language, Action and Interpretation.* Trans. J. Thompson. Cambridge: Cambridge University Press.

Rouch, J.
1960 *La religion et la magie Songhay.* Paris: Presses universitaires de France.
Sahlins, M.
1985 *Islands of History.* Chicago: University of Chicago Press.
1981 *Historical Metaphors and Mythical Realities: Structure in the Early History of the Sandwich Islands Kingdom.* Ann Arbor: University of Michigan Press.
Scheffler, Harold
1966 "Ancestor Worship in Anthropology; or, Observations on Descent and Descent Groups." *Current Anthropology* 7(5):541–48.
Scott, J.
1985 *Weapons of the Weak: Everyday Forms of Peasant Resistance.* New Haven: Yale University Press.
Searle, John
1969 *Speech Acts: An Essay on the Philosophy of Language.* Cambridge: Cambridge University Press.
Silverstein, M.
1976 "Shifters, Linguistic Categories, and Cultural Description." In *Meaning in Anthropology,* ed. K. H. Basso and H. A. Selby. Albuquerque: University of New Mexico Press.
Simpson, George
1978 *Black Religions in the New World.* New York: Columbia University Press.
Sklar, Richard
1963 *Nigerian Political Parties.* Princeton: Princeton University Press.
Smith, M. G.
1979 *The Affairs of Daura: History and Change in a Hausa State.* Berkeley: University of California Press.
1975 *Corporations and Society: The Social Anthropology of Collective Action.* First published 1974. Chicago: Aldine.
1960 *Government in Zazzau, 1800–1950.* London: Oxford University Press for the International African Institute.
1957 "The Social Function and Meaning of Hausa Praise-Singing." *Africa* 27:26–45.
1956 "On Segmentary Lineage Systems." *Journal of the Royal Anthropological Institute* 86(2):39–80.
Smith, R.S.
1969 *Kingdoms of the Yoruba.* London: Methuen.
1964 "The Yoruba Wars, c. 1820–93." In *Yoruba Warfare in the Nineteenth Century,* ed. J. F. A. Ajayi and R. S. Smith, 9–58.
Snead, James A.
1984 "Repetition as a Figure of Black Culture." In *Black Literature and Literary Theory,* ed. Henry Louis Gates, Jr., 59–79. New York and London: Methuen.

Soyinka, Wole
 1988 [1972] *The Man Died: Prison Notes of Wole Soyinka.* New York: Noonday Press.
 1984 "The Critic and Society: Barthes, Leftocracy, and Other Mythologies." In *Black Literature and Literary Theory,* ed. Henry Louis Gates, Jr., 27–57. New York and London: Methuen.
 1981 *Ake: The Years of Childhood.* London: Rex Collins.
 1976 *Myth, Literature, and the African World.* Cambridge: Cambridge University Press.
 1963 *A Dance of the Forests.* London: Oxford University Press.

Stepto, Robert
 1984 "Storytelling in Early Afro-American Fiction: Frederick Douglass' 'The Heroic Slave'." In *Black Literature and Literary Theory,* ed. Henry Louis Gates, Jr., 175–86. New York: Methuen.

Stocking, G., ed.
 1983 *Observers Observed: Essays on Ethnographic Fieldwork.* Madison: University of Wisconsin Press.

Swayne, A. C. C.
 1936 Intelligence Report. Ayede District of Ekiti Division, Ondo Province. Nigerian National Archives.

Sylvester, Christine
 1986 "Zimbabwe's 1985 Elections: A Search for National Mythology." *Journal of Modern African Studies* 24(2):229–55.

Talbot, S. A.
 1926 *The Peoples of Southern Nigeria.* Vol. 1. London: Oxford University Press.

Tambiah, S.
 1968 "The Magical Power of Words." *Man,* n.s. 3(2):175–208.

Tempels, P.
 1959 [1945] *Bantu Philosophy.* Reprint. Paris: Presence africaine.

Thieme, D.
 1969 "A Descriptive Catalogue of Yoruba Musical Instruments." Ph.D. diss., Catholic University of America.

Thompson, J. B.
 1981 *Critical Hermeneutics: A Study in the Thought of Paul Ricoeur and Jürgen Habermas.* Cambridge: Cambridge University Press.

Thompson, R. F.
 1983 *Flash of the Spirit: African and Afro-American Art and Philosophy.* New York: Random House.
 1976 [1971] *Black Gods and Kings.* Reprint. Bloomington: University of Indiana Press.
 1974 *African Art in Motion.* Berkeley and Los Angeles: University of California Press.

1973 "An Aesthetic of the Cool." *African Arts* 7(2):41–67.
1971 "Aesthetics in Traditional Africa." In *Art and Aesthetics in Primitive Society*, ed. C. Jopling. New York: Dutton.

Thompson, V. B.
1987 *The Making of the African Diaspora in the Americas, 1441–1900*. New York: Longman.

Turner, V.
1982 *From Ritual to Theatre: The Human Seriousness of Play*. New York: Performing Arts Journal Publications.
1974 *Dramas, Fields, and Metaphors: Symbolic Action in Human Society*. Ithaca: Cornell University Press.
1969 *The Ritual Process: Structure and Anti-Structure*. Ithaca: Cornell University Press.
1967 *The Forest of Symbols: Aspects of Ndembu Ritual*. Ithaca: Cornell University Press.
1957 *Schism and Continuity in an African Society*. Manchester: Manchester University Press for the Rhodes-Livingstone Institute.

Tutuola, A.
1982 *The Witch-Herbalist of the Remote Town*. London: Faber and Faber.
1958 *The Brave African Huntress*. London: Faber and Faber.
1954 *My Life in the Bush of Ghosts*. New York: Grove Press.
1953 *The Palm-Wine Drinkard*. New York: Grove Press.

van Binsbergen, Wim M. J.
1981 *Religious Change in Zambia: Exploratory Studies*. London and Boston: Kegan Paul International.

van Binsbergen, Wim M. J., and Scholffeleers, Matthew
1985 *Theoretical Explorations in African Religion*. London: Routledge and Kegan Paul.

Van Gennep, Arnold
1909 *Les rites de passage*. Paris: E. Nourry.

Vansina, Jan
1983 "Is Elegance Proof? Structuralism and African History." *History in Africa* 10:307–48.
1964 "The Use of Process-Models in African History." In *The Historian in Tropical Africa*, ed. J. Vansina, R. Mauny, and L. V. Thomas, 375–89. London: Oxford University Press for the International African Institute.

Verger, Pierre
1982 *Orisha: Les dieux Yorouba en Afrique et au Nouveau Monde*. Paris: Editions A. M. Metailie.
1957 *Notes sur le culte des orisha et vodun*. Dakar: Institute français d'Afrique noir.

Weber, Max
1968 *Economy and Society*. Vol. 2. Ed. G. Roth and C. Wittich. Berkeley: University of California Press.

Weir, N. A. C.
    1934 "The Broad Outlines of Past and Present Organisation in the Ekiti Division of Ondo Province." Ado: Ekiti Div. Office.

Wells, Rulon S.
    1977 "Criteria for Semiosis." In *A Perfusion of Signs,* ed. Thomas A. Sebeok, pp. 1–21. Bloomington: Indiana University Press.

Wescott, Joan, and Morton-Williams, Peter
    1962 "The Symbolism and Ritual Context of the Yoruba *Laba Sango.*" *Journal of the Royal Anthropological Institute* 92(1):23–37.
    1958 "The Festival of Iya Mapo." *Nigeria Magazine* 56:212–14.

West, Cornel
    1982 *Prophesy Deliverance: An Afro-American Revolutionary Christianity.* Philadelphia: Westminster Press.

Williams, Raymond
    1977 *Marxism and Literature.* Oxford: Oxford University Press.

Wilmsen, Edwin
    1989 *Land Filled with Flies: A Political Economy of the Kalahari.* Chicago: University of Chicago Press.

Wittgenstein, Ludwig
    1958 *Philosophical Investigations.* trans. G. Anscombe. New York: Macmillan.

Young, Crawford
    1982 "Patterns of Social Conflict: State, Class, and Ethnicity." *Daedalus,* Spring, 71–98.

INDEX

46, 51, 56, 69, 74, 94, 153; organization of, 60–65, 62 (fig.); and
other cults, 64, 67, 68, 161, 234n.8
Culture-hero, 150–54

Daramola, O., 154
Day of Carrying Water (*Ijọ Iponmi*),
104–6, 112, 125–36, 175, 234n.5
Deconstruction, 7, 125, 134, 148,
155, 190, 216
Deep knowledge: and cosmology,
149; and discourse, 5, 210–11,
228n.7, 239n.11; and hegemony,
223; and hermeneutics, 31; and
power, 7, 9, 214–18; in ritual, 94,
97, 98, 107–8, 110–11, 122–23,
148; and sociopolitical change, 7.
See also *Awo;* Secrecy
Deep truths. *See* Deep knowledge
Deities: Ado, 56, 57; Agiri, 67;
Ajaloorun, 123; Aramfe, 123; associated with Yemoja, 61, 63
(fig.), 64, 100; Bayoni, 61, 63
(fig.); and Crowther, 199–200; of
Ede, 28–31; Eleejigbo, 30; Elekole, 56; Ereo, 67; Erinle, 61, 63
(fig.); Erugba, 22; Eshu, 28–30,
59, 61, 100–101, 147, 231n.26,
233n.13, 234n.2; of Ibadan, 36;
Ibeji, 106; identified with
Catholic saints, 224; Idiya, 67; Ifa,
26, 28–30, 32–33, 75, 118; Igbo,
29; Iroko, 67; Iyagba, 54, 66; Iya
Mapo, 22; Iyelola, 61; Konkofo,
61; Obatala, 16, 28–30, 67, 123,
151, 154, 155, 200, 224 (*see also*
Deities, Orishanla; Deities, Osalufon); Ogbon-Ilele, 67; Ogiyan,
30; Ogun, 29, 61, 63 (fig.), 100,
106, 122–23, 151, 159, 185, 224;
Ojuna, 59, 160; Oke, 61; Oke-
Ibadan, 36; Oko, 61, 63 (fig.), 100,
106, 123; Okutaaro, 67;
Olodumare, 15, 151, 207, 208;
Olokun, 51, 63; Olooke, 67, 128;

Oloye, 67; Olua, 54, 56; Oluofin,
231n.29; Ore, 67; Orishaeguin,
231n.29; Orisha Igbo, 29; Orishajaye, 231n.29; Orishakire,
231n.29; Orishako, 231n.29; Orishanla, 67, 154, 155, 231n.29 (*see
also* Deities, Obatala); Orisharowu, 231n.29; Orishagiyan,
231n.29; Osalufon, 28–30,
231nn. 26, 27 (*see also* Deities,
Obatala); Osangin, 56; Osanyin,
61, 75, 237n.5; Oshun, 61, 63
(fig.), 100, 106; Oya, 61, 63 (fig.);
Pupupupu, 16; Santo, 22; Sino,
22. *See also* Cults; Deities, festivals of; Deities, shrines to; *Orìṣà*
—Oduduwa: in classification of
òrìṣà, 151, 154; descendents of,
24, 25, 39, 40, 207, 232n.2; in
founding myths, 19, 24–26, 40; in
migration myths, 15–17, 229n.6;
and myths of origin, 207, 208; in
ritual practice, 25–26, 29, 123,
231n.25, 232n.2
—Shango, 28–30, 61, 63 (fig.), 64,
100, 106, 217; Ajaloorun compared to, 123; and definition of
òrìṣà, 151; devotees of, within
Yemoja cult, 63; and Eshu,
231n.26; identified as Catholic
saint, 224; *oríkì* of, 134, 140; and
Osalufon, 231nn. 26, 27; and politics, 230n.19; propitiations to, in
Iya Mapo festival in Igbeti, 22;
and the ritual language of possession in the Yemoja festival, 136–147
—Yemoja: identified as Catholic
saint, 224; and the Iyagba festival, 160; *oríkì* of, 109, 111, 115,
125–36; relationship with other
deities, 61, 63 (fig.), 64, 100
Deities, festivals of, 14, 21, 23, 98,
114–16; Agemo, 235n.13;
Agunlele, 234n.4; in Ayede under Eshubiyi, 52; *Bééré*, 25;